Cultural Reality

CULTURAL REALITY

by

Florian Znaniecki

with

FOREWORD from PHILOSOPHY by DAVID L. MILLER

FOREWORD from SOCIOLOGY by ROY G. FRANCIS

Cap and Gown Press
Houston

First published in 1919

Reissued 1983, by Cap and Gown Press, Inc.

CAP & GOWN PRESS, INC.
5244 Fredericksburg Road
Suite #130
San Antonio, TX 78229

Library of Congress Catalog Card Number 82-73820

ISBN 0-88105-009-1

Printed in the United States of America

Editor's Note

The only time I personally met Florian Znaniecki occurred purely by chance. In late August of 1954, while attending the annual meeting of the American Sociological Association being held on the campus of the University of Illinois in Urbana, I happened to pass through the lobby of the student union building, the site of these sessions, when I noticed the presence of an elderly, distinguished looking gentleman sitting all alone in the spacious lobby area. I recognized Znaniecki from older photographs and took the liberty of approaching him and introducing myself. This intrusion on his privacy was accepted graciously by Znaniecki, even though he seemed tired and drawn, no doubt from the heavy demands made of him during the sessions usually required of its officials as Znaniecki was the outgoing president that year.

In surveying the empty and unusually quiet lobby, I commented, by way of starting the conversation, that apparently everyone else but us were probably in the auditorium attending an address by Talcott Parsons. Znaniecki smiled and remarked in his soft voice that there would likely be nothing new in Parsons' talk that Herbert Spencer had not already written. Responding to my puzzled expression, he said he was referring to Spencer's ideas on social institutions and principles of ethics.

I then decided to take advantage of our being alone and Znaniecki's friendly and relaxed mood, and asked him some questions I had for a long time wanted to ask if given the opportunity, and here it was.

In my earlier graduate studies in sociology and philosophy, I had noted some intriguing parallel thinking of Znaniecki and George H. Mead, particularly between Znaniecki's *Laws of Social Psychology* (1925) and Mead's *Philosophy of the Act* (1938) on the subject of "the stages of the act." Appearing much earlier, Znaniecki presents four stages of the unit act as does Mead. Both formulations are very similar for the first three stages but differ in the fourth and final stage.

The four stages of the act by Mead are: Stage of Impulse; Stage of Perception; Stage of Manipulation; and Stage of Consummation; (Essay I). Znaniecki's stages of the act were: The Social Tendency, which he defines "At the beginning of every social action we find an *impulse* to act in a certain way, a subjective motion to do something which gradually defines itself.." (p. 67), which closely resembles Mead's stage of impulse. Next comes the "social object," which Znaniecki defines as "every social action purposes to influence, to modify an individual or a group, and although a social tendency (impulse) on its first appearance may have no definite individual or group in view, yet the action cannot go on unless the object of its purposed influence is chosen and determined.." (p. 81) and this resembles Mead's second stage of perception. The third stage was termed by Znaniecki as the "instrumental process," (p. 87), and resembles Mead's third stage of manipulation. Finally, Znaniecki argues that no social act ever "ends" but, rather, continues indefinitely, depending upon the *reaction* of others to the on-going act (pp. 92-95), which opposes Mead's fourth and final stage of the act when it is consummated. Thus, while very similar in their formulations of the stages of the social act,Mead and Znaniecki differ in the final stage.

Realizing this parallel in thinking and knowing also that Znaniecki was a post-graduate scholar and research associate in the philosophy department at the University of Chicago from 1915 to about 1920, I deliberately asked Znaniecki in the lobby if he had had any contact with George Mead at Chicago while active in the same department during that time, and pointed out these similarities in their writings. He promptly informed me that he had absolutely no contact nor interaction whatsoever with Mead while at Chicago, that he came to Chicago to study primarily under John Dewey and others to get a first-hand knowledge of American Pragmatism of which Dewey was, of course, a prominent exponent. Indeed, while Znaniecki has acknowledged the strong influence of pragmatism on his work, he has given his intellectual debt to other individuals such as W. I. Thomas and Charles H. Cooley. After reviewing all of Znaniecki's works in English, I noted that he makes hardly any mention specifically to Mead other than a journal article by Mead, "The Psychology of Primitive Justice," and a short reference in the appendix of his *Social Actions*, on the general problem of "the process in which the biological individual is made into a cultural personality through the agency of the social milieu...—already implied in Comte's conception of the relation between the biological and the social—was formulated in various terms at the beginning of this century by Dewey, G. Mead, and (W.I.) Thomas.'' (p. 652f). The ironic point in this last citation, to me, is that of the three thinkers he mentions, all were at Chicago concurrently while Znaniecki was also there, yet Mead is the only one cited here with whom he had no personal interaction at all, and despite these remarkable similarities in their philosophical and theoretical formulations on social actions, interaction, *et al.*

Another interesting comparison is that while both had similar interests in what Professor Don Martindale would categorize as "elementarism" (see Martindale's *Personality and Milieu* and *The Scope of Social Theory* published also by Cap and Gown Press), and both were academically and professionally educated in philosophy, yet took somewhat divergent intellectual paths toward their explication and goals for a better understanding of these aspects of human actions. Znaniecki differed from Mead in his academic career by eventually joining the academic and intellectual circles of sociology while Mead remained academically in philosophy while pursuing his ideas and theories about sociological subjects. Thus one might say that both Mead and Znaniecki carried out personally and professionally their different conceptualizations of the final stage of their own "academic act!''

While there were these and other similarities in Znaniecki's and Mead's works, there were also differences as would be expected of such seminal thinkers, even on the same elementaristic subject. I therefore felt that a Foreword to our reissued edition of Znaniecki's *Cultural Reality* by a philosopher who was a scholarly authority on George Mead would be both appropriate and useful in focusing on these key similarities, and the Foreword from Philosophy herein by Professor David L. Miller is a stimulating contribution to this edition. Dr. Miller has not only indicated some of these major theoretical conceptualizations but has also pointed out that this earlier work of Znaniecki has provided the necessary philosophical foundations for the entire discipline of sociology. And the cross-fertilization of ideas and theories of Mead with Znaniecki provide a profound intellectual challenge to sociology that no serious sociologist can ignore!

Because of Professor Roy G. Francis's more recent work we recently published as *Sociology in a Different Key* in which his concept of *Idergy* would be compatible with Znaniecki's (and also with Mead's) work, we have also included a Foreword from Sociology by Dr. Francis. These dual forewords should illuminate the tremendous value of this work to both fields of sociology and philosophy, since *Cultural Reality*, while largely a philosophical treatise has profound implications for sociology, as both Drs. Miller and Francis have indicated.

Indeed, both forewords are contributions in themselves as well as to this reissued edition of Znaniecki's *Cultural Reality*. Although first published 64 years ago, this work is still uniquely relevant and essential to a fuller appreciation not only of Znaniecki's significant contributions to sociology throughout his productive lifetime but also to the basic structure and foundation of the discipline of sociology. Needless to add are the noteworthy contributions to philosophy as well.

Cap and Gown Press is privileged to reissue this new edition of Florian Znaniecki's monumental but too often ignored work with two notable and valuable forewords that comprise a most significant contribution to sociology and to philosophy, and which should further enhance the status of Florian Znaniecki in his adopted discipline and country.

E. Gartly Jaco
Social Science Editor

Selected Bibliography:

Florian Znaniecki

(The complete bibliography of Florian Znaniecki totals 88 items of which 18 (20 percent) were books, half of which were in English. Prior to publishing *Cultural Reality*, Znaniecki had published 5 books and 7 articles, thus suggesting that his move to sociology stimulated an even more highly productive scholarly career.

For a complete listing of the 88 items of Znaniecki's bibliography, see his *Social Relations and Social Roles: The Unfinished Systematic Sociology* below, pp. xx-xxviii; and *Florian Znaniecki: On Humanistic Sociology - Selected Papers*, edited by Robert Bierstedt, Chicago: University of Chicago Press, 1969, pp. 303-309.)

Books in English

Cultural Reality. Chicago: University of Chicago Press, 1919.

The Polish Peasant in Europe and America (with William I. Thomas). Boston: Badger, 1919-1920. Second edition, 2 volumes, New York: Alfred A. Knopf, 1927.

The Laws of Social Psychology. Chicago: University of Chicago Press, 1925.

The Method of Sociology. New York: Farrar & Rinehart, 1934.

Social Actions. New York: Farrar & Rinehart, 1936.

The Social Role of the Man of Knowledge. New York: Columbia University Press, 1940.

Cultural Sciences. Urbana, IL.: University of Illinois Press, 1952.

Modern Nationalities. Urbana, IL.: University of Illinois Press, 1952

Social Relations and Social Roles: The Unfinished Systematic Soc iology. San Francisco: Chandler Publishing Co., 1965.

Foreword from Philosophy

David L. Miller

Professor Emeritus of Philosophy

University of Texas at Austin

Prior to the existence of the Department of Sociology at the University of Chicago (1892), Sociology was a mixture of ideas gathered from the history of philosophy and political theory. Its subject-matter was not clearly defined. The early work of Florian Znaniecki represents a transitional period between, on the one hand, more abstract theoretic speculation and, on the other hand, empirical observation and factual studies of social problems, such as are involved in crime, delinquency, personal adjustments to new situations, and so on. *Cultural Reality* is, therefore, understandably mostly theoretic, philosophical, and deals especially with problems in epistemology and axiology. More specifically, it deals mainly with how systems of thought emerge and how individual members of society, through new experiences and new insights, enter into the business of helping to construct and modify systems already in existence. Through this approach Znaniecki shows how the real is constructed in relation to human cultures. Although Znaniecki was trained in philosophy in Poland and came to the United States in his mid-thirties (cir. 1915), he was influenced tremendously by pragmatism, which was flourishing in America at that time. He says: "Of all my later debts none is so great as the one I owe to pragmatism, of which, in fact, I am inclined to consider myself almost a disciple."(p. iii-iv) Apparently the influence of pragmatism was mainly through his association with John Dewey and W. I. Thomas. It is clear that Znaniecki subscribes to and

uses basic ideas held by William James as well as by George H
Mead. Although he does not mention Mead in *Cultural Reality* an
apparently had little if any personal contact with him, nor does Mea
mention Znaniecki in his writings, there probably was a tremendou
influence by Mead through Dewey and Thomas, who were Mead'
close friends and colleagues. It is clear that later Znaniecki becam
aware of Mead's theory of the social self and role-taking and that h
agreed with Mead, (see Znaniecki, *The Social Role of the Man o
Knowledge*, New York: Columbia University Press, 1940, p. 14). A
any rate, problems discussed in *Cultural Reality* are treated in
manner that is more like Mead's than any other pragmatist. Here
will discuss *Cultural Reality* primarily in relation to Mead's view.

Neither Mead nor Znaniecki are determinists. Both reject environ
mental determinism, social determinism, cultural determinism, and
both would reject technological determinism and socio-biologica
determinism. Behavior of which one is conscious is preceded by
reflective intelligence, by ideas that control overt action. Both me
reject idealism, which assumes that Man is born into a fixed physica
and moral order with objective values given. Both reject rationalism
which assumes that the natural order of events is rational and struct
ured prior to human culture and reflective intelligence. Neither ideal
ism nor rationalism leave room for the cultural construction of system
of thought nor for the social construction of reality. With all pragmat
ists, Znaniecki stresses that in constructing complexes and systems,
we must start with experience. "Experience" is rather difficult to
define. Znaniecki says it "is the presence of elements of a plurality
now and here."(P.27) James speaks of pure experience or of what is
presented to one in a specious present, what is unanalyzed, not known
in terms of descriptive categories, but by direct acquaintance. It is
what C. J. Lewis and Dewey call *the given*. For Mead it is that element
in immediate perception used as a basis for inferring something
beyond here now. It enables one to become aware of the oncoming
distant object, and is used as a means of breaking out of the present. It
is, as for Znaniecki, raw, undifferentiated, uninterpreted data that
belongs to the biography of individual members of society. It does not
at first belong to a complex or to a system; it is non-rational. Speaking
for both Znaniecki and Mead, if the datum—the raw "given"—is to
become rational and systematized, an individual must, through
reflective intelligence, interpret it, and every interpretation, even of
the most meager kind, at once relates the data in a systematic lawful
way to what is not given in immediate experience. To interpret is to

give a *meaning* to what is in experience. If in my immediate exper-
ence there are certain shapes and colors and I say, "I see a hammer,"
I have interpreted the given, I have indicated how what is here now in
experience is related to what is not here now, how it, "the hammer,"
is related to the hand, to nails, to lumber, and so on. I have indicated
how it functions in a complex, and it is now systematized.

Now the word "hammer" is a language symbol, a linguistic gest-
ure, which requires that its meaning be shared by other members of
society. Its meaning is socially and culturally bound. Its meaning for
each and every individual who understands it is rooted in a historical,
cultural, social milieu. Here the influence of Wilhelm Dilthey on both
Znaniecki and Mead is clear. Both studied the works of Dilthey and
Mead studied under Dilthey's direction in Berlin (1890-91). The main
claim of both these men is that whatever structure or rationality the
world has for us is furnished by the human mind. This applies not only
to mores, ways of living and making a living, including all of our social
institutions. It applies as well to the structure of the natural world of
physics, chemistry, cosmology, and so on. The real world, or simply
the real, is socially and culturally constructed. It consists of that
rational order, that system of actual and possible events that results
from an interpretation of the raw data of experience. The bare uninterpreted datum may be called subjective, but when it is rationalized, it
is "objectified;" it becomes objective and real.

As stated above, originally Man was born into an unstructured
world. However, once there are human societies and culture, the
world becomes structured and that structure is inherited by new
members of society. As Znaniecki (with W. I. Thomas, his collaborator
in authoring *The Polish Peasant in Europe and America*)stated in
"The Definition of the Situation," many situations are already defined
for the child by society. But in every culture new situations arise for
which there are no definitions and new kinds of experiences (new
data) happen to individuals, experiences not yet systematized nor
objectified. At such times there are occasions for restructuring the old
system in order to systematize the new data. The (subjective) data
then become rational and real. "By 'reality' we mean here anything
that is the passive object-matter of active thought..." (P. 44) Empirical objects are constructed and reconstructed from personal data. (P.
55) In *The Social Role of the Man of Knowledge* Znaniecki says: "The
definition of a situation raises the practical problem of how to achieve
the purpose under the given conditions." (P. 27) Thus reality must
have two characteristics: it must be given or possibly given in actual

experience, and it must be reconstructed or systematized throug[h] reflection. When a personal datum becomes an object of reflection, [it] has become impersonal content. (P. 61) It has become socialized [or] culturalized and, *ipso facto* rational and objective.

Here we see a close similarity between Znaniecki and Mead. Th[e] process by which data are rationalized and objectified is the same fo[r] both. For Mead, to rationalize or systematize new data (experience[s] exceptional to the accepted laws, habits, mores of the community) i[s] to modify the generalized other in some way, either by deleting ol[d] beliefs or by enriching the system of beliefs in some manner. Thi[s] systematization or rationalization of a datum requires an adjustmen[t] of the new (the datum) to the old system and vice versa.

"The new object must be adapted to the pre-existing reality in orde[r] to become real itself....the pre-existing reality must be adapted to th[e] new object in order to be able to include the latter." (P. 165) I[n] defending this same claim, Mead says: "The new objects enter int[o] relationship with the old...and the old objects enter into new relation[s] with what has arisen [the new]"(*The Philosophy of the Present*, p[.] 47). Hence in the objectivization of any new datum there is a mutua[l] adjustment between it and the old and, in general, between new idea[s] and the old generalized other. Thus there is historical and cultura[l] continuity between the past, the present and the future. Through thi[s] reconciliation of the new idea with the great body of historical know[-] ledge and values, there is an interpretation of the old and the new, [a] break within the continuum, but not of the continuum. But what i[s] objective and real is so only in relation to human society and culture[.] This is a new definition of "objective." Previously most philosopher[s] assumed that if anything exists objectively, it must not depend on any[-] thing outside itself for its existence. For example, George Berkele[y] held that since color depends upon a perceiver for its existence, o[r] exists only in relation to a subject, it is not objective. Both Znanieck[i] and Mead subscribe to what might well be called "objective relativ[-] ism." This has tremendous implications for epistemology, psycholog[y] and sociology. It applies not only to apparently insignificant cases bu[t] also to very important ones. For example, color exists only in relatio[n] to organisms with chromatic vision, but the color green, say, is in th[e] leaf, not in the subject. Environments exist only in relation to livin[g] organisms which in fact confer characters on their environments[.] Wood is food only in relation to such organisms as termites. A knife i[s] what it is only in relation to how it functions in connection with othe[r] things. Data are real only in relation to a system. There are no stimul[i] apart from responses. There can be no self except in relation to society. Nor can we have minds if we do not share beliefs and meanings with others. Data, which are at first personal, become impersonal and objective only in relation to a system in which they are related, usually causally, to other items in the system. Human beings through reflective intelligence confer new meanings on the world and are responsible for modifying old systems and creating new ones, whereby in fact they create new objects. This offers a justification for the claim of the sociology of knowledge: "Symbolization constitutes objects not constituted before, objects which would not exist except for the context of social relationships wherein symbolization occurs." (Mead, *Mind, Self and Society*, p. 78). Znaniecki means by "cultural reality" precisely what Mead means by "social reality." In his later book, *The Social Role of the Man of Knowledge*, Znaniecki deals mainly with the sociology of knowledge thesis and works out in detail what is implicit in his *Cultural Reality*.

Cultural Reality is profound in establishing the philosophic basis for Sociology; there Znaniecki justifies the empirical experiential foundation as essential for methodology in the social sciences. Were the implications of his thesis more fully worked out by him he would, I believe, have come to the same conclusion as did Charles Horton Cooley and Mead about the social nature of the self, the mind, and reflective intelligence. According to Mead, thinking is a conversation between the "I" and the "me," between the "I" and the other, the "I" and the voice of the community which consists of attitudes and beliefs established by culture with its history. "The empirical world is entirely a world of historically evolved objects and can contain nothing but that which has been gradually added to it actually by the active thought of empirically manifested conscious individuals..." (P. 133-4)

Another important claim held in common by Znaniecki and the pragmatists James, Dewey and Mead is that we live in an open universe and an open society of open selves. They were all opposed to the claim by the idealists that all relations are internal and, consequently, as James expressed their view, that we live in a "cut-and-dried" universe, in a "seamless whole." Also they were opposed to the rationalists' claim that the world is pre-structured, thus resulting in determinism and leaving no place for the creativity either of nature or individual members of society. Emergent and creative evolution are subscribed to by both Znaniecki and the pragmatists, and this includes the creativity of individual members of society, which is the source of new ideas, new structures, which in fact confer new characters on both the physical and the social environment. All subscribe to the belief that through symbolic interaction, reflective intelligence and creative thought, Man, by using nature as means, can justifiably hope to improve his lot and to control both one's environment and one's own destiny.

Implicit in *Cultural Reality* is Znaniecki's theory of the place of individual members of society in directing and re-directing the social process. This idea was developed more fully in *The Social Role of the Man of Knowledge*. The problem is this: If, as Znaniecki and the pragmatists claim, the old rigid religious, political and social idealistic and rationalistic systems are inadequate and inapplicable to our contemporary social problems, how are we going to free ourselves from them, and what will be our new method and our new philosophy to be substituted for these restraining systems of thought? In breaking away from old unwarranted doctrines, Znaniecki held that the first step was to acknowledge that the source of new knowledge is based on new experiences had by individual members of society. "The next step was due perhaps to the general exaltation of creative individualism which, since the days of Humanism has gradually permeated all domains of cultural life... Empirical reality gives the scientist inexhaustible material for creative thinking; new theories are products of scientific creativeness." (*The Social Role of the Man of Knowledge*, p. 185.) Znaniecki as well as Mead say in effect: We cannot go to public opinion or to common sense or to the generalized other or to old theories or systems for new knowledge. The innovation must come from an individual. Reflective intelligence, symbolic interaction, is carried on by individuals only. Through the dialectic process of a conversation of the "I" (the personal component of the self) with the "me" (the voice of the community), new hypotheses, new theories, new proposals for social action emerge, and they are relieved of their subjectivity when they are accepted by the group.

Here let us do no more than indicate that this conception of the interrelationship of the individual and society has tremendous implications for a new theory of individual freedom, for individual capacities and responsibilities, for the meaning of individualism, for the correct belief that the "me," the generalized other, is servant to the "I" as the "I" has new ideas, for a new conception of morality and loyalty for a fuller justification of the sociology of knowledge claim, for the responsibility of society to the individual, and, finally, for the claim that the locus of dignity and worth is in individual members of society and for the belief that although we are severally many, we are members of one body. It is in the great historical and contemporary cultural sea of humanity that each of us lives and moves and has her/his being.

Foreword from Sociology

Roy G. Francis

Professor of Sociology

University of South Florida

The second scene of Act II of *Hamlet* contains a remarkable exchange between Hamlet and his friends Rosencrantz and Guildenstern. They have been enlisted by the king and Hamlet is beginning to put some ideas if not plans together. As Polonius exits, they enter and greet Hamlet.

Hamlet: My excellent good friends! How dost thou, Guildenstern? Ah, Rosencrantz! Good lads, How do you both?

Rosencrantz: As the indifferent children of the earth.

Guildenstern: Happy, in that we are not over-happy. On Fortune's cap we are not the very button.

Hamlet: Nor the soles of her shoe?

Rosencrantz: Neither, my lord.

Hamlet: Then you live about her waist, or in the middle of her favors?

Guildenstern: Faith, her private we.

Hamlet: In the secret parts of Fortune? O, most true; she is a strumpet. What's the news?

Rosencrantz: None, my lord, but that the world's grown honest.

Hamlet: Then is doomsday near: but your news is not true. Let me question more in particular: what have you, my good friends, deserved at the hands of Fortune, that she sends you to prison hither?

Guildenstern: Prison, my lord!

Hamlet: Denmark's a prison.

Rosencrantz: Then the world is one.

Hamlet: A goodly one; in which there are many confines, wards and dungeons, Denmark being one o' the worst.

Rosencrantz: We think not so, my lord.

Hamlet: Why, then, 'tis none to you; for there is nothing either good or bad, but thinking makes it so: to me it is a prison.

We may see in this a literary expression of a basic sociological proposition enunciated in W. I. Thomas and Florian Znaniecki's *Polish Peasant*: if something is believed to be true, it is true in its consequences. While phenomenological theory and symbolic interactionism, alike, are predicated on it, its truth is neither immediate nor can be taken for granted.

For one thing, the meaning of "consequences" is obscure. Clearly, one may believe himself to be Superman who can leap off buildings without any personal danger. All that such a belief could do would be to warrant an initial effort; the individual may leap in confidence but the act would not be completed as intended. The proposition does not mean, "wishing will make it so;" it is not a justification for "rationalization" in the psychological sense of substituting credible motives for real ones.

This example is a mere individual instance, and the rule is often held to be *social* in character. Much of phenomenology and symbolic interaction appear to be based on a collective sense of societies acting out shared understandings. In this view, sociological research can be done respecting what people believe without raising the question of what is real: we can study the behavior of church members without determining whether there is or is not a God.

Yet the rule does not warrant a linguistic study of a people's language to determine their view of a limiting external reality. Were this so, one might quip that a people's "ontology recapitulates philology." Though that might prove to be so in certain selected instances, it, too, is misleading. For Znaniecki's *basic* problem is epistemological: how do we know what we know we know?

Until we come to grips with his solution of that fundamental issue, we will continue to make incorrect judgments of his better known works, as *The Method of Sociology, Social Actions,* and *The Laws of Social Psychology,* or try to infer from his use of the term "system" that he is a "functionalist" in the sense represented by Robert Merton and Talcott Parsons.

Positivists and other empiricists who begin their work with hypotheses may never see "analytical induction" as a source of precisely stated hypotheses. The materialist may be baffled and repulsed by his "humanistic coefficient" as some mystic dodge. His *Method*, then, may be ignored by those who need it most.

Similarly with his most widely cited effort, *Social Actions*. Those who subscribe to a deterministic "naturalism," based on a rejection of an idealistic metaphysics, would not accept his insistence on consciousness as integral to the social act. Since a social act takes place in a social situation, the underlying process of human behavior is that which generates a definition of the situation.

Logically, and, it happens, in sequence of publication, Znaniecki's *Laws of Social Psychology*, precedes his *Social Actions*. The latter may in many ways be regarded as an extension of the former, granting the right of an active mind to modify earlier positions. As with so many creative scholars, Znaniecki is best apprehended in the sequence of his effort. For one thing, the enormous struggle, the truly human part of inquiry, is revealed. For another, we get a sense of his intellectual problem and its relation to our own.

This suggestion implies that the person is more important than 'method' if we are to accept and understand critically creative inputs to science. It suggests that scientific method is not an empirical accounting of how the creative scientist proceeds; rather, it is normative, containing those 'oughts' which 'ought to be acted out' if the results obtained are to be accepted by others. Method may tell us how to test and possibly to validate the consequence of a creative intellectual act and neither affirm their place in inquiry nor their place in human affairs.

If this is so, or, to the extent that this is so, Znaniecki's effort, *Cultural Reality*, first published by the University of Chicago Press in 1919, and almost never cited among his contributions, is a critical 'missing link.' Not only does it bear an enormous contribution to sociology and its philosophical underpinnings, and as such is related to many diverse developments in sociology itself, it is a key to understanding much of society itself. That it is requisite to understanding his other works is, of course, interesting—but of validity only to the extent that his other works are held to be significant. My point here is that *Cultural Reality* makes its own dramatic contribution and can generate a new interest in his other writings with a new and clearer understanding of them. That he was a giant in the area of the *Sociology of Knowledge* would be manifest and the relation of that part of sociology to the rest would be more fully appreciated.

Florian Znaniecki was born in Poland in 1882 and died in America in 1958. He first came to the United States during World War I after having started a career in philosophy, with every intention of continuing it there. At that time, W. I. Thomas was seeking a research associate who was conversant in the Polish language; and the two collaborated in producing the classic *Polish Peasant in Europe and America*.

This happenstance was a critical point in Znaniecki's life and in his thinking. He was introduced more fully to sociology than he had been in Europe, and especially the empirical work of Thomas. The research device of the personal document relates closely to his commitment to Man, the human being. Perhaps had Herbert Blumer's question of how much we read into or out of the personal document been addressed as it appropriately can to the questionnaire instead of to letters and diaries, the development of sociology may well have been quite different; certainly, the status of Znaniecki would have been enhanced.

Be that as it may, *Cultural Reality* was published in 1919, and, during the 1920's, Znaniecki returned to Poland. On occasion, he served as visiting professor, as at Columbia University. But he never lost his feelings about Thomas, crediting him with support, help, and, importantly, as a tutor who improved his English writing. However difficult his closely reasoned argument may be to those deficient in critical philosophy, it is in impeccably correct English. Znaniecki was loyal to his benefactor and repeatedly repaid kindness with kindness.

Znaniecki's problem emerged from the intellectual climate of his day. Evolution was clearly the dominant intellectual idea. It pervaded and justified the idea of progress. It underlay the posture of white supremacy, especially on a world-wide scale where "our primitive contemporaries" were seen as anthropological evidence of early Man. Whether seen in the continuity of progress or in the zig-zagging of the dialectic, naturalistic evolution dominated thinking. Certainly, Comte's accounting of the emergent 'positivistic stage' is a special case of that mode of thought.

But the dialectic can be seen in "idealistic" or "materialistic" form. Now, the dialectic is *not* of great moment to Znaniecki; its idealistic or materialistic presuppositions are. In tight syllogistic reasoning, he rejects them both, while acknowledging much of what is attractive about each. The idealistic position, reduced to mere outside criticism, shows how the natural realism moves in a "vicious circle" — that it presumes the validity of the principles of thought it seeks to deduce from its data.

On the other hand, the idealist position simply has not generated a set of studies which flows from its presuppositions. In contrast, "realism" has. Further, in response to idealistic criticism, the naturalist position has generated an internal "things as substance and mathematical functions" system of great consistency. Yet, if it presumes its philosophical underpinnings as factual, it contradicts itself. If, on the other hand, it validates itself by extended application, it must be based on human values which, in turn, must have objective status independent of human evolution.

His objection goes further, and is in his *Method* buttressed by the humanistic coefficient. Here he says,

> Yet it is clear that we cannot accept the naturalistic view of the world without violating most of our highest standards of intellectual, moral, aesthetic, validity, standards which have been reached after innumerable centuries of constructive and critical activity, at the cost of incalculable efforts and sacrifices. (p. 6)

Anticipating Skinner's *Beyond Freedom and Dignity*, Znaniecki notes we might "train ourselves to become satisfied with naturalism by lowering our standards and limiting our aspirations." (*loc. cit.*) He credits idealism with at least being a consistent bulwark against the "self-satisfied intellectual philistinism" to which "scientific realism" inevitably leads.

Znaniecki later carries the attack further by calling attention to the paradox of modern evolution:

> individual consciousness has developed exclusively as instrument of adaptation to objective reality, and it is quite unadapted to objective reality, leading all the time human beings, *with the rate exception of a few modern scientists*, to various absurd notions about reality and to a very irrational behavior. (p.267)

(I added the italics.) Znaniecki recognized that many intellectual conservatives, especially in religious organizations, would find support in his criticism of scientism. This was unfortunate, to him, for that was not the intent nor the problem.

The problem was to account for knowing without committing inquiry to either set of presuppositions. Znaniecki acknowledges, sometimes awkwardly, that there is an empirical reality which in some ways limits mankind. But our knowledge is never the same as that reality. Indeed, it is a part of our experience, and the fact is we are more or less conscious of having experience. Moreover, as creative active creatures, we reflect on our experience. These are the fundamental starting positions of his argument; and he, essentially, dares anyone to deny them.

It is important to note that here he shares a basic predilection of European scholarship: to account for human knowledge. Znaniecki refuses to do this in terms of formulae for logic; for appealing to the 'mind' as either the idealists or the naturalists do. Indeed, he does not really appeal to the mind as such. Instead, he invites us to study human culture.

Znaniecki's definition is denotative; it is consistent with mine which is to say that "culture is the enduring consequences of human behavior." Perhaps it would be more consistent to say "the enduring consequences of the social act." In any event, he stresses cultural relativity and requires us to notice this will require a relativity of values as well as relativity in science itself. He thus notes that culture includes science; and any accounting of culture must account for science as well.

He notes that the human being can be both subject and object, and uses 'subjectivity' basically as meaning that which is private to any individual. It would be better, I think, had he used private instead of subjective as it would have freed him to dismiss a concern about the "concrete empirical" reality.

This can be done by acknowledging that 'things' making up whatever external world there may be can be 'subject' as much as Man can. More importantly, anything is an object to another by virtue of having a relation to it. Thus, a cow makes grass an object by relating to it as food; and the lizard makes the same grass shelter by relating to it in that way. In either case, it has its own subjective status independent of what we say about it or how any other thing may relate to it.

Mutatis mutandis, however, his argument can be generally accepted. In particular, it is important to note the underlying sense of process in Znaniecki's reasoning. Words are carefully defined and restrictively used. Something can be actualized — made actual; something can be objectivized — made objective; something can be realized — made real.

That reality encompassed by the act of knowing is simply the collective experience of it at the time of the putative knowledge. Thus, when the only life-form was that of unicellular organisms, the 'reality' was simply the sum total of their experience. Clearly, they did not experience 'mountains' or 'sunsets' as we say we do.

Though the 'mountain' was not experienced as mountain, Znaniecki does not suggest that some physical mass was not there, that it emerges in the act of being experienced. Whatever it was, its 'mountain-ness' is in how it is experienced by those creatures for whom 'mountain' has meaning. Note, in particular, that 'mountain as meaning' does not pre-exist the experience of mountain; rather there is a processal sequence of experiences and reflections such that as an end-product its mountain-ness is apparent. At some intermediary point there is a "what's-it?" meaning and when that is the case, that is its reality.

The sense of process requires pause. We experience only 'now.' The argument of reality is always located in a particular 'now.' Philosophically, he excludes a concept of "absolute space" and a concept of "absolute time," finding presuppositions about them flaws in either an idealist or realist form. For the key to the process of meaning is conscious reflection: thought. Objective meanings develop as thoughts are connected, such that awareness of a part generates an awareness of the rest.

This requires an interactive process; and that process is such as to generate changed meanings. His examples may begin in the case of extant objective meanings, but since communication of thought is the mechanism both of cultural existence and of objectification, the attempt at communication may result in new connections and hence in new meanings.

Again the element of process is involved. Again the implication is one of 'time.' Though he rejects absolute time, he is aware that it can have culturally objective status: it can have meaning. This he allows for by the notion of *duration* and "succession." There is no time except as experience endures, that is, as experiences succeed each other.

Things are not communicated; thoughts are. Things are not interconnected; thoughts are. Words are not thoughts; they are instruments by which thoughts are expressed, are communicated. It is at this point that the relation between his argument and symbolic interaction becomes clear, and, indeed, necessary. Thus one conceives of the sphere of experience of an individual and a sphere of reflection which are constructions, or will be constructed, from the linking 'here.'

Similar processes obtain for all individuals capable of interaction. Concrete realities are not merely actual, in the sense of participating in the spheres of experience and reflection, but trans-actual in the sense of enabling interperson exchanges. That the basic element is that of thought, not concrete empirical things, makes this possible. Moreover, the trans-actual character, making collective constructions of reality essentially transactions, leads to the conclusion that all knowledge and all systems by which knowledge is understood and exchanged is social.

Znaniecki more than allows for creative thought; he requires it in the process by which any experience takes on meaning. Yet, in his

ormulation of successions, there is relatively little new that can be
brought in any creative act. Much of the past must persist, indeed,
most of the new is presupposed: his thinking tends to require relative
continuity and no essential breaks with the past.

His relation to Frederick Teggart's three processes of history is not
quite apparent. That the element of persistence is contained in historical experience is clear, as is the process of slow change. Teggart's
insistence on 'events' is left more to methodological differences of
differing rates of change rather than an explicit acceptance. Thus
Znaniecki, while rejecting absolute time, maintains a traditional view
of its continuity; but human history reveals instances in which social
reconstructions of institutional patterns have taken relatively little
calendar time.

Thus, we accept, in some sense, the existence of a chaotic and
concrete empirical world. We experience it in moments located here
and now. Successive experiences are partially reconstructed in a sense
of time. Out of the real world we construct actualities which exist in
what becomes historical fact. Man, to Znaniecki both subject and
object, experiences an empirical world but knows the actualized historical one; one does not know ultimate reality. Nor does one impose
philosophical presuppositions of it without leading to contradictions,
either from a realistic or idealistic perspective.

Part of his effort to distinguish between a subjectively real world
and the objective world known through statements about it leads him
to connect the latter to 'history.' History, after all, is indeed experience mankind has reflected about. Thus he says,

> The continuity in duration of the concrete empirical world is thus historical,
> not natural; is a continuity of growth by the agency of creative thought, not a
> continuity of changes determining one another.(p. 121)

After all, to Znaniecki, the world of experience is a chaotic one, a
buzzing sea of what psychologists would call stimuli. A reasoning
reflective, if not a rationally ordered, mind strives to make sense of it.
The collective judgment of a society is *imposed* on the world, not
created by it.

His ultimate intention appears to place applied (social) science in a
context of values. His argument contains the same structure as he
sees in the general process of knowledge as becoming. He carefully
develops a point and attaches a commanding label to it. Each such
discussion leads to a broader formulation, resting on, if not implied
by, what has gone before.

Moving from a generalized accounting of knowing to an analysis leading to a discussion of the social situation, he notes, remembering the use he makes of 'objectivity,'

> The objectivity of biological or geographical phenomena is an objectivity of things and processes; the objectivity of social phenomena is an objectivity of rules. (p. 287)

Rules and the systematic organization of rules become the key to his analyses of cultural reality.

The locus of every act, including the individual pondering the application of scientific knowledge, is in a situation. While we can identify the aim of the situation and distinguish it from the instrument, the difference is more analytic than real. In the natural world the future cannot be *given*, for that requires things to exist prior to their being; but in the social world, unless the situation is organized in advance of the action, the result cannot be the required one. Therefore, the process by which situations become defined is the definitive one and the mechanism by which a society imposes order on a chaotic world.

The interactive and reflective process by which agreements are made regarding the aim and the instrument by which the aim is to be realized is the process of defining the situation. Indeed, a situation is defined when such a determination has been made. The interconnected decisions and subsequent rules of all constituent parts of the situation (including how concrete individuals get involved in it) constitute a scheme. Once a scheme, as a set of practical rules, is determined, the situation is defined "once and forever," all essential elements of the intended action are also set. In a subsequent "Here and Now," however, a reconstruction may well begin.

Two very important points must be noted. One is his insistence on practicality, on things leading to practice, to actual concrete historical behavior. The other is that rule-making is a form of thinking and "the mere thinking of a certain organization of objects is already organizing these objects"(p. 196). Further, the selection is that of a creative act, no more imposed by natural conditions "than is the artistic style of a painting determined by its object-matter"(p. 287).

Znaniecki is nothing if he is not a pragmatist. Yet his pragmatism is not the simple-minded kind that leads to situational morality. He refuses to abandon those fundamental human values—"our highest standards of morality"—as mere conventions. To him pragmatic utility is not merely of the moment; there must be more durability an that. The question of values becomes his paramount concern. "Pragmatic" leads to practice; and practice is a form of human ehavior. Everything ends up in the world of human conduct. His eory of values and his theory of knowledge is relative in substantive ntent, depending upon the process of the construction and re-con- ruction of reality.

> A thing, a practical situation, a scheme, a system of schemes, a scientific idea, a theory, the entire body of science, may become an aesthetic, a hedonistic, a religious, an economic, a political object, or all of these, by becoming the object-matter of various individual activities. (p. 341)

his leads both to his noting that, therefore, each increase in rational- y is correlated with an increase of historical chaos—witness the nsequence of the computer and of programs to retrieve programs to trieve or process data—but to the question of values. For know- dge, the social construction of reality, is the stuff out of which bsequent behavior emerges. While it may become an "aesthetic bject," that is simply one way to use knowledge. All knowledge is to e used.

His bridge between accounting for the apparent appeal to values by dividuals and collectivities and a theory of behavior is to introduce e concept of "appreciation." Since the consequence of actual eflection about historical objects is not the same as those objects but omething imposed on them, each object becomes or leads to a posit- e or negative appreciation. Man, Znaniecki presumes, is a normat- ely judging creature as well as a reflective one.

He differs from George Mead in his understanding of values. To Mead, a value is the character of an object to satisfy a human interest; o Znaniecki that would be presupposing the consequence of an inter- ction. Thus Znaniecki holds that the objective reality is by itself either positive or negative. By using it for some active purpose—if nly mental (e.g., scientific)—we make it positive or negative depend- ng upon how it aids or impedes the fulfillment of the purpose.

What happens, Znaniecki says, is that as a situation becomes lefined, the system of schemes (or a collection of systems) making it p become dogmatic assertions of what ought to be done; at least the ssertion is implied if not always articulated. And,

> every dogmatic system of schemes, political, economic, moral, aesthetic, religious, theoretic, is empirically used as a standard of appreciation by all the individuals who accept it as the basis of the practical organization of their experiences in a certain line. (p. 349)

Thus, objects are not good or bad as they give pleasure or pain rather, they provoke pleasure or pain from the intentionally construct- ed scheme invoked at the moment of action.

Here Znaniecki comes close to a major difficulty: the object-matter may be accepted as a friend but turn out to be a mugger. But "if something is believed to be true, it is true in its consequences" holds only for the most immediate here and now. A subsequent 'here and now' may be materially different. The judgment, "whoops! I erred!" would be a reconstruction of the later, not the initial, moment.

His scheme embraces the individual act. More importantly, and more to the issue of modern sociology seeking to make academic sense of "applied" work, his argument is mandatory reading. Nothing appears to be more akin to his sense of the situation, how it is defined, and how a scheme of action is imposed than in the sense of "scientific method." His argument of how the plan can be implemented, on the one hand illustrating the process of research, illustrates as well what Rural Sociologists have determined in their studies of changing farm practices. It is a virtual handbook required of those who would go beyond theoretic sociology and speak of its use.

When that happens, Znaniecki points out, scientific thought be- comes a part of a system of schemes and inevitably meets the "problem of appreciation." This goes far beyond the question of values regarding the conditions which generated the putative use of sociology; it includes the contribution of sociology as something in itself which must be judged in terms of the larger scheme of action.

Cultural Reality is an imposing *tour de force*. It is not a book of easy reading. The subtleties of his syllogistic argument are likely to be missed by those who pride themselves on speed reading. One must continuously take care not to impose one's own definition of terms on Znaniecki. "Words," Hans Gerth used to tell us, "are like tooth- brushes: we do not like to put other people's words in our own mouth." However, if role-taking is indeed the basis of *verstehen*, then to read Znaniecki, one must be Znaniecki. The momentary difficulty is worth the effort.

There appears to be no segment of contemporary sociology which would not find some significant contribution in this book. That phenomenologists, symbolic interactionists and ethnomethodologists virtually depend on his careful philosophical criticism is almost appar- ent. Those functionalists who, following Durkheim, are serious in understanding their own argument would do well to recall that to Durkheim, culture's basic property was that it was ideational and ence internalizable. For them, Znaniecki's version of social institutions is a bridge between 'structure' and how one becomes "like the system."

For those who recognize the significance of the social process of election, his argument on communication, requiring each individual at any moment of action to have the logical integrity of his accumulated past, serves as a bridge. This part of his argument is directly related to social change, and carries with it implications for those who seek statistical verification of an argument. As with Durkheim's articulated concept of "cohesion," Znaniecki's discussion of change implied that the process of defining a situation is one in which variance is reduced. And this can be tested, if the constituent parts can be measured, by an F-ratio of variances independently obtained.

For those who feel that the proper study of Man is man, *Cultural Reality* is a must. He simply refuses to surrender ultimate human values. While our *knowledge* of them flows from our use of an organization of scheme, since he accepts an existential real world independent of our knowledge of it, he invites a continuing reconstruction of our sense of values. Here it must be remembered, he holds that values must have an existence independent of their position in evolution, or they may not be proper standards of judgment. Thus, he implies, the quest for values is as real as any other part of the quest for knowledge.

But he also holds that knowledge is and must be continuously reconstructed. And this is as true of value statements as it is of any other collective judgment. Thus he does not stand pat with the entrenched moralists, no more than he does with classical "idealists" or "natural realists." Rather, Znaniecki takes his stand with mankind, who are, individually and collectively, creatively reflective and valuing creatures.

He dares to dream; and though his is not the yellow brick road to the Land of Oz, he invites us to walk, if not to dream, with him.

PREFACE

The present study of cultural reality constitutes the first part of a general introduction to the philosophy of culture, to be supplemented soon by a second part bearing upon the fundamental principles of creative activity. As will be clear from the first chapter of the present volume, in calling the body of knowledge for which this introduction intends to lay the formal foundations a "philosophy of culture," I do not mean to say that it is a mere branch of philosophy in general, but to indicate by this term a standpoint and a method applicable to the entire field of research which has belonged or can belong to philosophy. This field is incomparably wider than, not only scientists, but even professional philosophers are now inclined to admit. There can be hardly a more paradoxical situation found in the history of knowledge than that of modern professional philosophy, which is slowly waning for lack of material, whereas at no other period was there such a wealth and variety of ready materials at hand.

We find the question quite seriously discussed whether philosophy has or not a subject-matter of its own, while innumerable concrete problems, as vital, as positive, as important, as those which any theoretic discipline ever had to deal with, are waiting to be adequately formulated and solved by a well-organized and self-conscious philosophy. We see philosophers trying to put an artificial life into old systems, or attempting to synthetize the ready results of special sciences, or reducing their discipline to a mere investigation of the methodological and ontological presuppositions of these sciences, or even resigning all unity of philosophical purposes and methods and dissolving philosophy into a multiplicity of partly philosophical, partly scientific or practical, monographs.

Things have gone so far that philosophers are almost ashamed of their profession and seriously try to justify the fact that they are still doing some philosophical work by limiting this work to what in their opinion may be directly useful to the scientist or practitioner. They do not seem to realize that in the division of scientific labor each branch of knowledge can be useful to others only if it has an independent significance of its own; if, instead of merely reflecting about the problems of other sciences, it can by its own power draw from our empirical world—the object-matter of all theory—problems which no other discipline can state and solve. But philosophy is officially denied such a power; it is supposed to have no vitality of its own. Interesting illustrations of this view can be found in the attitude of philosophical faculties. Thus, the Faculty of Paris decided about ten years ago that students of philosophy who intended to do systematic (not only historical) philosophical work should be advised to take a degree in mathematical and physical sciences. A similar attitude prevailed in Vienna under the influence of Mach, in Cracow where a prominent biologist was appointed associate professor of philosophy, and at many German universities, particularly in Leipzig. The same lack of confidence in philosophy shows itself in the emphasis that in America is put upon psychology as a discipline which, having more positive problems than it can embrace at its present stage, may give the poor philosopher who lacks material something to work upon.

While such conditions prevail in professional philosophy, simultaneously, an incalculable amount of philosophical work is being done by men who profess to be scientific specialists and classify their philosophical theories as belonging to the domains of their respective special disciplines. The literature of sociology, psychology, political and economical sciences, history, philology, aesthetic criticism, contains not only fragments of works, but whole voluminous works whose proper place is not at all indicated by their classification; for whatever may be the field from which they take their raw materials, their methods of research, the content of their concepts, the types of their systematization are certainly not scientific, but comply with philosophical standards, though often rather imperfectly.

The chief reason why such theories are not definitively excluded from the domains of the respective sciences is the insufficient methodical development of the latter; the sciences of culture have not yet elaborated and applied their criteria of scientific validity as perfectly and consistently as the sciences of nature have done in their own field. In fact, in the measure in which the consciousness of scientific aims and methods progresses in the domain of cultural knowledge, we see a growing tendency to get rid of all influences popularly called "metaphysical," just as natural science did long ago. This tendency has been for more than one generation manifest in psychology and has since the beginning of the present century shown itself very clearly in sociology and economical science.

But the interesting point is that the non-scientific types of problematization, justly excluded from these sciences, do not lose their vitality as did most of the old "philosophy of nature" when supplanted by positive scientific investigations. They return continually, impose themselves upon the attention of both the theorist and the practical man. We see, for instance, innumerable particular and general problems formulated in terms of values—moral, aesthetic, religious, political, intellectual, hedonistic—surviving all scientific analysis of valuations, reappearing sometimes most unexpectedly in the midst of purely scientific researches, disturbing their methodical perfection, and impairing the positive validity of their results. We find the tendency to put concrete problems from the standpoint of liberty and creativeness persisting in spite of the extension of the principle of causality to all fields of activity, and frequently influencing even men who want to remain pure scientists. And so on. The very progress of scientific method in the domain of culture limits the possibilities of its application; by showing how to put scientific problems, it shows that there are problems in this domain which, however vital, cannot be scientific, and thus forces us to recognize the existence and the importance of a completely different problematization.

It is certainly time to proceed to a more critical and systematic elaboration and application of this non-scientific methodological standpoint which we continually take, intentionally or unintentionally, with regard to the cultural phenomena. This will help cultural sciences in their efforts to reach a perfect scientific method free from disturbing factors, and will permit us to supplement their investigations by a completely different but equally necessary philosophical type of studies. For the standpoint which cultural sciences have to exclude is precisely that which has most commonly been accepted by philosophy as its own. Logic, ethics, aesthetics, often even metaphysics, have been essentially concerned with problems of values, and the acceptance of freedom or creation in some form or other, as against the exclusively causal scientific viewpoint, has been a characteristic feature of most of the great philosophical systems. Modern philosophy is conscious that these are the two points to which its existence is attached, that in the domain of values and in that of creative freedom there is something left for it to do independently and outside of science. The two relatively most vital philosophical schools are precisely those which took these two points respectively for their fundamental object-matter—the philosophy of values in Germany, with Windelband, Rickert, Münsterberg, in some measure perhaps also Meinong, Husserl, and the American new realists, though their terminologies are different; and the philosophy of creation in France, with Renouvier, Guyau, Bergson, and his followers. And pragmatism, which is rather a current of thought than a school, is continually, even if unsystematically, working on both of these problems.

The great mistake which modern philosophy committed in this line was to treat the problems of values and of creative freedom in their general formulation as ultimate and self-sufficient, instead of taking them only as starting-points of future investigations, as mere problems of philosophical methodology. All a philosopher usually attempted to do was to show that there are values or that there is creative freedom in spite of science which ignores or rejects both. Sometimes he tried to classify and define the fundamental types of values or to indicate where and how creative freedom manifests itself in the world; with this, he thought his task accomplished, the philosophical problem of values, the philosophical problem of creation, all solved. Accustomed to the fact that philosophy in the technical sense of the term has progressively limited itself to the most abstract, formal problems, he could hardly realize that there was in the subject-matter of his study a new opening by which his discipline might pass from the narrow inclosure of formal discussions into the wide, inexhaustible field of concrete empirical materials.

The importance of the problems of values and of creative freedom does not lie merely in the fact that they permit us to believe in something more than scientific data and laws. Their significance for philosophy is exactly parallel to that which the problem of causality has for science. They are simply problems of philosophical method. In putting and solving them philosophy might have reached something incomparably more important than a few more or less new metaphysical conceptions: it could have critically established a methodological foundation for future investigations, thanks to which it might have begun to develop an independent, empirical, philosophical knowledge, bearing on the same raw materials as science, but obtaining from them, by a radically different and original treatment, an indefinitely growing and systematically organized body of theoretically and practically vital truths, which science by the necessary limitation of its standpoint can never reach. This possibility was occasionally foreseen by some philosophers. Thus, Bergson has thought of a philosophical and yet empirical knowledge supplementing science, but his mystical doctrine of intuition and his narrow conception of logic preclude any possibility of future development. The pragmatists, particularly Dewey, had at one time a much clearer conception of what might be done in this line; but their lack of faith in philosophy in the technical sense of the term and their mistrust of systematization have prevented them up to now from developing organically and consistently this empirical philosophy which their principles seem to require, and makes them often leave to non-philosophical disciplines empirical problems which can be attacked only by a thoroughly and critically elaborated, completely original, philosophical method.

The work of which the present book constitutes the first part was originally, years ago, meant to be nothing but a methodological introduction to a philosophy of cultural activities to which I was led by a study of some general historical and sociological problems. But new difficulties arose at every step of this methodological investigation, and with every difficulty the field widened. The main point was how to reconcile the conceptions of reality as a world of practical values and of thought as empirically creative and yet objectively valid human activity, which an adequate philosophical treatment of cultural problems seemed to demand, with the naturalistic view of reality prevalent in science, and the idealistic view of thought found not only in systems of philosophical idealism, but in almost all classical logic. For at first I did not even dare to touch these most fundamental problems in their general significance and hoped to construct a methodological viewpoint sufficient for the purpose of what I thought then a special branch of philosophical investigation, without going too far into ontological and logical discussions. This hope proved vain; it became more and more evident that a philosophy of culture, if it wanted to take seriously and thoroughly into consideration the empirical problems concerning cultural values and activities, had to revise the whole traditional philosophical problematization. I tried to clear the ground for my methodology in several philosophical monographs published in Polish (*The Problem of Values in Philosophy*, Warsaw, 1910; *Humanism and Knowledge*, Warsaw, 1912; *The Significance of Evolution*, Warsaw, 1914) and a series of articles between 1909 and 1915 in the *Philosophical Review* of Warsaw. The results of these studies seemed to indicate, first, that a philosophy of culture, if fully and adequately treated, must become a complete empirical theory of all activity in its bearing upon reality, and must thus include the totality of the subject-matter of all existing philosophical disciplines and much more besides; secondly, that the methodology of a philosophy thus conceived must be based on a systematic and complete treatment of the formal characters which all empirical reality acquires as object-matter of activity and of those which all empirical activity assumes when taking reality as its object-matter—a treatment which, unlike most of the existing philosophical theories of reality and active thought, would not pretend to give a self-sufficient and complete ontology and logic, a body of ultimate truths about the world, but merely to prepare the formal ground for future studies. According to this plan, I published in 1915 in the American *Philosophical Review* an article, "The Principle of Relativity and Philosophical Absolutism," which outlines the field of philosophy from the standpoint of the universal relativity of all values, and have been trying since to reconstruct for the fifth or sixth time my methodological introduction on a wider ground than before.

I give all these biographical details here in order to explain and to justify the imperfection of the present work, of which I am painfully aware. The reader has the right to expect of a study that attempts to construct a new positive formal foundation of our whole view of the world a much more exhaustive treatment of problems, a more perfect systematic organization, and a clearer exposition than this book can offer. But it would require many more years to raise it to the highest philosophical standards, while I am more eager than ever to pass from introductory investigation to the main work. I hope to be able to develop during the latter a part at least of the points which have been only suggested in this introduction; in particular, I have postponed almost all historical and critical discussion of other philosophical theories, past and present, in order to treat them more completely and adequately when studying in detail theoretic activities as historically manifested in systems of science and philosophy. Meanwhile, I hope that the kind reader will hold me justified in publishing this book as it is and will supplement himself such deficiences as he may find in it.

There is also an objective consideration which emboldens me to proceed at once with the publication of the present work instead of endeavoring to make it more perfect from the standpoint of traditional philosophical criteria. Our most pressing intellectual need at the present moment is an adequate knowledge of the cultural world as a basis of a rational technique for the practical control of the immediate future of our civilization. The Great War has, apparently, opened a new historical epoch which promises to be more eventful than any period of the past. The traditional lines of cultural evolution are changing with an astonishing rapidity; new currents are appearing whose direction we are unable to calculate and whose power we only begin to suspect. Do these changes imply some wonderful future progress or are they the symptoms of an incipient disorganization similar to that of the

Dark Ages? The old and established types of cultural investigation give us no methods for the understanding of the present in its bearing upon the future. Nor do they help us to decide what we should do in order to influence this future in accordance with our aspirations, in order to incorporate our highest ideals into the cultural reality which is evolving under our very eyes. It seems to me, therefore, the duty of all intellectual workers to concentrate their efforts for years to come upon problems whose solution may give the statesman and the moral reformer, the practical economist and the educator, the religious idealist and the artist, instruments with which to foster cultural progress. In the light of this emergency, it is evident that many of the traditional problems and methods of philosophy, while preserving their importance as historical facts, products of theoretic activity, should be systematically discussed and utilized at the present moment only in so far as they have a bearing on the construction of a critical methodical foundation of cultural studies. If therefore I have not given in this work as much attention to certain issues as their deep elaboration in modern philosophy seems to demand, it is because I feel that they should be temporarily subordinated to a more vital task.

I do not hope therefore to contribute much to the solution of the already defined technical, philosophical problems. My highest hope is that the philosophy of which this book is the necessary starting-point will, when developed, be of some significance for the progress of culture. If it is, only a small part of the merit will be mine, for I know that I am only continuing to develop viewpoints for which I am in a large measure indebted to others. Among our intellectual obligations the greatest are usually those which we owe to the ideals we have accepted in our youth; the primary source of the views on which I am trying to build a philosophy of culture lies, therefore, in Polish historical idealism. Of all my later debts none is as great as the one I owe to pragmatism, of which, in fact, I am inclined to consider myself almost a disciple. I shall not be surprised if the masters disown me, since I cannot share most of the established pragmatic views on special philosophical problems, such as the biological conception of activity, the instrumental definition of truth, and several others. It seems to me that the general current of thought which pragmatism has started is too powerful, too wide, and too deep to be regulated in advance by the few formulae already accepted in the schools. To become an orthodox pragmatist now would mean to sacrifice the spirit for the letter. On the other hand, though it was not only useful but necessary for such a movement to start by a sharp criticism of traditional, dead doctrines and to avoid in the beginning any far-reaching attempts of systematization, the time has come when criticism should give place to positive construction, and instead of scattered, fragmentary, often conflicting, monographical sketches, a self-consistent, internally unified, organically growing body of new knowledge should be created.

While speaking of my obligations, I am glad of this opportunity to express my deepest gratitude to Dr. William I. Thomas, who, from the very first day of my arrival in this country, has given me invaluable assistance in intellectual and practical matters. I am greatly indebted to him for the training in sociological investigation which I have acquired by collaborating with him, and for the help which I have continually received from him in trying to master the English language, in particular for his kindness in correcting the most important of the many stylistic imperfections of the present work. I must also thankfully acknowledge the large part which my wife had in the definitive formulation of this work by discussing critically almost every important point and offering numerous positive suggestions, particularly for chapters ii and iii, some sections of which without her help would be almost unreadable.   F. Z.

CONTENTS

CHAPTER I

CULTURALISM

The predominant feature of intellectual evolution during the last hundred and fifty years has been the growing separation and struggle between realism, representing the relatively new and common ground of all sciences of nature, and idealism, representing partly a survival, partly a development of the fundamental points of that view of the world which was achieved by the synthesis of mediaeval religious doctrines and ancient philosophy. And—a curious historical problem— the faction which, from the standpoint of logical consistency, was and is decidedly and irremediably in the wrong has been continually victorious in this struggle, has gradually wrestled away from its opponent its whole domain, appropriated all the vital intellectual issues, and left to the spoiled, though not subjugated, enemy nothing but the empty and practically useless consciousness of his eternal right.

It is not difficult to see how this process went along. The triumph of realism, in any sphere of investigation, has not consisted in a successful logical demonstration of the validity of its claims and methods, but simply in an actual growth of the number and importance of the concrete particular problems which it set and solved, without concerning itself much as to the philosophical justification of the standpoint assumed in these problems. The defeat of idealism, in any sphere of investigation, was not due to a logical inferiority of its general philosophical doctrine, but simply to the fact that it failed to develop a large and continually growing body of positive empirical knowledge based on idealistic premises.

Thus realism grew stronger with every step and no efforts could prevent idealism from losing ground continually in the wide field of intellectual life covered by empirical science, and popular reflection. Every particular realistic science, in its beginnings usually despised by idealistic philosophy for its lack of logical perfection, became more and more self-consistent as it developed, and some of these sciences have reached a level where idealism itself is forced to treat them as models of systematic construction. And it can scarcely deny to them this tribute, because it has in its past days emphasized the importance and the rational perfection of those very *organa* which realistic sciences use in systematizing their investigations, i.e., the logic of things-substances and the mathematical theory of functions. Idealism has become thus unable to attack the internal organization of realistic sciences; it can criticize only their foundations, their explicit or implicit epistemological and metaphysical presuppositions. Of course, as long as a realistic science claims an absolute validity for its foundations, idealistic criticism has an easy task in showing the absurdity of such claims, in demonstrating, for example, that the assumption of an absolute objectivity of geometrical space is self-contradictory· or that the reduction of all sensual qualities to movements of matter is not a substitution of reality for illusion but merely an expression of all kinds of sensual data in terms of one particular kind of sensual data, a combination of certain sensations of sight with certain sensations of touch and of the muscular sense. If, however, a realistic science begins to base its claims not on the abstract philosophical justification of its presuppositions, but on the practical applicability of its results; if it concedes that its assumptions cannot be demonstrated a priori but that they show themselves valid a posteriori by the growing control of reality which they permit, the attacks of idealism lose much of their force. For in this line also idealism itself has unconsciously strengthened in advance the position of realism by bringing forth, in order to defend traditional religion and morality against realistic theoretic analysis, the idea that practical claims can have an objective validity of their own, independent of theoretic criteria; it can therefore hardly reject now the test of practical applicability to which realistic science appeals.

This is not all. During the first three centuries of its development scientific realism was practically unable to reach any general view of the world. Not only did a large part of experience remain for a long time outside of realistic investigations, but the connection between such investigations as were pursued in various sciences of nature was not close enough to become the foundation of a consistent realistic conception of the entire empirical world. The rise of a realistic psychology and sociology on the one hand, the doctrine of natural evolution on the other, obviated these difficulties and led to modern naturalism—the most comprehensive and consistent realistic doctrine ever reached. The application of positive realistic methods to individual consciousness and to social institutions brought within the scope of naturalistic science a domain from which idealism drew most of its materials; at the same time the theory of evolution not only gave a general foundation on which all sciences of nature could hope to attain their metaphysical unity, but bridged over the chasm between man as thinking subject and his object, the inorganic and organic natural reality which he studies and controls. By putting concrete problems concerning the development of human consciousness out of the elementary needs of organic life and up to its highest rational manifestations, modern naturalism claims to have actually and definitively incorporated man into nature. Reason itself, as manifested in science, is then only a continuation of the natural evolution of the animal world, the latest stage of adaptation of living beings to their environment; and all the forms of thinking on which idealism constructs its systems are products of the natural reality and, as instruments of adaptation, dependent both on their natural object-matter and on the natural organization of the living beings who use them.

On the other hand, indeed, idealism preserves some of the old arguments which enable it to prove that the naturalistic conception of the world as a whole moves in a vicious circle. It is clear that natural evolutionism presupposes for its own validity the ideal validity of those same principles of thought and standards of practical valuation which it tries to deduce genetically from natural reality. Ideas may be, indeed, instruments of real adaptation of the living being to its environment, but only if used not as realit es but as ideas referring to reality and logically valid or invalid in this reference. The system of ideas constituting the evolutionistic theory itself certainly claims to be a valid *theory of reality* and not a mere *part of reality*. The entire content of evolutionism as a rational system is subjected to ideal criteria, to these very criteria which it wants to deprive of their ideality. In the measure in which it succeeds in reducing thought to biological functions it will make itself and this very reduction devoid of objective significance; that is, its claim of objective significance for its form proves it is false in its content.

An analogous reasoning can be used with regard to the practical test of natural science. If this test is to be objectively valid, it presupposes objective standards for appreciating practical activity as successful. But since the practical test is by hypothesis independent of theory, we cannot take as the standard of success the adaptation of the active being to its natural environment, for the conception of the active being as a living being, the conception of natural environment, and the whole conception of adaptation have been reached by a purely theoretic study subjected to criteria of theoretic validity. Therefore, the standards of practical success must be sought in the sphere of practical human values, and they can guarantee the objectivity of the practical test only if they are themselves objective as values, not merely as existential data; that is, if they are not merely reactions of living beings to their environment, as the biologist in his character of a theorist conceives them, but objective ideal values as the moralist, the artist, the religious man, etc., assumes them. The practical success of the applications of the natural sciences can be thus a proof of the objective bearing of these sciences as instruments of adaptation only if we accept, besides theoretic reason, some objective values, of the type of the moral values of Kantianism, which are not the products of biological evolution and by which the practical results of our activity can be measured. If there are no objective values independent of those produced during the biological evolution of the human race, the test of naturalism by its practical applicability has no objective significance.

But however binding the criticism which idealism opposes to the theory of natural evolution, and we have here merely schematized the two central arguments among the many found in idealistic literature, its weak point is that it has no positive doctrine to oppose to it which can solve the problems put by the theory of evolution. While naturalism has made an enormous progress and undergone deep changes during the last fifty years, idealism has remained on the same ground on which it stood in the beginning of the past century; instead of nature as a dynamic and changing process it is still facing nature as a changeless substance or a system of substances, as it did when the timeless evolution of the Hegelian Idea seemed the limit of dynamism. Is idealism merely unwilling to enter into the heart of evolutionistic problems, or is it not rather essentially incapable of doing it? The fact is that it has lost all touch with modern science, that the present scientific issues are unable to move it, and that Platonism, mediaeval realism, Kantianism, and Fichteanism still continue to be revived and accepted as if nothing had happened since their first promulgation, as if our intellectual life were the same as a hundred, a thousand, or even two thousand years ago.

Yet it is clear that we cannot accept the naturalistic view of the world without violating most of our highest standards of intellectual, moral, aesthetic, validity, standards which have been reached after innumerable centuries of constructive and critical activity, at the cost of incalculable efforts and sacrifices. We cannot voluntarily and consciously resign ourselves to a doctrine which in the light of theoretic criticism proves irremediably self-contradictory; we cannot voluntarily and consciously accept as guide of our moral life a view which considers free creation a psychological illusion and proclaims the impossibility of bringing into the world anything that is not already virtually included in it; we cannot admit an interpretation of our aesthetic life which treats it as nothing but a play. Above all, we cannot consciously agree to look at these our highest standards as mere by-products of natural evolution, instruments of adaptation of one particular species of living beings to their natural environment, having no other objective validity than the one derived from the success of this adaptation; we cannot resign ourselves, in spite of all realistic argumentation, to be nothing but insignificant and transient fragments of a whole which, while transcending us infinitely, remains almost unaffected by our existence, absolutely indifferent toward our claims, and absolutely inaccessible to our valuations. We might, indeed, train ourselves to become satisfied with naturalism by lowering our standards and limiting our aspirations, forgetting the general problems of life and knowledge for the sake of the many and various particular problems which confront us at every step of our personal and social activity. Such a course would be identical to that which Pascal prescribed against religious doubts by advising the doubter to follow in detail the ceremonies and prayers of the church instead of raising any fundamental problems of dogma and morality. Or we might, like James, accept as a matter of personal belief any doctrine we need to supplement, for our individual use, the deficiencies of naturalism, an attitude which has a curious analogy with the attitude of the workman who, dissatisfied with his everyday job, instead of trying to learn a wider and more interesting speciality, supplemented the monotony of his work by the excitement of day-dreams.

However insufficient and lacking in concreteness and vitality the idealistic philosophy may be, it certainly has the merit of being a permanent protest against these two extremes of powerless pessimism and of self-satisfied intellectual philistinism to which the naturalistic view of the world alternatively leads. Weak, inefficient, and unfruitful when brought into connection with concrete problems of actual life, idealism preserves nevertheless some vestige of its old importance in the abstract domain of the highest theoretic and practical standards, and this explains the attraction which it still has for all those who, while realizing the vitality of naturalism in particular fields and not wishing to intoxicate themselves with some rationally unjustifiable faith, still refuse to resign those aspirations of which Greek and mediaeval philosophy were the expression, and cling desperately to what is left of the old values in modern philosophic abstraction.

This is, or rather was still a few years ago, the predominant situation of our intellectual life. The opposition of idealism and naturalism has completely absorbed the attention of scientists and philosophers. More than this: it has been carried over into practical fields and more or less consciously identified with the fight between social and religious conservatism and synthetic traditionalism on the one hand, and progressive radicalism and analytic rationalism on the other.

By one of the most curious failures of observation ever found in history, neither the theorists nor the men of practice involved in this great struggle have ever noticed how, along-side with the gradual development, unification, and systemati-zation of naturalism, there had grown slowly, but ceaselessly, an independent domain of concrete theoretic and practical problems at least as wide as that covered by natural science and technique, but remaining completely outside of the entire opposition of idealism and realism and implying a view of the world entirely different from both. We mean, of course, the domain of investigations and practical problems concerning human culture in its historical past and its actual development —politics, economics, morality, art, language, literature, religion, knowledge. Certain schools of psychology and sociology have tried indeed to reduce cultural evolution to natural evolution; but, as a matter of fact, this reduction remains only a postulate and, as we shall see in detail later on, the essential and objectively significant side of cultural life remains forever inaccessible to naturalistic science. On the other hand, certain idealistic currents appealed to history for help in determining the content and the meaning of the absolute values which they exposed and defended; but they did not see that the historical and absolutistic standpoints are irreconcilable by their very logical essence and that to search in history for a justification of any absolute values is simply self-contradictory.

We can, however, hardly wonder that neither the realistic scientist nor the idealistic philosopher sees the full significance of the great problem of cultural evolution, since even those who are most immediately interested in this problem—the historians and the active and conscious builders of culture—scarcely begin to realize that their work has a much more general and fundamental intellectual meaning than a mere description of some past cultural happening or a mere modi-fication of some present cultural situation. The reason is easy to understand. Whatever new and original contribu-tions the cultural workers ever brought to our methods of studying and controlling the world were produced and offered in connection with particular problems put within the limits of special cultural sciences or special fields of cultural practice. Thus the wider meaning of each such contribution was seldom seen at once and the fundamental unity of standpoint underlying all cultural sciences and reflective cultural practice was very slow to develop, slower even than in natural sciences and technique, for as a matter of fact, there has always been a more far-going specialization in the sciences of culture than in the sciences of nature and the intellectual connection between special problems has been therefore more difficult to establish in this field. Moreover, the sciences of culture, for many reasons, have been so far unable to reach the same relative degree of methodical perfection as the sciences of nature, and this has prevented them from becoming as conscious of their own significance as the latter. Finally, as we shall have many opportunities to see, the entire logical and metaphysical foundation of both natural science and idealistic philosophy represents a more primary stage of intellectual activity than that required by cultural science, so that the statement of problems of knowledge in terms of natural realism or idealism seems so much simpler and easier in this relatively early period of theoretic evolution in which we live as to appear almost self-evident and to exclude any attempt to transgress its limitations.

But if all these reasons explain why the theoretic implications of cultural sciences have been scarcely noticed and intellectual interest has concentrated during the past century and a half on the various phases of the idealism-realism controversy, no reason can justify at present a continuation of this policy. Naturalism has reached the summit of its power with the theory of evolution and, while always still able to extend its presuppositions and methods to new data, it can no longer produce, at the present moment at least, any fundamentally new standpoints; it may still change in detail but

not in its essential outlines as a general view of the world.   It
has become a complete system with definite foundations and
a definite framework in a great measure filled out.   There is,
indeed, a very large place left for new content, for new results
of particular scientific investigations, but the framework
cannot be modified any further without ruining the whole
building.   This may come some day, but certainly not now,
when there is still so much to do before the building is completed.   On the other hand we have seen traditional idealism
unable not only to develop any fundamentally new standpoints, but even to extend its old doctrines to any new data.
It is evident that the time has come to search for some new
view of the world, more comprehensive, more productive, and
more able to grow by creative additions.

   By a view of the world we mean here not merely an abstract
philosophical doctrine, but a complex of concrete intellectual
functions manifested in numerous particular acts of investigation and reflection in various fields of theoretic and practical
life and culminating in an intellectual ideal.   As examples we
can quote, besides modern naturalism, the Greek rationalism
of the fourth century B.C., the later Stoicism and Epicu-
reanism, neo-Platonism, mediaeval Aristotelism.   It is evident that a view of the world in this sense cannot be created
by a single thinker: it is the accumulated product of whole
generations; it arises slowly, thanks to many efforts of
synthesis, out of innumerable scattered activities, and, after
being unified and formulated as an explicit ideal, goes on
developing by many various and unexpected applications.
It is clear therefore that no new view of the world can be
substituted at the present moment in the place of naturalism,
however unsatisfied we may be by the latter, unless such a
view has already been gradually developing in concrete intellectual life and is sufficiently mature to find its explicit expression in an intellectual ideal.   This makes it evident that a
revolution of our intellectual life such as is demanded by the

present situation cannot come from any other source than from the domain of cultural science and practice, because this is the only field outside of naturalism where a creative intellectual development has been going on in modern times. The only question is whether the synthetic activity in this domain has already reached the point where we can formulate the fundamental aims of cultural science and practice and attain thus an intellectual ideal sufficiently unified and sufficiently wide, not only to take the place of naturalism, but to include, besides the positive elements of naturalism itself, all those important principles of our intellectual life for which naturalism found no place.

Whether this is possible to fulfil only actual attempts can show. Certainly such attempts are now, if ever, indispensable. Not only is a new ideal needed to satisfy the demand for a harmonization and modification of our complex and scattered intellectual activities, but the time has come when, for all actual human purposes, the most intense reflection must be concentrated on the field of culture. It is more and more generally recognized, particularly since the outbreak of the present cultural crisis, that we have permitted ourselves to be blinded by the successes of natural science and material technique and have failed to bring a consistent, self-conscious, and critical intellectual attitude into the domain of cultural science and practice, so that the results attained in this domain, however important by themselves, are very insufficient if compared with the number of failures at the cost of which they have been reached and if measured by the scale of demands which can and should be put in the name of cultural progress. At present our attention is forcibly attracted to this domain, and it is clear that we shall have to face, for the next two or three generations at least, such problems of cultural construction as will require all our creative and critical powers. Needless to say that we are very inadequately prepared for this task, particularly in so far as theory is concerned, in spite of the enormous accumulation of materials during the past few centuries. This inadequacy manifests itself chiefly in two respects. First, we lack laws of cultural becoming which would give us means of controlling the cultural world as we control the natural world. Secondly, we lack objective and applicable standards of appreciation of cultural values which would permit us to organize the aims of our constructive activities so as to avoid wasting our energies in useless fights and destroying almost as much as we create.

Now, while laws are found only by empirical investigation of particular problems and aims are created only in particular actual pursuits, the history of cultural science and practice shows with a perfect evidence that the present unsatisfactory situation in both lines is directly due to the lack of a *general* understanding of culture, to the lack of a *view of the world* based on cultural experience. The theorist of culture associated scientific laws with naturalism, so that when he found that the laws of natural sciences did not apply to culture, his immediate reaction was to proclaim cultural becoming to be essentially inaccessible to any method which tries to determine laws of becoming. The builder of culture associated objective standards of appreciation and selection of aims with the idealistic search for absolute values, and when he saw that absolute valuation could not be applied to cultural experience he proclaimed concrete cultural life to be inaccessible to any standardization and hierarchization of values, to be a chaos of valuations whose only justification is their existence.

The fundamental and distinctive characters of cultural data which were discovered in the course of positive empirical investigations or found in concrete constructive activities were thus formulated negatively, in terms of opposition to naturalism or idealism, instead of being formulated positively in terms of their own. The scientist and the practical man were accustomed to see no other possible order of becoming than the order of nature, no other possible order of appreciation and aims than the idealistic order of absolute values, because their *world as a whole* was the world of material things and of individual or social conscious processes, subjected to laws of natural causality and, eventually, to principles of ideal finality. Cultural data had to comply with this double causal and final order as well as they could; they were not supposed to have any positive order of their own, because they did not constitute the world, because in reflecting about them, in philosophizing about them, the theorist or the builder of culture saw in them, not a unified and ordered totality of experience, but only a plurality of detached phenomena, each separately rooting in the consciousness of human beings and in their natural environment and each separately drawing whatever objective meaning it might possess from its reference to the "kingdom of ends," to the absolute order of super-worldly values.[1]

If thus, on the one hand, the predominance of idealism and naturalism in modern thought has prevented the new view of the world implied by cultural knowledge and practice from developing more rapidly and manifesting itself explicitly in a conscious intellectual ideal, the lack of such an explicit formulation of this view has, on the other hand, contributed to keep cultural knowledge and practice under the domination of idealism and naturalism and prevented them from becoming more efficient and from developing consciously and methodically along their own independent lines. This shows with

---

[1] There were, as we know, attempts to conceive the totality of cultural phenomena as constituting a unified and ordered world, not *the world*, indeed, but *a world* at least, distinct from the world of nature. But the Hegelian historical school to which these attempts were almost exclusively confined was completely dependent on idealism. By treating culture as gradual manifestation of absolute values, by exaggerating its unity, and by assuming an entirely arbitrary order of cultural becoming, it had discouraged subsequent efforts in this line even before realism extended the theory of natural evolution to this field and attracted general attention by this attempt to absorb definitively culture into nature.

particular clearness the necessity of collaboration between philosophy and particular sciences, a collaboration which has become lately very imperfect. The rôle of philosophy in the past has been certainly incomparably more important than it is now. This importance was due to the fact that philosophy was a special discipline, with its own field of investigation, its own perfectly elaborated and efficient methods, and at the same time from its own standpoint was able to supervise the entire field of knowledge and practice and to outline general intellectual ideals which scientific and practical activities could follow with a profit to themselves. Now, the peculiar modern intellectual conditions sketched above had, among other consequences, the effect of almost entirely separating philosophy as a special discipline from philosophy as a synthetic, dynamic unity of other disciplines. As a particular branch of knowledge, with its own aims and standards, philosophy is idealistic and critical; it has preserved or even increased its methodical perfection, but, as we have seen, it has nothing new to say, no vital ideals to give to science and practice. As a dynamic unity of other disciplines, philosophy is realistic and constructive; it has, indeed, given new and vital ideals; without it natural science and social life would not be what they are; but these ideals, as we have seen, are narrow and uncritical and represent a striking lowering of philosophical standards as compared with the past.

If we claim therefore that it is time to substitute a new culturalistic philosophy for both idealism and naturalism, it is because we believe that a systematic and explicit philosophical study of culture will both regenerate philosophy, in the same way as in the sixteenth and seventeenth centuries contact with nature regenerated it when it was slowly dying between scholasticism and occultism, and give us the most powerful instrument possible for the progress of concrete cultural sciences and concrete cultural creation. Our scientific knowledge and reflective control of culture can reach a level superior or even equal to that of our knowledge and control of nature only with the help of an independent, systematic, and productive philosophy of culture.

THE THESIS OF CULTURALISM

We shall use the term "culturalism" for the view of the world which should be constructed on the ground of the implicit or explicit presuppositions involved in reflection about cultural phenomena.   Let us try to formulate first of all the most general of these presuppositions.

The progress of knowledge about culture demonstrates more and more concretely the *historical relativity* of all human values, including science itself.   The image of the world which we construct is a historical value, relative like all others, and a different one will take its place in the future, even as it has itself taken the place of another image.   Yesterday man conceived himself as part of an invisible, spiritual society, and regarded the visible material nature as an instrument created exclusively for his purposes; today he conceives himself as part and product of the visible material nature; tomorrow he will reject this conception as naïve and uncritical and find a new one, and so on.   More than this.   The methods with which he operates in studying and controlling the natural world; the principles which he applies, consciously or not, to his material environment; the logic which he uses in isolating and determining things and their relations; his very ways of perceiving the sensual reality, have changed more or less slowly, but perceptibly, even during the short historically known period of cultural evolution, and will change still more. History of culture is the only field in which we can follow directly and empirically at least a part of the evolution of the human "mind," and the only theory of mind which can be directly based upon empirical data is therefore a theory which takes mind as a product of culture.   The theories of the old type of idealism are in disaccordance with experience, for they conceive mind, individual consciousness or super-individual reason, as absolute and changeless, whereas history shows it relative and changing. The theories of modern naturalism are not empirical, for the pre-cultural evolution of consciousness, whatever it was, has left no historical traces by which it can be directly reconstructed; the entire genetic conception of biological evolutionism is based on indirect inference and cannot be accepted even as a metaphysical doctrine, since it leads, as we have seen, to a self-contradiction.

Hundreds of thousands of years of cultural life have agglomerated such an enormous mass of habits and traditions that man is absolutely unable to perceive or to conceive any other nature than the one he sees through the *prisma* of culture, absolutely unable to act upon nature otherwise than in culturally determined ways. Our whole world, without any exceptions, is permeated with culture, and we can no more imagine what was the world of our pre-human ancestors than we can imagine the fourth dimension. There is no way out of culture. The study of the animal or of the child? But we must either interpret their consciousness by analogy with our consciousness, identifying the world as given to them with the world as given to us, or else we study their behavior as a part of the processes going on in our world and their behavior is seen by us as is everything else, through the prisma of culture. Our own childhood remembrances? But we found ourselves from the very beginning in a cultural world, and our cultural training began much earlier than our memory can reach; moreover, every later addition to our cultural stock has modified the form and content of our first memories. The study of the organism? But the organism, our own or that of any other being, as seen by us while studying it, is also a part of our culturally conditioned world. Its sensual image, all the meanings of this image, all the connections that we find between it and the rest of material reality, all the connections between the elements of this image, even the manual acts by which we prepare it for anatomical or physiological studies, even the acts by which we turn our attention to it, are products of culture to a degree which we are unable to determine—and how much more the theory which we construct on the basis of all this!

Naturalism will here interpose the argument that the practical efficiency of our adaptation to nature guarantees some kind of accordance between nature in itself and our images of it. We cannot avail ourselves of the opposite argument of idealism, as that presupposes the existence of absolute values, whereas we reject absolute values, both in the explicit claims of idealism and in the implicit assumptions of naturalism. But the argument from practical success does not prove anything in favor of naturalism or against culturalism, for it justifies as well any one of the images of the world which have been advocated and discarded during the process of cultural evolution, and it may be used in the future to justify quite different images from the one which modern naturalism defends.[1] Our success depends on our claims and on the part or side of reality to which we apply those claims: our claims are one-sided and limited, and the range within which we attempt to realize them does not include the entire empirical world, but only relatively few phenomena taken from a certain standpoint. Therefore to the savage his magical technique seems as successful as scientific technique seems to the modern engineer.

The argument becomes more serious when it appeals not to the mere fact of the relative success of a certain technique at a certain period, which must be always appreciated from the viewpoint of those who use the technique, but to the absolute growth of the range of control which we exercise over nature. Our savage ancestors may have

---

[1] The very concept of adaptation of the conscious being to its environment is, as we shall see later on, philosophically unacceptable.

been as successful in attaining things which they wanted as we are in attaining things which we want, and the proportion of their unsatisfied claims to those which they could satisfy may not have been any larger than ours, but we want and attain incomparably more than they did. This is clear; but in order to conclude from this that our image of the world has grown more objectively true than theirs we should have to assume that man and nature as given to man have remained essentially unchanged: the growing range of our control of nature would then have no other explanation than a more perfect adaptation of our image of the world to the world itself. Now, such an assumption would be manifestly false. Our knowledge has indeed become much wider and more methodical, but its development is only a fragment of the general development of man and of the world, and it would need a special and long investigation to show what part of our present wider range of control is due to the higher stage of our knowledge and what part to other factors. Besides, the relation between knowledge and practice may be quite different from that which naturalism assumes. Whatever it may be, it is clear that if we want more and attain more than our ancestors did, it is not merely because our knowledge is more perfect, but because our whole personalities are richer, better organized and more creative, and because the world contains for us more and means to us more; in a word, because our selves and our world are products of a longer cultural development.

However, if an investigation of the history of culture shows the relativity of any naturalistic view of the world, it does not lead to idealism in any sense. We have above referred to mind, and to our ways of perceiving and conceiving the world, using the traditional terminology, but we do not mean to imply that, the world of things-in-themselves remaining unchanged, only the mind has evolved in its ways of perceiving and conceiving them, or that the world is not a world of real nature at all, but only immanent data of individual or super-individual consciousness. The point is *not* that the world as men see and conceive it is not the world as it really is, but that the world as men see and conceive it and as it really is changes during cultural evolution, and that therefore our present nature, being objectively such as we see it, is quite different from pre-human nature, for it is, in a measure which it is impossible to determine a priori, a product of cultural evolution.

We may agree that human culture has not brought it out of nothingness, that it found a pre-human world ready as material for further development, but it has modified it so deeply, not only by technical invention, but by sensual and intellectual, social and economic, aesthetic, religious, and moral activities, and in modifying it has evolved so many and various types of these activities, so many new ways for future modifications, that whatever this pre-human world may have been, none of the generalizations of our knowledge based on our now existing world can be true of that distant past. Our science of nature is valid when applied to our present natural reality, but not valid if extended to nature as it was before the appearance of humanity. Our astronomical, physical, geological, biological theories hold true of nature only for the relatively short historical period during which the character of reality has not fundamentally changed. When projected into a more distant past, our scientific conceptions lead to more or less fantastic images of the world as it might have been if it had been and remained continually as it is now, except for those changes which, according to the present character of natural reality, should have occurred between the imagined moment of the past and the present moment. An analogous limitation makes all scientific prophecies about future states of the world appear the more fantastic, the more distant the imagined state. In other words, our science of nature is in its proper field when it searches for abstract definitions and for the laws of the present reality, and when it uses them to reconstruct and to control this reality, but it transcends its domain and is mere imagination whenever it tries to reconstruct the unique concrete evolution during which the world and man have become what they are or to foresee the concrete unique course of the future evolution of the world or of man. This means, for example, that all attempts to understand the pre-human evolution of the solar system, of earth, of the organic world, of consciousness, etc., are irremediably devoid of objective validity if pursued, as they are now, exclusively by naturalistic methods and based upon the naturalistic view, for they can never, not even hypothetically, reconstruct the past as it really was, but only as it might have been if certain impossible conditions had been realized. The only merit of the theory of natural evolution, aside from its particular applications to specific present happenings, is that in its extension over the entire past of nature it satisfies the philosophical aspirations of the modern scientist by permitting him to construct a monistic system of the universe. But this merit is a doubtful one, for naturalistic monism prevents the application of a more adequate standpoint to the history of the world.

If we want, indeed, to understand the past of the world as it really was, assuming that we may take for granted at this point that there is a possibility of developing proper methods of reconstructing past phenomena, we shall evidently first of all study the nearest and most accessible past, that is, the historical period of evolution. By careful analysis of the history of culture we can determine the gradual additions brought during the historical existence of humanity to its own consciousness and to the world as given to it at various moments. We cannot tell in advance how far into the past we shall be able to go, nor how much will be left of our world when we have subtracted all the cultural additions the origin of which we can determine directly from historical traces. We can only hope that this investigation will bring to our hand principles which will permit us to extend hypothetically our theories beyond the historical past, into the pre-historical period; we can obtain materials for this hypothetical indirect determination of the past from ethnographical studies of still existing lower stages of culture. Then, and only then, by a still more hypothetical extension we can try to reach the still more distant period of pre-human evolution, and at this point only we may be able to use the data of natural sciences as raw material. Our method should then be a special analysis subtracting from these data everything which has been proved to be an addition posterior to that moment of the past that we are trying to reconstruct.

How this investigation can be done in detail is a complex problem of methodology. For a general view of the world the fundamental points are that the concrete empirical world is a world in evolution in which nothing absolute or permanent can be found, and that as a world in evolution it is first of all a world of culture, not of nature, a historical, not a physical reality. Idealism and naturalism both deal, not with the concrete empirical world, but with abstractly isolated aspects of it. Idealism continues to treat evolution as a merely phenomenal matter and tries still to find some immovable ground above the moving stream without seeing that to have any significance at all in the development of knowledge it must remain in the stream and move with it: that is, it must cease to be idealism. Naturalism wants indeed to reconstruct evolution, but it takes an abstract cross-section of the concrete becoming and attempts to understand the becoming by studying this cross-section. If therefore modern thought intends to avoid the emptiness of idealism and the self-contradictions of naturalism, it must accept the culturalistic thesis. It must maintain against idealism the universal historical relativity of all forms of reason and standards of valuation as being within, not above, the evolving empirical world. It must maintain against naturalism that man as he is now is not a product of the evolution of nature, but that, on the contrary, nature as it is now is, in a large measure at least, the product of human culture, and if there is anything in it which preceded man, the way to find this leads through historical and social sciences, not through biology, geology, astronomy, or physics.

But it is much easier to formulate the culturalistic thesis and to show in the abstract the necessity of its acceptance than to develop its consequences in concrete application to the empirical world. The better we understand what a radical revolution of all our intellectual dogmas the realization of such a thesis would demand, the greater appear the difficulties. For, on the one hand, naturalism seems to be simply a systematic and logical development of a view of reality which is implied not only by our common-sense reflection, but by our practical activity, by our language, by the very logic which our knowledge has to use. On the other hand, idealism with its search for the absolute, with its tendency to rise above the relativity of historical becoming, seems to express a necessary and fundamental condition of our thought which cannot conceive itself as being a fragment of a dynamic development, cannot immerge itself back into the stream from which it has just emerged by the very act of constructing or accepting a truth, a good, a beauty, or any other value.

In order to overcome these apparent difficulties, we must go to the very bottom of the problem of reality and thought and try to determine their general empirical character as independently as possible of the implicit or explicit assumptions which common sense, practice, language, science, and philosophical tradition tend to impose upon our conceptions of the world. This does not mean that we should attempt to build a philosophical theory by intentionally ignoring all those assumptions and starting *ab ovo* as if nobody had philosophized before. On the contrary, the history of philosophy shows that such attempts at absolutely new beginnings involve the danger of accepting uncritically many assumptions which a less pretentious method would avoid. There are no absolutely new beginnings, no fundamental original truths which a philosopher can find at the outset of his reflection and which would make him independent at once. The only way to avoid the undesirable influence of past or present uncritical prepossessions concerning the problem which we are studying is to find them out by critical research, to understand their proper significance, to keep them continually in mind, and to use them in their proper connection. For there is no conception in the history of knowledge which does not have some validity, no methodical assumption ever used which does not have some sphere of application; the only question is, Within what limits is the conception valid? For what purposes can the method be utilized?

CHAPTER II

EXPERIENCE AND REFLECTION

THE ELEMENTARY EMPIRICAL FORMS OF EXPERIENCE

The primary problem of all philosophy is the problem of the most general characters of experience and of reflection. For no object-matter of knowledge can escape the necessity of being given in individual experience and no theory can escape the necessity of being the product of logical reflection. Though this double necessity does not impose any permanent limitations upon the content of the world and the meaning of knowledge, though the former can indefinitely transcend the data of individual experience, and the latter leads far beyond the significance given to these data in the course of any present reflection, yet the fact of experience and the fact of reflection which the philosopher finds in constructing any theory whatever about any object-matter whatever constitute for him the most immediate and the most certain starting-points, though, of course, only relatively certain and relatively immediate.

Both facts have not only a formally methodical, but assume also a particular material importance if we remember that modern philosophy must be a philosophy of culture. As long as the world remained for philosophy a world of pure ideas independent of the individual's experience, or a world of pure natural reality independent of reflection, starting with experience or reflection was merely a methodical trick used in order to reach something entirely different. But if we realize that the concrete world is a world of culture, the situation changes. For we know culture only as human culture and we can think of it only with reference to concrete conscious beings which experience it; whatever else a cultural object may be, it certainly must be at some time and in some connection experienced by somebody, and thus the fact of experience has a universal importance with regard to the cultural world. On the other hand also, we know that the world of culture is a world in evolution, and that cultural evolution involves active thought; and in so far as it does this—a point which we shall determine presently—reflection becomes also a general characteristic not only of philosophy, but also of its object-matter.

If the starting-point of the philosophy of culture is thus more or less in accordance with philosophical tradition, this very fact should keep us aware of the dangers of our beginning. In order not to accept unconsciously premises which may vitiate the further development of our theory, we must limit our admissions, both with regard to experience and with regard to reflection, to the absolutely necessary minimum. With regard to the former, we cannot accept as a general basis the results of the individual's reflection about himself as subject opposed to objects, because the "subject" is both a form of experience, when we consider the course of experience as a "subjective" activity, and a matter of experience, when we take him into account as a personality who can be apprehended by himself or by others in the course of experience. In the first character, it is the condition of all experience; in the second, it is conditioned by other experiences. The concept of the subject cannot therefore be used in discussing the problem of experience, for the latter, as primary problem, as starting-point of philosophical investigation, should not depend on the previous solution of other problems; and the concept of the subject, since it has to be qualified either as active thought of which the matter of experience is the object, or as an object-matter among others, presupposes both a theory of active thought and a theory of objects. Furthermore, in studying reflection we cannot identify it with theoretic thought, for the concept of theoretic thought implies also a dualism. On the one hand, indeed, we know that theoretic thought has for object-matter the entire world, including all types of human activity; on the other hand, it is itself only one of the types of activity which are found in the cultural world, and thus becomes its own object-matter. In its first character it claims an absolute validity for itself in reference to its object-matter; in its second character it has to deny to itself any absolute validity, since it finds its theories changing, multiform, and conflicting. This seeming antinomy can be solved only on the ground of a general study of both the systems of ideas, the "theories," as products of cultural activity given alongside other products, and of the thought which creates these systems, alongside other types of creative activity.

Thus the chief problem in the determination of the most general characters of experience is to find a characteristic which would be indeed the most general possible, would not involve a priori any limitation of experience to some particular object-matter to the exclusion of others. The initial definition of experience must be, in a word, purely formal; and in this respect it is clear that any character of experience found in our own direct reflection about the course of experience, experienced itself in a retrogressive or progressive act of attention, must lack the necessary generality, being itself, in this act, a matter of experience, no longer a pure form, and in so far given from a certain standpoint, the definite standpoint which we have taken in performing our reflection. The most various and often contradictory theories of experience have been reached by this method.

On the other hand, we evidently cannot avoid basing ourselves on those characters of the course of experience which are themselves empirically given in the course of reflection, for our determination cannot be pure invention, but must actually apply to experience if it is to be used in philosophy of culture. Thus, we must resort here to a special method. We must find the most general of those forms of experience that can be given in an act of reflection, and then try to reach beyond them, by means of a rational construction, the primary ground from which they are derived and which cannot itself be given.

Those most general forms of experience that can be yet ascertained empirically will be found if we ask ourselves what are the conditions which, on reflection, seem to be necessary and sufficient to have an object given in experience. We emphasize the point *to have an object given*. For we are not investigating here *consciousness*, that is, the way in which the concrete individual sees "himself" experiencing, but merely the form which the data of experience assume in the course of experience; our problem is not psychological, but phenomenological.

If we try now to define experience in the most general terms which yet have an empirical meaning, we must say that *experience is the presence of elements of a plurality now and here*.

All the parts of this definition, which is evidently still a description, are indispensable; that is, every one of them indicates a condition of experience which applies to any matter of experience, independently of its intrinsic diversity. At the same time there are no other indispensable parts of an empirical definition of experience; any other condition of experience which may be added can apply only to certain data to the exclusion of others.

By saying that experience is the *presence* of something we imply the possibility that this "something" may be also absent, non-present, if it does not satisfy the other conditions enumerated above; in other words, we assume that "being experienced" is not a priori identical with "being," that it may be a determination which would only partly or occasionally belong to those objects about which we think as being experienced. This assumption is indispensable for the empirical definition of experience, because with regard to every matter of experience we empirically assume this possibility of its not being experienced. This applies to every matter, but, of course, not to the fact of experiencing.[1] It does not involve any affirmation as to the nature and degree of modification to which any matter of experience may or may not be subjected by being experienced.

Every present datum of experience is *an element of a plurality* whose other elements are not present. This means (*a*) that the whole matter of experience is not given at once, but in parts; (*b*) that any present part of experience is empirically isolated from the rest, given as a distinct unit; (*c*) that every such unit is empirically associated with other parts of experience and in so far given as an element of a plurality, not as an absolutely isolated entity.

Our first affirmation contradicts the theory of absolute experience, according to which it is the essence of the matter of experience to be experienced and therefore the whole of it must be present at once and always. But this is not, of course, an empirical theory, since we can never ascertain empirically that the whole matter of experience is present at once; such a theory can be only a rational inference from an empirical definition of experience. Such an inference involves one of two groundless assertions, either that the essence of the matter of experience is exhausted in its being present, or that there is an absolute subject, timeless and spaceless, to whom the matter of experience is always given. The first assertion is groundless, because it contradicts a priori the assumption, empirically found in all experience,

[1] Thus, for example, my past "feeling" as object of experience (if we suppose that there really are such objects) can exist without being now the datum of my experience, whereas if treated as merely the way in which some other object is given to me, it exists only as long as this other object is given. Evidently, we do not touch here at all the pseudo-problem of objects existing without ever being given to anyone.

that every matter of experience may be present or not. As to the idea of the absolute subject, historically and logically it is based not upon an investigation of experience itself, but upon an analysis of the systems of human knowledge which, granted certain presuppositions, leads to the concept of a unique reason, manifesting itself in the many individual minds. We cannot accept the conclusions of this analysis as valid beforehand, and still less permit them to be applied in advance to the problem of experience.

In saying that every element of experience is a distinct unit we are in disaccordance with the conception of the matter of experience as a primary continuity, out of which only our perceptive or rational activity cuts distinct elements. We cannot accept this theory because it cannot be ascertained in experience. And even this theory is obliged to admit that a certain discontinuity is empirically given; it can only put absolute continuity as a limit of a certain synthetic process; but the question is, then, whether this synthetic process is returning to a primitive unity or creating a new unity, and any answer to this question must be entirely arbitrary at this stage of investigation.

For an analogous reason we cannot accept the contrary theory that the matter of experience is primarily given as an absolute discontinuity and only our synthetic activity establishes a connection between the disconnected elements. No element is ever given to us absolutely isolated, but whenever we try to grasp it in itself, we find that we take it already in connection with other elements. Even as the limit of an empirical tendency, an absolute dissociation cannot be admitted, for here again the question arises whether it is not our reflective act itself which has artificially individualized the given element more than it was individualized when first given. In general, it is a vain effort to try to go back to an unreflective, pure experience by the way of experiencing, since every act of a conscious "becoming aware" of the process of experience involves already reflection and thus modifies the original nature of this process.

As metaphysical, non-empirical theories of experience, both the theory which conceives experience as primarily a continuous stream and that which treats it as primarily a discontinuous series of data can be equally well accepted without in any way influencing our empirical reconstruction, for the first must acknowledge that there are waves upon the surface of this stream and that we see always this surface only with the waves, while the second must agree that we always find before us associations which make a more or less continuous chain of the series of data.

In answer to another possible objection, that the field of individual experience contains always many simultaneous data, we need simply to point out that this is a psychological, not a phenomenological problem, and to repeat that we are interested here not in the way in which the concrete individual sees himself experiencing, but in the conditions under which objects come to be experienced by the concrete individual. From the purely formal and phenomenological viewpoint, the question whether for the individual many data are present at once has no more importance than the question whether many individuals are experiencing something at once; it is merely incidental. In order that the process of experience may go on it is sufficient and necessary that always some matter, however simple or complicated, be present and referring to other, non-present matters. If there were no single, isolated matters present, we should not have anything empirically given; if the present matter did not refer to non-present matters, we should not be able to go beyond the present datum.

The affirmation that experience is the presence of something *now* will probably find least opposition. The temporal character of experience can hardly be denied, and we postpone for awhile the question whether it is due to the temporal character of the matter of experience, or of the experiencing subject, or perhaps to something else. In any case the elements of the plurality of experience succeed one another in the sense that each in succession is "now given." The *now* may be defined from the standpoint of various theories, as a passing moment of the absolute time, or as a timeless present through which the course of time goes on, or as the limit of the past, or the beginning of the future, or as still something else. Empirically it is absolute, not relative to any other moment; it is an ultimate unanalyzable form. Therefore, with any definition of the time the fact holds true that the element given *now* is one definite member of a successive series, is passing through the form of *now* after some element and before some other; and therefore, as a general empirical form of experience, duration, whatever else it may mean, means a succession of elements in the present; these elements with regard to the present have to be considered as arranged in a one-dimensional series, externally to one another, and still associated with one another so as to make the series continuous.

We are perfectly aware of the difficulty which such a definition presents to our reason, which cannot conceive externality and continuity together. But both are universal components of the form of experience as far as it can be ascertained empirically, and we can reject neither of them only for the reason that they seem to disagree logically. This disagreement is the result of that fundamental difficulty of the problem of experience, that the form of empirical data must be turned into an empirical datum itself in order to be determined; when we succeed in overcoming this difficulty, the irrationality will disappear. Certainly the modern reduction of externality to continuity and interpenetration is no more a rational solution than the ancient reduction of continuity to externality.

Of course, we can only repeat here what we have said already about the distinction of the form of experience and the form of consciousness; there may be many parallel temporal series running in the individual consciousness, as there may be many data present at once, but this is only a complication of the elementary form of experience in determined empirical conditions.

The formal temporal character of experience does not involve anything concerning the matter of experience. The temporality which we define is extrinsic, not intrinsic; the empirical data themselves may or may not have the empirical feature of duration. One of the current errors of empiricism is to assume duration as belonging to the matter of experience universally, while absolute idealism tends rather to ignore or to deny the time as empirical datum. Both theories lead to one-sided and evidently insufficient theories of reality. Empiricism is unable to account for the possibility of experiencing timeless data, such as mathematical relations; idealism is finally obliged to deny the objectivity of duration. Our way of stating the problem makes a future admission of temporal data of experience (for example, changes) and of untemporal data (for example, theories) equally possible, without presuming anything beforehand.

More doubtful than the universality of the *now* seems at first that of the *here*, particularly as, since Kant, so much emphasis has been put upon the theory that extension is not a universal form of experience like duration, but characterizes only the "external" experience. But we must again distinguish two problems: the intrinsic spatiality of data of experience and the extrinsic extensiveness of experience. Spatial extension and localization may be included within the data of experience, in the sense that single objects may be spatially extended and that among the data of experience there are groups of objects spatially localized with regard to one another. Of course, in this spatial sense extension is not a universal form, only a matter of experience, since there are data of experience which are neither spatially extensive objects nor groups of objects spatially localized with regard to one another. But this is not our present problem. We omit completely the question of an intrinsic spatiality of data of experience in the same way as we have omitted the question of their intrinsic temporality. We affirm now only the formal extrinsic extensiveness of experience, the fact that any datum whatever, spatial or not, whenever it is given, is given *here*. This does not mean that data of experience are localized here; if localized at all, they are so in some place determined by their relative spatial position with regard to other objects within a certain section of reality, and this place and these other objects are then one complex datum of experience, one spatially arranged group. Nor does it mean that some copies, some "images" of objects are *here* in my mind or *here* in my brain; this would be pure nonsense. The *here* is an absolute point of extension in the same way as the *now* is an absolute moment of duration. The empirical *here* as an ultimate form of experience does not depend upon any definition of space any more than the *now* depends upon any definition of time; nor does it involve any localization of the body of the experiencing subject with regard to other data, nor even the representation of the subject's spatially extended body. On the contrary, the *here* is the point around which the data of experience are centered, and thus it is a primary condition of any extension of the empirical world. But it is not a sufficient condition of the spatial order, for only those objects are taken by us as spatially localized with regard to the *here* which are spatially localized with regard to the particular object called my body, and of course, this can apply only to spatial objects, that is, to those with regard to which spatiality is a matter of experience.

The extension implied in the *here* is not space just as the duration implied in the *now* is not time. Both are only the last, the poorest, the most elementary forms which can yet be experienced. The pure *here* only completes the determination of experience in the *now* by limiting it. Even the *now* of an element of experience leaves its presence yet incompletely determined, for the *now* has many contemporary *here's*, many elements can be given *now* in many different *here's*. On the other hand, of course, it is not enough for an element to be *here*, for the *here* has many successive *now's*, and many different elements can be present in the same *here* at different *now's*. The question could be made seemingly clearer by recalling that the individual's experience is limited both in extension and in duration, that out of the extensive wealth of the empirical world at a given moment various data are present in the experience of various individuals, and that in the experience of the same individual various data appear at various moments. But such a formulation would lead us to problems which at this stage of investigation must be avoided, for it introduces concepts which are not those of the primary form of experience. Empirically it is the individual limitation of experience which presupposes the intersection of duration and extension, and not reciprocally.

ACTUALITY FROM THE STANDPOINT OF THE EMPIRICAL ANALYSIS OF EXPERIENCE

Presence, extrinsic plurality, succession with regard to the *now*, and concentration with regard to the *here* are the most formal determinations of experience that can be drawn from empirical data by direct analysis. But, as we have said, they are still empirically given, they still preserve a minimum of "intuitiveness," and in so far have some of the character of matter of experience. They are not given, indeed, as independent elements of the plurality of experience, nor as components of other elements; but, when we reflect about the process of experience, we can experience them as external characteristics of every datum in its relation to other data. Their universality distinguishes them positively from any datum which is only a matter, not a form of experience. This universality has been denied to each of them separately by some philosophical theories; every one of them separately has been treated somewhere as a mere datum of experience, which may accompany or not other data and has no importance beyond that of being given within the realm of experience. The plurality is rejected by the mystics; the succession in duration is considered illusory and explained as an illusion by absolute idealism; the concentration in extension is ignored by subjective idealism.

The possibility of denying the universality of any one of these characters of experience is, of course, only apparent; in further development every form must be reintroduced in some way or other, if experience is to be accounted for. The difference between philosophical theories of experience lies mainly in the metaphysical presuppositions from which experience is deduced and in the manner in which its forms are presented. If each of them separately has ever been denied, it is because they are the result of the analysis of a more fundamental and general ground of experience, which is not empirically manifested, cannot become a matter of experience, because it underlies both the acts of reflection about experience and the process which is the object-matter of this reflection. While rejecting singularity or plurality, duration or extension, a philosophical theory does not reject the really primary ground of experience, but only a part of the entire product of its analysis. Therefore the error of denying one of these empirical forms does not lead at once to the negation of experience in general, but only to an incomplete conception of it.

We call *actuality* the primitive ground of experience which is the common root of presence, unity and plurality, succession and concentration. We use the term "ground of experience" because of its vagueness; none of the precise philosophical terms could express adequately the rôle which actuality plays with regard to experience, actuality being absolutely unique, not to be put into any class of forms, principles, etc.

Our definition of it must be clearly a genetic one; that is, we have to define actuality precisely with regard to those forms which arise from its analysis. They cannot be contained in actuality as fully and explicitly as we find them when they are analytically isolated from the data of experience, for then actuality would be nothing but a simple sum of these forms and empirically ascertainable, which is impossible. But they must be virtually contained in actuality, for otherwise reflective analysis of experience could not have found them.

In order to pass now from empirical forms to the pre-empirical ground of experience, we must know the effect of this reflective analysis, the modifications which it was bound to introduce into its object-matter, the original course of experience, in order to change it into data. This is easy to determine. The reflective act which analyzes the course of experience is an act of isolation and objectivation; it abstracts single aspects of the entire concrete process and stabilizes them as definite and ready forms. In thinking about our experience we necessarily take as complete that which is only a part of the total process, as achieved that which is only becoming; we substitute the limit for the tendency and the result for the act, because the experiencing about which we are reflecting is no longer the experiencing as it is going on. Thus the conclusion which we have reached in the preceding paragraph—that the empirical forms of experience are virtually contained in the pre-empirical ground of experience—can only mean that when not reflected upon these forms they are only becoming, not achieved, are tendencies, not limits, acts, not results.

When we say therefore that the presence of an element of a plurality which the act of reflection finds in experience is only virtually contained in the primary ground of experience, this means that in actuality there is a becoming of a plurality. The two sides of the extrinsic plurality of experience which we have treated as coexisting statically in various proportions, the isolated elements, and the association of these elements in actuality can only express the limits of two tendencies, one of which increases the isolation and the other of which develops the association.   Actuality is not a presence of ready elements of a ready group, but a formation of both elements and group, a process of isolation of elements out of a relative continuity and of connection of elements relatively isolated.   When we consider the static results of this process, the limits of both tendencies, whatever these limits may be for any matter in particular at any moment of reflection, we have precisely a present element, more or less ready in its isolation, and a non-present plurality, more or less ready in its association.

Likewise, in the temporal succession of empirical data passing through the *now* there is something which appears to our reflection as ready and accomplished, that is, the definite direction in time and of time.   Only in so far as such a direction is attained, can we consider a present element given *before* some and *after* other elements.   This definite direction is one from the past through the present into the future, if we view it from the standpoint of pure time; it is one from the future through the present into the past, if we take it from the point of view of the data which pass through the *now*.   But both of its aspects can be only virtually contained in actuality.   Actuality has in itself the fundamental condition of the directed succession, the condition that is common to both of its aspects and that is necessary both for the direction of the time and for the direction of the data in time: it has the *becoming*.   In this becoming of actuality the definite direction of the time-succession is not ready; it only develops.

We must understand that without this principle of becoming there would be no directed succession of data.   The data

themselves as passing through the *now* would be evidently
unable to produce direction, since their passage does not
preclude the possibility for a past datum to become future
once more.   This essential point has been too much neglected.
If we leave aside a pre-existing order of things and ideas and
limit ourselves to the conception of experience as a plurality
of data passing separately through the present, directed succession is a difficult problem.   A datum is past from the
standpoint of the present if it was experienced; it is future
from the standpoint of the present if it will be experienced.
And since there are a multitude of data which return in the
present more than once, they are by themselves either past or
future, indifferently—past in so far as they already were
experienced, future in so far as they will be experienced.
There is no datum of experience of which we could say
a priori that it cannot return; it does not matter from the
standpoint of pure experience whether we qualify this datum
ontologically as an image or a thing.   Thus neither a direction in time nor a direction of time can be deduced from the
data as passing through the *now*.

There must be therefore in the course of experience some
factor which makes an irreversible series of data in spite of the
fact that each of these data can reappear an indefinite number of times in the series.   This factor must be inherent in
the primary ground of experience, not be produced by reflection alone.   Actuality must be a becoming in which the
definite direction in time and of time itself becomes; this
direction is not pre-existent to the course of experience, but
is gradually created in it.   And as without a definite direction
there is no time in the traditional sense of the term, from the
standpoint of experience time is never ready; it is continually empirically created.   We shall see later that from the
standpoint of the objective world time also preserves this
incomplete and dynamic character, that it is not primary and
independent, but derived and gradually, indefinitely produced.

Only our reflection which generalizes the indefinite progress of actuality raises thereby the indefinitely progressing creation of time to the absolute, carries the continuous tendency to its ideal limit, and accepts this limit as if it were real.

The extensive concentration of experience around the *here* exists virtually in actuality in the same sense as the preceding forms; it becomes actually, but is never stabilized and ready. We can distinguish here also two sides of the question. The data are concentrated around the *here*, but at the same time they are independent in some measure of the *here*, they are *in themselves;* not all the matter of experience present *now* is also present *here*. The becoming of actuality is concentrating them and at the same time limiting their concentration; it refers various elements to a common center, but at the same time eliminates others which formerly were concentrated, moves them away from this center. The entire matter of experience, or any part of it, is never effectively centered *here* and never fully independent from a reference to the *here;* only partly and gradually it concentrates itself in the actual becoming, and in the same course of experience it becomes partly and gradually diffused. If I suppose the complex result of the indefinitely progressing actuality definitely achieved, I reach the conception of some elements of the total plurality of experience constituting my experience, of other elements being outside of my experience, or of a certain side of all experience being mine, other sides remaining not mine. But the concept of an individual part or side of experience determined for any moment of time marks again only the ideal limit of a tendency that can never attain any limit. The world as experienced is neither concentrated around me nor self-existing independently of me; it becomes simultaneously both, datum by datum, moment by moment, in an indefinite dynamic development.

Actuality can be thus reconstructed from the standpoint of the empirical forms reflectively found in experience, as a continuous, simultaneous, and parallel *subjectivation* and *objectivation* of the elements of experience. In so far as an element of experience becomes present and refers to a non-present plurality, in so far as it becomes past and refers to the future, in so far as it is brought *here* and refers to others as being *there*, it acquires a subjective character; in so far, on the contrary, as it becomes the element of a non-present plurality, as it becomes the future datum referred to from the past through the *now*, as it becomes *there* while others become *here*, it acquires the features of objectivity. This is only a becoming, relative and varying; no element of experience ever is subjective or objective, and every element of experience can pass from the tendency toward subjectivity to a tendency toward objectivity and vice versa. For subjectivity and objectivity are not ready forms of experience; we do not find them directly in our reflection. They become themselves, together and in reference to each other, in the concrete pre-reflective course of actuality in which they are both unified dynamically. Unprejudiced observation of experience cannot detect them as achieved and opposed to each other. If they were isolated and made static and definite by philosophy, it was because philosophy did not take the unprejudiced standpoint of simple observation of experience, but tried to make experience fit into the ready mold of the ancient ontological dualism of soul and body.

ACTUALITY FROM THE STANDPOINT OF THE ACT OF REFLECTION

The definition of actuality which we have reached is still incomplete, since it is only valid from the standpoint of the results of reflection about the process of experience; though it goes beyond the immediate product of this reflection and reconstructs the original ground of experience, it reconstructs it with reference to these secondary, empirical forms which the act of reflection draws from it. Therefore we must supplement our definition by trying to reconstruct actuality from the second possible standpoint. We must now remember that our act of reflection itself is going on in actuality, like all acts of reflection ever performed, and we must therefore reconstruct actuality no longer as object, but as source of reflection, as the ground upon which any reflection, including the reflection about actuality itself, originates.

Every reflection implies a fundamental distinction without which it would be impossible—the well-known distinction of *thought* and *reality*. This distinction is not limited to theoretic reflection; it characterizes every conscious activity of whatever kind. In so far, now, as every conscious act is actual, actuality must be the ground upon which, for the experiencing individual, the distinction between thought and reality arises, just as it is the ground upon which the distinction of subjectivity and objectivity arose.

In order to demonstrate these propositions with all the relative certainty which they can possess at the present stage of our investigation, we must point out, first of all, that the distinction of thought and reality is not at all implied in the empirical forms of experience as outlined above, and not even in the distinction of subjectivity and objectivity, whose becoming has been found the ultimate and most general characteristic of actuality as reflected upon. Relatively subjective data, and even the pure form of subjectivity—the ideal limit of the subjectivation of all data—can be a reality given to thought in the same way as the relatively objective data and the form of objectivity. On the other hand, thoughts and realities alike can become both subjectivated or objectivated. When viewed as mere data, the elements of experience are neither thoughts nor realities, though they can become more or less subjective or objective. Therefore from the standpoint of the results of a reflection about experience it is impossible to understand how any rational or logical systems can arise in the course of individual experience, how there can be any meaning, any systematization, any standards of validity where observation shows us nothing but an associative organization of data. On the other hand, when we look upon the empirical world as upon a world of thoughts and realities, we find neither subjectivity nor objectivity and it is impossible to understand from this standpoint how there can appear within this world a partial organization of realities and thoughts as data and associations of data with regard to indefinitely becoming individual centers of presence, duration and extension, how there can be any subjectivity or objectivity. The assumption of an ontological subject, at the same time receptacle of data and author of thought, permitted philosophy for a long time to close its eyes to these problems, but they reappear at every step in the chaotic relations between subjectivism and objectivism on the one side, idealism and realism on the other.

It is clear that, if actuality is the source of the distinction between thought and reality, this gives it a completely new character, not included in the characters discussed in the preceding section. The act of reflection about the course of experience is indeed, in a sense, going on in the course of experience and can be viewed as an association of data continuing the very series about which it reflects; but it is also something entirely different. It is a *conscious activity* of which the course of experience analyzed by it is the *passive material*. These, the consciously active character of thought and the passive character of reality as material of thought, are evidently new and independent features of the concrete development of actuality; they could not have suddenly appeared out of the associative organization of data which implies no distinction of passivity and activity and is not conscious of itself. The act of reflection about experience, as act, must be a continuation of other acts, even though as association of data it is also a continuation of the preceding series of data. With regard to its present performance it roots in the course of experience, but with regard to its significance it transcends experience immeasurably. Its object-matter is, as we know, a reality which is a part of an objective, real world, and as active thought this act has a logical form by which it participates in some objective ideal order of the cultural systems of science or art, morality or religion, etc. Therefore its results lead us at once beyond all limitation of individual experience and reflection, into the entire development of culture, for they can be understood only as parts of a super-individual, trans-actual world.

Of course, even reflectively analyzed experience cannot be limited to "individual consciousness." We have seen that it involves a plurality of elements in duration and extension without any positive, determinable limits. But this lack of limits is purely negative; there is no positive transcendence of experience in the course of experience as reflectively viewed, and the subjectivity and objectivity of data is not only always becoming, never ready, but is relative, belongs to these data only with regard to each other. Therefore no conception of the world whatever can be deduced from the reflective analysis of experience. If there is a world transcending any experiencing individual and yet common to all of them and experienced by all of them, it is because every individual is not only a center toward which data of experience converge from the trans-actual, common world, but a center from which trans-actual thoughts and realities radiate to the common world. By the organization of data in the course of experience the super-individual world becomes empirically given; by the opposition of thought and reality the empirically given world becomes super-individual. And while, viewed from the standpoint of experience, the most common characteristic of the concrete world of culture is that all that it contains can be given in the course of individual experience, from the standpoint of reflection its most common characteristic is that all that it contains is either a real object-matter of active thought or a valid thought acting upon reality.

By "reality" we mean here anything that is the passive object-matter of active thought, natural objects and happenings, social institutions, language, products of art, religious myths, etc., and even thoughts themselves when they become the object-matter of other thoughts. By "thought" we mean any conscious activity which handles these real materials, isolates them, and connects, modifies, and organizes. Not only theoretic reflection, but also moral, aesthetic, religious, social, technical, hedonistic, activities are thoughts by the active and conscious organization of given materials which they produce. Whenever, in whatever field, actuality leads to a trans-actual result, which thus becomes incorporated into the super-individual world, whenever we have not a mere, more or less subjective or objective, datum or association of data, but an ideal significance or a real object of this significance, we must assume a distinction between thought and reality of the same fundamental character as the one which has been usually ascribed only to theoretic reflection and its object-matter. And we find trans-actual significances and real objects of these significances, whenever there are any criteria, any standards, for the existence of a standard shows that we are beyond the simple organization of data, that there is an opposition of thought and its object-matter and a trans-actual standpoint taken with regard to the validity of thought and the reality of its object-matter. Since all cultural activities involve standards, every cultural activity implies an opposition of thought and reality. If we use the term "logic" to indicate not exclusively the Aristotelian logic of knowledge, but every system of standards which thought must follow in order to reach an ideal validity and an objective reality, we can say that, in the same way as the existence of theoretically valid theories demands that our knowledge be not a mere process of association of data but have a logical bearing, the existence of an aesthetically valid art demands an aesthetic activity following the specific ideal standards of a logic of artistic production and contemplation, the existence of morally valid moralities demands a moral activity which follows the criteria of a particular logic of moral creation; even the existence of technique, language, or political organization cannot be explained by a dynamic organization of data, but require specifically standardized thoughts, and to these thoughts must correspond a reality which is rational precisely in so far as it is the proper material of logical thoughts, however imperfect and however different its rationality in different fields may be.

The peculiarities of the past development of philosophy resulted in the fact that, whereas it is almost universally recognized that the organization of data in the course of experience is a necessary condition of anything's existing *for us*, there is no general recognition of the opposition of thought and reality as a necessary condition of there being any self-existing world at all. On the one hand, indeed, the rationalists, who were inclined to recognize this opposition, treated thought as subjective and, reducing reality to data, absorbed reality in the subject; on the other hand the empiricists, treating reality as objective and unable to deduce rational thought from the association of data, absorbed thought in the object. After having emphasized the essential difference between subjectivity and objectivity as becoming in the course of experience reflectively considered, and thought and reality as implication of reflection itself, we must now emphasize as against both rationalists and empiricists the impossibility of there being in the empirical world thought without reality or reality without thought.

There can be no thought without reality, for this would be possible only if thoughts were inherent in the subject and defined as subjective processes. As they are not, as thought is characterized in its very essence not by its psychological occurrence, but by its logical bearing, it is clearly correlative to some reality with regard to which it is logically valid, which is its material. It must be recalled once more that reality, for philosophy of culture, does not mean merely material or even psychological reality, but includes all cultural products whatever, among others even ideas, i.e., thoughts which have become the object-matter of other thoughts. Nor can we accept the common contention of naturalistic empiricism that there are realities without thoughts corresponding to them. If reality were identified with objectivity, with existence independent of actual subjective associations, this contention would be, of course, perfectly justified, at least as marking a limit. But reality is characterized as such not by its reference to the subject, but by its reference to thought, as object-matter of thought, and it would be evidently self-contradictory to point out any reality as not being the object-matter of thought, for it would be an object-matter at least of this very thought in which we have denied its connection with thought. And of all realities none shows as distinctly the influence of logical thought as the reality of naturalism, the rational product of a long and complex development of scientific theories. Of course, to give our proposition its full concrete application we must recall again that logical thought is not only theoretic thought, but all kinds of conscious activity, and from the fact that any concrete reality within the empirical world seems never to have been the object-matter of theoretic reflection it does not result that it has not been the object-matter of some thought.

The opposition of thought and reality is evidently not enough to make thought in any particular way logical, reality in any particular way rational. It is simply the most elementary and universal condition of all standardized activity of whatever kind, all standards being either standards of thought as applied to reality or standards of reality as object-matter of thought. What will be the specific standards applied depends on the systematic organization of thought and reality; but no specific standards can be applied otherwise than on the ground of this opposition.

Therefore this opposition must be assumed as universally characterizing individual reflection, just as the presence of elements of a plurality *now* and *here* characterizes universally individual experience. Without the latter nothing could be given; without the former that which is given would never transcend individual experience; individual reflection would never rise to a super-individual trans-actual world.

Having thus defined actuality on its active side, as course of reflection, by the opposition of thought and reality, we meet now an analogous problem to the one we met before, when trying to define the fundamental form of experience on its passive side, as object-matter of reflection. Indeed, the distinction of thought and reality cannot ultimately characterize pure actuality, because we have reached it by considering the developed results of actual reflection as they appear in logically organized thoughts and rationally organized realities. The opposition between thought and reality is completed only when thought is already connected with other thoughts, reality with other realities, and it is only in these connections that we can reach them as ready and opposed. Meanwhile, a thought when first arising in the course of individual reflection is not yet incorporated into a logical system, its object-matter is not yet for the reflecting individual a part of a wider reality, and their opposition is not complete. There could be indeed no thought and no reality within the world as given to us, there could be no trans-actual and yet empirical world at all if actuality did not contain the opposition virtually; the opposition must have in actuality its ultimate source, for if the world is a world of culture, a human world, all systems of thought and reality, however highly rational and objective, must be constructed or reconstructed from human actuality. But actuality cannot contain the opposition in a definite form, for precisely by producing it, it leads beyond itself, to the trans-actual world. The only possible conclusion is that actuality is the *becoming* of both thought and reality in their reciprocal determination.

SYNTHESIS OF THE TWO DEFINITIONS OF ACTUALITY

We have constructed our two definitions of actuality from two standpoints which usually have been considered irreconcilable: the standpoint of the epistemological evidence, based on the ground that anything that is given in any character whatever must be experienced as a datum, and that of the logical evidence, based on the ground that any theory or any criticism of a theory must presume the logical validity of thought and the—at least relative—rationality of its object-matter. We have found that these two standpoints in their traditional form were not exactly equivalent. That of the epistemological evidence was really much broader, for it could be extended over the entire empirical world and did not include any limitation as to the nature of data, whereas the standpoint of logical evidence—for reasons which it would take too long to expose—was usually limited to a portion of the entire domain of validity, to the field of theoretic logic. Having once removed this unjustified limitation, we find the two standpoints exactly counterbalancing each other, equally one-sided, and incommensurable with each other, if taken as ultimate. Meanwhile, they evidently must be unified; actuality in its concrete development does not show this duality of standpoints. Both the organization of data in experience and the opposition of thought and reality have a common ultimate ground. This community is comprehensible when we remember that neither the organization of data with regard to their relative subjectivity and objectivity, nor the opposition of thought and reality are ready and achieved, but both only become in actuality, and that the latter must be therefore conceived as a common becoming of both, not as a common existence of both.

The development of the individual's experience and reflection is, indeed, not isolated from the empirical trans-actual world of thoughts and realities, but goes on within this very world, is an integral part of it. If we imagine "consciousness" as a closed receptacle or even only a closed series of specific phenomena, then, everything in this receptacle or series is a datum or empirical association of data in the full and exclusive sense of these terms from the very moment it enters into consciousness; everything outside of this receptacle or series is a reality or a logical thought, and there is no possible bridge between them. But actual experiencing is not a ready series, only an ever-becoming series, not a ready consciousness but an indefinitely created consciousness of which every datum and every association is at the same time in some measure a reality or thought, part of the trans-actual world of systems of reality and systems of thought, because it never exclusively *is* but always only *becomes* a datum or a connection of data. The process of subjectivation by which the subjective series is continually created without ever being achieved as subjective, is thus not simply making subjective data out of objective data, but making subjective data and subjective associations out of something that was not data nor associations of data, that was realities or logical thoughts. A reality or a thought becomes subjective and becomes a datum of experience or an association at the same time, but it is never entirely subjective, never entirely ceases to be reality or logical thought. Experiencing as process of subjectivation is thus turning pre-existing realities into data, thoughts into associations, without ever reaching the limit of pure subjectivity and without ever destroying entirely the logical character of the thought or the rational character of the reality, which thus becomes given by becoming subjective and becomes subjective by becoming given.

On the other hand, the world of thoughts and realities is not a pure *absolute* system or systems, absolutely self-existing and developing absolutely independently of the individual's experience. The interrelation between the experiencing individual and the world is double. The individual not only turns realities into data and thoughts into associative processes, but turns his data and associations into realities and thoughts. The process of objectivation, going, as we have seen, along with subjectivation in experience, is not merely, as it seemed to us from the standpoint of pure experience, giving objectivity to data and associations which were subjective, but changing data and associations into realities and thoughts, giving them a rational order and a logical significance. The limit here also is never attained; the realities and thoughts of which actuality is the source never entirely cease to be data and associations, and as far as they still remain data and associations, never can become *absolutely* objective with no subjectivity attached to them. But the limit can be indefinitely approached, thought can become indefinitely more and more logical, reality more and more rational, while becoming more and more objective.

Actuality is thus a dynamic center toward which in a process of subjectivation realities and thoughts converge by becoming data and associations of data and from which in a process of objectivation realities and thoughts radiate by ceasing to be data and by becoming rational and logical.

ACTUALITY AND PERSONALITY

This definition of actuality makes us understand the double relation between the individual and the world of objective reality and objective thought. On the one hand, indeed, we see how the individual at every step assimilates, so to speak, pre-existing objects and thoughts, changes them into personal experiences by taking them out of the systematic rational or logical order of which they are elements, and incorporating them into the subjective series of his data, but without ever entirely destroying their rational or logical character, so that even as components of his personality they remain in some varying measure trans-actual and super-individual, and his personality, as gradually realizing itself in the complex series of data, always is somewhere between subjectivity and objectivity, partly existing within the objective world itself, partly organized into a unique development of experiences. This is the experiencing individual as receptive personality and this is the side which was chiefly, if not exclusively, treated in all theories which presumed the world to be an absolute system of reality or an absolute system of thought, existing and developing without any active participation of conscious individuals, whose only rôle was to be adequately receptive. But there is another side, indispensable to the explanation, not only of the evolution of the objective world, but even of the progress of the individual's personal adaptation to this world. For a merely receptive individual not only could not contribute anything to the world of realities and thoughts, but could never reach a sufficient degree of objectivity to understand it adequately. Receptive assimilation is a passage from objectivity to subjectivity, and the more it progresses, the more personal realities and thoughts become, the more they also acquire the character of data and associations and lose their rational or logical connections and their objectivity. It is usually implicitly supposed that this disadvantage can be offset by having the individual assimilate continually new experiences. But this would not change the character of assimilation, only widen its range. Assimilation once begun would always tend toward subjectivity instead of approaching more and more to a reconstruction of the objective order. Therefore, whether we agree that the individual can contribute to the evolution of the objective world or not, whether we treat the objective realities or thoughts which the individual reaches as creations or merely reconstructions, as new objectively or new only for him, we must take the other, active side of the experiencing individual, the creative personality into account. The result, the reality or the thought produced by the individual, has not the same importance from the standpoint of the evolution of culture when it is merely a reproduction of something that already existed as when it is a new creation; but the mechanism in both cases is essentially the same. The individual can reach objectivity, can reconstruct an existing reality or reproduce a subsisting thought in their objective character, not by assimilating them merely, not by changing them into subjective data or associations, but, on the contrary, by depersonalizing his personal experiences, by changing his data into realities and his associations into objective thoughts. In other words, there are two ways for the individual to include any part of the objective world in his personality: the first is making this part of the objective world a part of subjective experience; the second, identifying a part of his own personality with this part of the objective world. By the first method the individual constructs his own subjective personality as component of the cultural world; by the second method he constructs it as creator or at least reconstructor of the cultural world. Therefore, when we want to understand the cultural world in general, we must take into account this objectivating creative activity by which the individual raises his data to the level of realities and his associations to the level of logical thoughts, whereas the subjectivating receptive process by which realities become personal data, and thoughts personal associations, acquires an importance only for the study of certain special domains of culture where the receptive personality is acted upon or studied as a specific complex reality.

CHAPTER III

THE CONCRETE, EMPIRICAL OBJECT AND HISTORICAL REALITY

THE METHOD

We have seen that actuality involves, in the course of objectivation, a growing distinction between reality as rational object-matter of thought and thought as logical activity handling the real materials. Absolutely objective reality and absolutely objective thought are only ideal limits of this actual objectivation, and since only that is empirically attainable which can be reached from actuality, the empirical world contains neither absolute reality nor absolute thought; any reality which can be empirically ascertained must preserve in some, however slight, measure the character of a subjective datum, any thought which can be empirically reconstructed must preserve in some, however slight, measure the character of a subjective association of data. Realities and thoughts are, indeed, objectivated and opposed to each other by being incorporated into systems of realities or thoughts, and, as we shall see later on, it is possible to consider them abstractly only within a given system, disregarding characters they may possess outside of it; it is by this abstract isolation that the concepts of pure or absolute reality, of pure or absolute thought, have been constructed. Once ready, those concepts have been used to reconstruct the full empirical, imperfectly objective realities and thoughts in their concreteness. But it is clearly an inversion of the proper method to deduce formally human experience and reflection in general from a theory of nature, or from a theory of absolute reason, or from a combination of both, since nature and absolute reason are attainable only by human experience and reflection.

Our method must therefore be entirely different. In studying reality, which is our present task, we must proceed from experience to more and more objective rational reality and not vice versa. Instead of assuming, as realism does, a maximum of objectivity and rationality as inherent in the real world and trying to show how this maximum decreases in personal experience, we must start with the minimum of objectivity and rationality which reality must have to exist at all as a plurality of objects transcending present experience and opposed to thought, and then show how this minimum can increase. For, even if we admitted provisionally that all reality as such possessed approximately that amount of rationality and objectivity which realism ascribes to it, it would be none the less continually experienced and reconstructed by experiencing individuals in the course of actual reflection. Therefore, even if the claims of realism were justified, empirical reality would still have to rise from that minimum of rationality and objectivity which is just necessary to make any personal datum a real object and to pass through many stages of rationalization and objectivation, before our actual reconstruction could empirically reach that highest level of rationality and objectivity which is postulated by realism. For a theory of empirical reality, the fact that the latter is continually reconstructed by personal reflection is at least as essential as the fact that it constitutes objective and rational systems which to the degree in which they are objective and rational are also assumed as independent in their constitution from personal experience and reflection. In a word, empirical reality moves between two limits: the limit of personal subjectivity and the limit of absolute objectivity and rationality, and we must determine the universal conditions, as a result of which it is raised above the first limit, before we attempt to show how it approaches to the second.

The necessity of such a method appears with particular evidence if we realize that, while all real objects must equally be reconstructed from actuality in order to exist for us at all, only some real objects approach near enough to the limit of absolute objectivity and rationality to permit us for certain scientific purposes to ignore their dependence on the experiencing and reflecting personalities; whereas many of them remain very far from this limit. Take, for instance, social institutions, works of literature, objects of religious worship, etc., in general all those objects which constitute cultural reality in the traditional, narrow sense of the term, as opposed to natural reality. It is clear that if we tried to study the former by the same realistic method which is applied by physical science to material objects and treated them as objective and perfectly rational, completely independent of personal experience and reflection, we would fail to understand them properly, for they are much too far from the absolute limit of realism to be sufficiently characterized from the standpoint of this limit alone. Thus, the provisional admission which we made above, that all reality may possess approximately the maximum of objectivity and rationality which realism ascribes to it, was too far-reaching. The fact that objects are continually reconstructed from actuality is not as much, but more fundamental for the purpose of a general characteristic of reality than the fact that they belong to objective, rational systems. Reality is primarily empirical and only secondarily rational; all real objects possess fully the empirical character, whereas their rationality is mostly imperfect, admits innumerable gradations, and can, as we shall see later, increase and decrease not merely from the standpoint of personal experience, but objectively, from the standpoint of their own real constitution. It is impossible to understand the objective rationality of the real world without having understood its concrete empirical character. We must therefore first of all study reality as empirical, leaving aside for the moment the question of its rational organization, and our first probem will be: how are empirical real objects constructed or reconstructed from personal data?

The two fundamental characters which reality must possess in so far as empirical are, as follows from our preceding discussion, the possibility of being given in actual experience and of being reconstructed by actual reflection. Whatever a real object is as a part of the self-existing reality in general can be empirically ascertainable only in so far as this object becomes a datum in the course of experience; whatever a real object is as object-matter of logical thought in general can be empirically reconstructible only if and in so far as this object becomes the subject-matter of actual reflection.

We call *content* that which, while constituting the object as subject-matter of reflection, is also given in the course of experience, or, in terms of experience, the content can be defined as a datum of experience which is also subject-matter of reflection and thus transcends the limitation of its own presence *here* and *now*.

The content is therefore free from any subjective or objective determinations. It is free empirically from subjective determinations, because, though in fact present *here* and *now*, it is not affected by its presence *here* and *now* with regard to that which objectively constitutes it as subject-matter of reflection; it is given, but taken not as personal datum, only as subject-matter of reflection. We can have reality empirically given to us only because it is possible for us actually to ignore the fact of the content's actuality and to take it exclusively with regard to what it is as subject-matter of reflection, neglecting its appearance in the course of personal experience. It is rationally free from objective determinations, because whatever may be the system of objects to which it belongs, we must have it first given to us in itself before we take it as component of a system of reality; its rational character as object, part of a system, does not exist for us until we have reconstructed it by ourselves, by our own logical thought, and therefore the content as such is logically prior to any objective determination which the object may possess as part of a reality. Since all the definitions and classifications of our theoretic reflection bear upon objects, the formal character of the content must be expressed negatively; we must exclude from the definition of the content all the particular real forms which various classes of objects possess, thanks to their participation in various systems. But this negation represents only one side of the problem; for, since the content is the basis of all objects, since every object must be a content before being anything else, the content in general must have the possibility of acquiring under certain conditions any determinations which objects as real possess. In denying every particular real determination which one might be tempted to ascribe to the content as such, we mean thus to say simply that the content cannot possess this particular determination because this would prevent it from acquiring other real determinations, and a priori, before having reconstructed the entire objective reality, we cannot say of any content that it belongs only to an object of some particular class, and not to one of any other class.

a) In this sense the content is neither perceived nor imagined; it is simply given as subject-matter of reflection. The contents "horse" and "centaur," the content given in a dream as well as the content given in a waking state, are formally, without regard to the connections of the respective objects as parts of various systems, equally contents and nothing more or less. The content may even sometimes include the character of being perceived or that of being imagined; this character may belong to its objective and empirical matter. For example, instead of the content "horse," we may have the content "the perceived, or perceivable, horse," instead of "centaur," "the imaginary being centaur." But the content "the perceivable horse" is not itself perceived, and the content "the imaginary being centaur" is not imagined; we have only here instead of the contents "horse" and "centaur," which we had before, new contents, composed of the contents "horse" and "centaur" taken together with certain contexts, with certain complex characters which we call "being perceptual" and "being imaginary," even as we may add to a content the character of "being a dream," or again the character of "being a common-sense reality," acquiring thus two new and different contents. Each such addition is then an empirical subject-matter of reflection and together with the other unqualified components of the content constitutes a new content. For the manner of existence of the content is not determined by the manner of existence of the object, but any determination of the object, any manner of existence that we ascribe to it, must be given as part of a content in order to become empirically given at all.

b) The content is neither particular nor general. Of course it is a unit, but it is neither the member of a class nor a class. "This oak" is a content and "the class tree" is a content, but the content "this oak" is not a member of a class and the content "the class tree" is not a class of which the content "this oak" is a member. Both contents are equally units, equally single subject-matters of reflection. We may indeed connect logically the respective subjects and include this oak in the class tree; but in so far as the contents are concerned, the result will be expressed by two new contents, "this oak as member of the class tree," which is different from the content "this oak," and "the class tree as exemplified by this oak," which is different from the content "the class tree." The determination of an object as belonging to a class must become a content in order to be empirically realized, and precisely therefore the content as such is independent of this determination.

c) The same holds true of the distinction between concreteness and abstractness. The content is neither a concrete object including all the special characters necessary to its full determination as empirical reality, opposed to the abstract concept, nor abstract in the sense of being a concept which includes only certain essential characters common to many empirical objects. The content "the Louvre" is not a concrete to which, together with other contents, the content "the French Renaissance" would correspond as an abstract, and the "principle of conservation of energy" as content is not more abstract than any particular change of one form of energy into another when given as empirical subject-matter of reflection. Of course, the material object "Louvre" can be taken as concrete as against the abstract ideal object "French Renaissance," and their synthesis may then constitute a new content. But "the French Renaissance" or "the principle of conservation of energy," as empirically given subject-matters of reflection do not contain other contents; they contain what is actually included in them, and this may be a simple formula expressed in words or other symbols, or the formula with several examples of its application, or the formula with a vague characterization of the common features of the objects included under the concept, or all this together. We can have thus several different contents, whereas the objective idea is supposed to be one and the same, however it is given, because it is supposed to have the same rational constitution and the same field of application. But the application of the abstract to the concrete must itself become a content in order to be given.

d) The content may include simple or complex objects, but neither the qualification of complexity nor the correlative one of simplicity can be applied to it, because the very distinction between simple and complex objects must be given as a content to be given empirically at all. The objective green color of the grass is, of course, simpler than the object grass; this chair is a simpler object than the furniture of this room. But the content "grass" is not a composite of the various contents including different characters of the object grass, the content "the furniture of this room" is not a composite of the contents including the different pieces of furniture separately; and reciprocally, the content "green" is not a product of an analysis of the content "grass" into simpler elements, nor the content "chair" a product of a division of the content "the furniture of this room" into parts. But we can have contents in which the comparative simplicity and complexity of objects is empirically given as subject-matter of reflection, for example, the "green color of grass," or "the furniture of this room composed of chairs, tables, etc."

e) In the same way, the content may include space and time as characters of objects: and perhaps even pure objective space and time may be contents. But the content itself is not spatially localized nor temporarily determined, precisely because spatial and temporal determinations must be given within a content to be empirically given at all. Neither, on the other hand, does it possess any characters which would make its incorporation as an object into a spatial or temporal system impossible; it is not positively raised above space and time as are the Platonic ideas, for it is not a component of any system of ideas. Thus, while the content "the dimensions of the Metropolitan Opera House" contains space but is not itself in space, and the content "the nineteenth century" contains a time-determination but is not itself in time, the content "the problem of the syllogism" contains no spatial characteristics but is not essentially raised above space, and "the equilateral triangle" as content is not essentially timeless, whatever may be the determinations of the respective objects.

f) One of the very important kinds of contents are those which contain changes of objects. But the content "movement of the street car" clearly does not move and the content "evolution of the state" does not evolve. Of course, the objective concept which we form of the evolution of the state can and does evolve as an idea, by being introduced into different systems of the ideal reality. What is there empirically given as subject-matter of reflection is either a series of distinct contents, "the evolution of the state as conceived at the moment A," ". . . . at the moment B," ". . . . at the moment C," etc., or this whole evolution is itself a new content, "the evolution of the theory of the evolution of the state," and this content does not evolve either. On the other hand, no content can be said to be by virtue of its objective essence changeless, for this would mean that we attribute to it a certain objective character excluding change from that which it contains. "The substance of Spinoza" will be changeless only when it is taken as part of the one ideal system of Spinoza; "two times two equals four" is objectively changeless only "by definition," that is, as an object-idea, as component of the system of mathematics.

g) Finally, a particularly good illustration of the nature of the content is found in contents including personal experiences. The content, as we have seen already, has no personal characters, because, though it is a datum of experience, it is taken not as datum of experience, but as subject-matter of reflection. Now, a personal datum of experience can become the subject-matter of reflection, but then it has an impersonal content. This is precisely what happens when I reflect about the course of my own experience. The course of experience becomes a content which is no longer mine, no longer taken as present *here* and *now*, though in fact present *here* and *now*. I can discuss it, analyze it, communicate it to others. I can also incorporate it reflectively into the course of my personal experience out of which I took it to objectivate it; it will then become an object, part of the reflectively constructed system of objects which I call my personality or my experience. Or, on the contrary, I can connect it with contents in which experiences of other persons have become subject-matters of reflection, and then it will become a completely different object.

In the examples quoted above we have tried to deny the
content of the most important characters which under the
influence of various philosophical traditions may be ascribed
to it; we do not pretend to have exhausted the list.   The
principle is clear.   All reality must be accessible as such to
our experience; the term reality is meaningless unless applied
to the reality with which we are empirically acquainted.
And all reality must be objectively reconstructed from actuality by our logical thought;   an agglomeration of data is not
reality.   Therefore, whatever there may be in reality must
be accessible to both our experience and thought.   Any
object must be able to become a content, an empirically given
subject-matter of reflection, for we cannot admit that there is
anything in reality which cannot become the material of our
reconstructive activity;   and, on the other hand, any content
must be able to become an object, for we cannot admit that
there is anything in reality which we cannot reconstruct out
of the given materials.

The problem of the reconstruction of objective reality
from individual experience should not therefore be put, as
it usually is: "How is a copy of the object, or a phenomenal
object, constructed out of contents?" but: "How does a
content become an object?"   The first question either leads
to the conception of the object as outside the field of experience, a transcendent nucleus of contents inaccessible in itself
and given only through its empirical copies, or supposes that
the object—the "natural thing"—is empirically given besides
its copies—the "psychological images."   In both cases the
essential problem is left untouched.   In the first case, besides
the transcendent object we must have an empirical, objective
copy of this transcendent object, and this objective copy
differs as much from the subjective contents from which it has
to be reconstructed as if there were no transcendent object;
and its reconstruction from individual experience demands
explanation quite independent of the existence or non-

existence of a transcendent nucleus. Even if we supposed that subjective contents were the product of the influence of the transcendent object upon the subject, the problem would remain, for the transcendent object by definition could not be given in the subjective content, and the subject would always have to pass from the content to the object, even though in this passage he would reconstruct only an empirical copy of the object. In the second case the possibility of the individual's experiencing the natural "thing" is simply postulated, and the postulate is in the most naïve way self-contradictory, since the primary assumption implied in the opposition between things and psychological images is that the individual can experience only the latter.

These difficulties led to the well-known attempt to maintain the traditional way of putting the problem by separating experiencing and thinking; the individual was supposed not only to experience either effects of the transcendent object or subjective images of the natural thing, but to reconstruct the transcendent object or the thing by theoretic reasoning. But theoretic thought, as defined by these rationalistic schools, is not supposed to create reality, but only to know it. If it knows only subjective elements, it cannot know objects. Only that can be empirically reconstructed which is both empirically given and logically thinkable as objective—that is, only a content can become an object.

THE CONNECTION

The object is real only as part of a system of reality. The content is precisely a datum viewed as ready to become a part of some system of reality, but not yet determined as to the system to which it will belong. The question, "How does a content become an object?" is thus equivalent to the question, "How is a content incorporated into reality?" or "How does a content become a part of a real system?"

Here we meet at once a difficulty. We have postponed provisionally the problem of the rational organization of reality as manifested in the existence of systems; we have found it necessary to study reality as empirical before studying it as rational. And yet we see that there is no possibility of avoiding the problem of the system of reality, since there can be no real empirical object except as part of a system.

This difficulty, however, will be easily overcome. As we shall see, there are many systems of reality and they vary within the widest limits with regard to the rational perfection of their organization. If it is necessary for an object to belong to a system of reality in order to be real, it does not follow from this that the system to which the object belongs must be rationally perfect; on the contrary, though there are probably no perfect systems at all in the empirical world, this world is yet objective and real. Therefore, at the present moment when we are investigating reality only as empirical, not as rational, we do not need to assume any degree of rational perfection in the organization of real systems; it is enough for objects to be real that they belong to any system whatever, however imperfect and chaotic. A system viewed in this way, without regard to the rationality of its organization, is a mere *complex;* therefore throughout this chapter we shall speak mostly of complexes, not of systems of objects, and our present problem will be formulated: "How does a content become a part of a real complex?"

Two points must be kept in mind while trying to answer this question. On the one hand, indeed, the objectivation of the content must go on in actuality, otherwise the object could not be empirically reached; on the other hand, it must have a trans-actual bearing, must manifest itself in some way beyond the actual moment, otherwise the object would not be real, would not transcend the course of individual activity. The content must actually acquire a *connection* with other contents which will trans-actually characterize it as object, part of a real complex.

The necessity of the object's being reconstructed in actuality makes the use of the category of *relation* here impossible. A relation exists between ready objects as such; it is already objective, it is an object-matter of logical thought and a link of a definite system; and its own reconstruction in actuality is as much of a problem as the reconstruction of the objects between which it exists. It cannot therefore be the factor of objectivation of contents. However ultimate it may seem from the abstract standpoint of the logic of things, from the standpoint of concrete experience it presupposes the more primary category of actual connection.

On the other hand, since the connection must have an objective significance, be the ground of objectivity, it cannot be interpreted subjectively, as a psychological process. The theory which wants to explain objectivity by a permanence and uniformity of psychological associations of data simply begs the question. For the psychological association either has no objective ground, is not founded in the objective order of the associated data, and then it cannot serve to reconstruct this objective order in experience, or it has an objective ground, and then it is independent of the psychological course of experience and is not an association but a logical thought.

The connection must therefore be objective, but both ideal and real. It is ideal, for it is established by active thought in the course of actuality; as such, it is conscious and dynamic, subsisting fully only in the very act of its establishment and not existing trans-actually as a relation does. It is real, for it modifies the character of its object-matter and turns the content into a real object. We must leave the investigation of its ideal, conscious, and dynamic aspect provisionally aside; here we can study only its real, trans-actual side, the static result it leaves with objects. This static result is double.

On the one hand, the contents which have become actually connected with other contents must in some way preserve empirically the character of objects which they have acquired, must in other actualizations appear as objects, as being already parts of a reality into which they have become incorporated; otherwise, reality would always appear to us as depending continually and exclusively on individual acts of thought, whereas even in the course of its actual reconstruction it appears usually as more or less imposing itself upon our activity. This character which the object preserves beyond actuality and with which it appears in every new actualization can be neither a part of its content, for then it would not make the content anything else than a content, nor a relation, for a relation presupposes both the reality of the object and its own objectivity. There remains only one possibility. The new empirical character which a content acquires when it becomes object by an act of thought connecting it with other contents, must be simply an objective and still empirical ground for repeating indefinitely this act of thought, for reconstructing indefinitely the connection in actuality. When we say that a content which has been actively connected with other contents has become real, this character of "being real" from the empirical standpoint can be only a special feature which becomes and remains attached to the content as object and by virtue of which its connection with other contents remains latent even when not actually reconstructed, and can be made actual, conscious, and dynamic, at any moment and by any individual. By calling it an objective ground of an actual connection we wish to have it understood that it is less than a relation, which is supposed to be always explicit, always the same whether actually thought or not, but more than a mere subjective possibility of thinking the same connection over again without anything in the object being the reason for the thinking it over. This distinction is rather difficult for our intellectual habits, for we

have been accustomed to think of objects either as not connected at all, so that the establishment of a connection is
absolutely arbitrary, or as fully related, so that our thought is
logically compelled by the relation to connect them. Meanwhile, in concrete experience what is left of a connection once
established is merely a *suggestion* of its actual reconstruction,
a suggestion which gives to our thought the ground for
repeating the connecting act without logically forcing it to
do it.

We call the *meaning* of an object this suggestion to reproduce actually a connection which has been established between this object and others, when this suggestion appears
as grounded in the nature of this object as such. It is the
meaning which makes the empirical distinction between the
content and the object persist, even when the act in which
the connection is established is not being actually performed;
it is the meaning which makes reality empirically transcend
the limits of present individual experience. It is not given
with the content nor is it a content; and still it is empirical, it
qualifies empirically the content as real. It is empirical in
this unique sense, incomparable with the empirical character
of the content, of being a qualification of an object as existing
within a certain sphere of empirical reality.

The meaning is only one static result of the connection:
it is the characteristic of the object with reference to the
actual thought which reproduces it. Objectively, in the real
complex, the reality of the object must also manifest itself
with reference to other objects. An object is a part of a real
complex only if it influences other objects by being connected
with them, if it determines their contents really and objectively. The connection by which a content is made an object
is real, not merely ideal, and introduces the object into the
sphere of existence, only because it in some way modifies some
other content with regard to the content that it objectivates;
the objectivated content becomes the ground, the starting-

point of some real determination of the content with which it becomes connected. This is what the real relation is supposed to produce absolutely and objectively, by its very existence, for the objects are supposed to be permanently determined by it in their content with regard to each other. Of course in concrete experience such a permanent reciprocal determination is impossible, because the primary connection, being established in actuality, can really determine a content only while it is actually being produced or reproduced; and, because it is directed in time, it passes from one content to another as they successively become actualized, and therefore can determine only one of them from the standpoint of the preceding one, not both simultaneously and reciprocally. However, the act which objectivates a content by connecting it with another leaves a double trace: a meaning acquired by the first, objectivated content and a new determination, a variation of the second. The suggestion involved in the meaning of the first content to repeat the connection is therefore also a suggestion to reaffirm, to fix the determination of the second.

If, now, the second content thus determined by the connection with the first, objectivated content becomes in turn the starting-point of a new connection which gives it a meaning with regard to the first content and determines the latter from the standpoint of the former, we have the most elementary possible complex of objects. The complexes which we really find are, of course, composed of much more numerous objects, each having several meanings and determined with regard to several other objects and all thus directly or indirectly connected with each other. And when a set of contents has become a complex of interconnected objects, the influence of each of these objects on the other objects of the complex, which constitutes the objective ground of its "being real," is explicit and effective only in so far as consciously and dynamically reproduced, but it remains latent and implicit beyond actuality. As we shall see more in detail later on, the greater the number and stability of the connections of which an object is the starting-point, the greater the complexity and fixity of its meaning and the sphere of its influence on other objects, the higher also is the degree to which it is real.

Let us take several illustrations.

a) The most popular example illustrating the meaning is a word. The word as mere sensual content—sound or written sign—is not an object, unless it is incorporated into the physical world; but this is a relatively complicated problem which we shall discuss later. But when we use it as *symbol* of another content, when we refer it to this other content by an act, it acquires the character of a specific object and preserves it even when its connection with the content symbolized is no longer actual. Its meaning, as we clearly see in this case, is neither a part of its content nor an objective relation between it and the content indicated, but merely a suggestion to perform the same act of thought as the one already performed, a suggestion which may lead to a repetition of the act when the content of the word appears in actuality. The more frequently the act is repeated, the stronger becomes the suggestion, the more fixed the meaning, though its essential character does not change; it does not become either a part of the content or a relation, and the only explicit manifestation of this growing fixity of the meaning is the growing probability that this objectively grounded act and not any other act of symbolization will be performed whenever the word appears in actuality. This relative stability and uniformity of the meaning is usually not limited to the experience of one individual, because the word normally is a social object, its meaning is approximately the same for everybody in the social group, everybody obtains a similar suggestion.

At the same time, the reality of the word manifests itself objectively by the fact that the content given with reference to the word acquires thereby a special determination, becomes given with a special character corresponding to the meaning of the word and conditioned by the word. Thus, it is isolated from other contents and stabilized, it acquires prominently the categorical characteristic of a thing, a quality, a state, it becomes more or less distinctly qualified as pleasant, good, important, or unpleasant, bad, insignificant, etc. It is hardly necessary to emphasize this well-known influence of words upon the contents symbolized by them, and we observe how this influence grows with the fixation of the meaning of the words.

The same field of language furnishes us with another type of examples. Besides the acts in which we pass from the word to the content symbolized, there are usually other acts in which it is the content symbolized that acquires in turn a meaning with reference to the word: its appearance "suggests the word." We see in the history of culture many interesting examples of how far this reference of a content to a word is able to give objective reality to the former; it has frequently been noticed that a content constituting an imaginary extension of the natural or social reality, when permanently called by a word, can become so vivid that no efforts of philosophical or scientific criticism can destroy the belief that it must exist somewhere in nature or society, since it has a name. The variations of content which the word then acquires by being referred to from the standpoint of the symbolized object are best illustrated by the examples of onomatopoeia and of the morphological assimilation to some other word used of a similar object.

b) The myth gives another interesting illustration. The meaning of the myth involves many and complicated suggestions. These suggestions are, first, those of the aesthetic or theoretic acts of thought by which the mythical personality is connected with other mythical personalities or happenings in the pantheon of the social group; secondly, those of practical or religious acts by which the mythical personality is connected with definite objects used in the ritual, temples, sacred vessels, sacred food, drink, incense, bodies of the priests, etc., and with such objects in the sphere of individual or social interest as are supposed to be affected by the interference of the mythical personality. It is this whole complex of meanings which makes the myth subjectively as real in the experience of the group as any sensual reality. This point appears with particular clearness when we compare the myth with the popular tale into which it often degenerates; the tale lacks all these complex meanings, and therefore its personalities are no longer treated by the group as real. Objectively, with reference to other objects, the myth is real by all the influence it exercises, through the acts in which its meaning is realized, over individual ideas and emotions, over social organization, and even over the material world, indirectly by putting certain demands on technique, directly by conditioning the view of the material world which prevails at the given period and in the given society; and certainly its objective reality is not less manifest than that of many a material object whose influence is not even approximately as wide.

c) Take now the bank note. Of course, it is an object as part of the physical world, but this character is almost completely ignored when we treat it as an economic object. Then we neglect its physical and chemical properties and pay attention only to its directly given sensual content. It is for us not a complex of atoms or electrons but a note of certain dimensions, certain color, with certain pictures and signs printed on it, etc. And this content has an economic reality because it suggests a plurality of acts which consist in planning or effecting economic exchanges and which establish connections between the note and other contents—those of objects that can be bought with the note. The meaning, and with it the reality of the note, lasts, even though no new acts are performed, as long as the objective ground is there, as we see from the example of the miser; the note loses reality only if these acts become limited or impossible, if, for example, paper money becomes depreciated. Objectively, the reality of the note expresses itself in all the modifications that its meaning determines in the economic and material reality— changes of property, production, transportation, and consumption of goods, etc.

d) The problem of consumption suggests another kind of reality which a content acquires when it becomes connected with our body by a reference to our needs. Thus, an unknown fruit, if we once more exclude by abstraction its objectivity as part of the physical world, which is in fact taken into account only on special occasions, remains a content without much objective character as long as we merely contemplate it with regard to its form, color, etc. But the acquaintance with its use, that is, the performance of the acts of observing, planning, or effecting the movements which will bring it into touch with our palate and throat, gives it immediately a meaning and makes it appear real. The connection between the fruit and the body is less fixed in the acts of observing or planning than in those of actual consumption, and therefore the object acquires a less definite reality in the first case than in the second—a difference which we shall be able better to understand later on. There is an interesting point here which shows that it is indeed the fruit as content which acquires a specific reality distinct from the material reality, not the ready material object which acquires a new subjective significance. When the fruit is consumed, the material object is no longer there; it is evident, however, that the content is not annihilated but preserves the meaning it thus acquired, perhaps for the first time. It remains an object of a specific kind, a hedonistic value. When it later returns in actuality, it suggests the same acts, even though the "thing," the material "fruit" is a new one, or even if the content is given only as an "image" or a "dream," for the specific object, the hedonistic value, is the same. Objectively, its reality is shown by the variations it adds to the content of our body, the new smell-, taste-, and touch-sensations which result from its being brought into connection with our body and which may be revived even if the connection is not fully, only partly realized, as in a hallucination or a dream.

e) But our body is not only an exceptionally rich content continually modified and determined by the objects which are brought into connection with it in satisfying our needs; it is also a prominently real object; we can say the real object *par excellence*, because of the active connections of which it is the starting-point, because of the modifications which we bring with its help into other objects. The type of these connections is different from the one discussed in the previous example; here the connections are "material" and it is the body itself which acquires through them the character of a material object, whereas in the previous case they were hedonistic and it was other contents which became hedonistic objects with reference to the body. But the mechanism of objectivation is the same; here the actual connection—the conscious and dynamic, though at the same time material, act—leaves after it a new meaning added to the body as "instrument" of this particular kind of activity (a question to which we shall return later) and a new determination of the content which became the object-matter of this activity, and both the meaning and the determination remain latent; the body appears later in actuality as able to perform this movement, the other content as determinable in the same way by this movement. The other content, we repeat, not the particular material object, for the material object that was the object-matter of the bodily activity may no longer be in existence, the movement might even have consisted in destroying its materiality. When this content reappears in actuality, whether as other material object or as "image," the possibility of determining it in the same way by the same actual connection with the body is always there, whether the connection and the resulting determination be performable materially or only "in imagination" (which is a later problem).

f) Not only the body but many other contents can be objectivated by the same type of connection, that is, by a conscious and dynamic, though at the same time "material," action which gives them the actual meaning of material objects and makes them objectively real by modifying other contents with their help. They are the material "instruments" in general. In order to understand the question properly, we must provisionally forget the fact that material instruments are already real even before being used for a particular activity. This is not very difficult, as we still occasionally find children, savages, and even ourselves testing the reality of given sensual contents by trying to use them as material instruments, that is, by trying to produce with their help materially some modifications in other contents, even if only in our own bodies. Moreover, whatever may have been the pre-existing "realness" of an artificial instrument, such as an ax or a sewing-machine, it is clear that this pre-existing "realness" of a lump of matter is relatively unimportant as compared with the highly specified and definite "realness" which it acquires by being particularly adapted to perform special activities. Thus, in the course of ordinary experience the material meaning of a piece of iron or wood is poorer than that of the sewing-machine or ax made of them; they appear less real in actuality because they count less for activity. They may indeed acquire a very complex meaning and appear as very highly real when the technician takes them as practical materials, or the scientist as object-matter of theoretic investigation, precisely because then they become actually connected with many other objects, become incorporated into systems; but aside from this, their average subjective "realness" in common-sense experience lacks much as compared with that of a ready and much-used instrument. Objectively their existence is also less effective, for the field of their actual influence is narrower; the number, variety, range, and definiteness of modifications which a piece of iron or wood can determine in other contents are normally much smaller than those which an ax or a sewing-machine can bring forth.

g) Passing now to this pre-existing real character of the material object as such, if we only exclude provisionally the naturalistic postulate of the absoluteness of the material world in general, we shall see that the empirical objectivation of a content as material object, even without reference to its use as instrument, has the same explanation as the objectivation of a content as symbol, as religious, economic, or hedonistic object. The material object appears real in actuality because the numerous conscious and dynamic connections—spatial, qualitative, causal—which have been established between it and many other contents have incorporated it empirically into a wide and intricate complex. The meaning of this object involves thus numerous suggestions of possible acts, particularly since many material things have similar contents and their suggestions agglomerate. These suggestions are usually more numerous, more fixed, and simpler than those offered by most of the objects of other types, though, as the example of a material object worked over into an artificial instrument shows, their number and definiteness are far from having attained any absolute limit and can greatly increase. And the real character of the material object is also objectively manifested by the influence which it has over other objects; only our naturalistic prepossessions make us assume that this influence is independent of the actual, conscious, and dynamic connections which we may establish between this object and others, that, for example, any modification which a material object can produce in other objects, aside from its being used as instrument by us, is due to relations of causality purely objective and independent of our thought.

But it is clear that, since the empirical existence of the causal relation, just as the empirical existence of any part or side of reality, depends on its actual reconstruction, whatever is empirical in the causal relation must be deducible from actual contents and connections. As a bond between actually given objects in which one of these objects *now* and *here* empirically influences the content of the other, it can be nothing but a very stable connection. It can be actually realized by any experiencing individual at any moment only if this individual actively connects the given objects; otherwise, in this individual's actual experience, these objects will not be connected at all, there will be no dynamic bond between them. Of course this bond is objective; it transcends any particular actuality, is not reducible entirely to the act by which a particular individual determines the objects as causally connected *now* and *here;* but it is reducible, as empirical objective connection, to the totality of actual and conscious acts by which various individuals at various moments have determined one of these objects from the standpoint of the other as causally modified by it in its content. Now, such an objective connection becomes a relation when we abstractly ignore its dependence on actuality in general and treat it, not as an objective possibility of acts which will actually connect the objects when empirically given, but as a trans-actual object-matter of logical thought, as a self-existing dynamic influence exercised by one object upon another in a rational order of reality. We shall investigate later on the origin and significance of this conception.

There is one important factor which makes it difficult for us to see that the material reality is as dependent in its empirical existence on actually established connections as any other reality; it is that material reality has been always the favorite object-matter of theoretic thought and no real connection can be reproduced in actuality by this thought;

reality imposes itself upon our knowledge as seemingly quite independent of the latter.   This is due, as we shall see later on, to the specific character of knowledge which never tends to reproduce pre-existing real connections but takes their results as given and reconstructs them in a new way.   But actually each real connection in particular can be reproduced by some other kind of activity—technical, hedonistic, aesthetic, etc.—and only in so far as thus reproduced by some activity can it be actually experienced.

h) There is one sphere in which even theoretic thought is able to produce or reproduce entirely the objective reality of contents: it is the sphere of scientific and philosophical ideas. "The principle of conservation of energy," "the binomial theorem of Newton," "the concept of substance," can be given by thought a double kind of meaning.   As formulae they have a symbolic character in reference to empirical contents; their own content is then merely the formula as set of sounds or signs; their meaning is of the same type as the meaning of a word; they are then not scientific, but philological objects.   But they can be taken, together with the postulate of their empirical application and eventual illustrations of this application, as forms of reality (we shall see later the significance of this term) and then objectivated as *ideas* with reference to other ideas.   In other similar connections, from the standpoint of other ideas, their own content becomes determined, acquires a higher degree of exactness, abstractness, and generality, and in this way they are incorporated into a system of ideas and acquire a specific real character, on account of which they can be called, in spite of the seeming contradiction of terms, the *ideal reality*.

As these examples sufficiently show, contents can become incorporated into any type of reality by actual connections. The more frequently the connections are reproduced, the more fixed become the meanings, the stronger the suggestions which they have in the experience, not only of the same, but of any individual whether acquainted or not with their former actualizations. We find innumerable gradations from the faintest aesthetic suggestion presented by a new combination of sounds down to the strongest and most definite suggestions of consumption offered by food or suggestions of resistance and weight given by material objects when we look at them.

Of course, we must always keep in mind here that the individual can actually experience a meaning only after having reconstructed the connection in actuality. But he can actually experience a previously unknown character of a content also only after having reconstructed this character in actuality by being brought to perceive the content from a certain particular standpoint. I must be trained to experience meanings, to realize suggestions; but I must also be trained to experience contents, to see in them such sides as I have not seen before. But this necessity does not permit me to conclude that every meaning begins to exist only when I experience it, any more than I conclude that every content begins to exist only when I perceive it. I know usually, when I experience a previously unknown content, whether I have just produced it by my own activity or merely reproduced it as it pre-existed in the cultural world, for in the latter case it has a definiteness and clearness which it seldom possesses in the first case. In the same way I distinguish a meaning which is given to an object for the first time by me from one which I have merely discovered and reconstructed in actuality and which the object had long ago, for the suggestion in the latter case is incomparably stronger. The distinction may be difficult in intermediary cases, when either the old meaning is not yet very fixed or the new meaning is merely a transference of some old meaning to a new content. There is also no doubt that some, though it is impossible to say a priori how much, of the relative objectivity with which many meanings appear when reconstructed is due to the consciousness of social sanction.

THE CONCRETE HISTORICAL OBJECT

On the ground of the content and the connection, as discussed in the preceding sections, it is thus possible to reconstruct any objective and rational reality from actual experience and by actual reflection; for in the content any rational determination of a real object can be actually experienced and in the connections any rational organization of a real system can be actually reproduced. We shall study in later chapters the problem how this reconstruction, or construction, of a rational and objective reality is actually performed, how complexes of objects by acquiring a rational organization become more and more perfect systems, and how objects included in these complexes acquire a rational determination which makes them more and more independent of actual experience.

But the problems concerning the empirical character of reality are not exhausted by our having shown how an object and a complex of objects is empirically produced or reproduced in actuality. For there are many possible ways of empirically determining and objectivating a content, many complexes into which an empirical object may be introduced in the course of actuality, and none of these ways of objectivation is, from the standpoint of experience, the only rational one to the exclusion of others; none of these complexes determines the object so perfectly and completely as to make other determinations of the same object, even entirely different ones, rationally impossible. There is hardly any object whose concrete reality is completely exhausted by any one system to which it belongs; in the examples which we quoted in the last section every object was found to belong to several different types of reality.

Moreover, there are, as we know, no absolutely objective and absolutely rational systems in the world as reconstructible from actuality and, on the other hand also, no actually produced complex of interconnected contents is

merely subjective and none is ever deprived of that minimum of rationality which it must possess in order to make
real objects of the contents of which it is composed. Once a
content has been actually connected with other contents, it is
no longer a mere datum, for it has become in some, however
small, measure independent of the course of personal experience: it may return indefinitely with the same objective
determination in other experiences of the same or of other
individuals, even though the set of data with which it returns
will always be more or less different. Once a number of
contents have been actually interconnected and have formed
a complex, this complex is no longer a mere association of data,
for it has become in some, however small, measure rational;
for each and all of the connections can be reproduced indefinitely in actuality as the same objective connections by the
same or other individuals, even though the associations in
which these contents will be given as data in the course of
personal experience will vary from case to case. This is
precisely the most elementary and fundamental difference
between a connection of objects and an association of data,
for the association of data is as such unique and irreproducible.
In so far as the individual connects objects to some degree
at least independently of the succession and centralization of
data in his present experience, by giving these objects meanings and determining their contents with regard to each other,
he is no longer a mere subject of data but a creator of reality.
Though the results of this conscious connecting activity, the
more or less imperfectly organized complexes, may appear
as relatively subjective and relatively irrational from the
standpoint of more objective, more rationally perfect systems,
they are not absolutely subjective, not absolutely irrational.
The difference of objectivity and rationality between various real systems is one of degree, not of nature. We shall
later on examine this difference as manifested in the rational
organization of various systems. Here we can discuss only its

manifestations in experience. And we notice that, in so far as empirically given, complexes of objects present indeed many gradations in two respects: with regard to their stability and with regard to their wideness.

Thus, the difference between a part of the common-sense reality, an imaginary construction of a poet, and a dream shows itself, first of all, in the various degrees of fixity with which the respective contents and meanings impose themselves upon the reconstructing individual. During the reconstruction of all three of these complexes, some part is still played by the individual objectivation of data and of associations of data into real objects and rational connections; for even the common-sense reality, the most fixed of the three, reaches the individual only as personal data and associations and must be reconstructed in actuality by this kind of objectivation in order to be empirically given as reality at all. But in the common-sense reality the channels of objectivation are so fixed, the meanings established, and the contents determined by such innumerable repetitions that the individual is hardly conscious of his reconstructive activity and every individual reconstructs it in nearly the same way. The imaginary construction of a poet or artist, without being irrational or subjective, is more personal and unusual; it can be repeated by others in the same form only because the poet or artist tries consciously to use for his construction a sufficient number of fixed meanings and determinations to make its reconstruction by others easy. Whereas in the dream the intention to communicate the new reality to others is absent and there is no limitation imposed by common sense or social tradition on the construction of the dream-complex, which thus appears as purely personal. And yet the dream is still an objective reality. It is a curious fact that dreams after having been treated for innumerable centuries as objective realities, were for a period considered as pure associations; but now their "meaningfulness," with the ancient mystical exaggerations excluded, once more begins to be taken into account. However great may be the difference of fixity between a dream, an artistic construction, and a part of common-sense reality, all of them are objective, because all of them are reconstructible.

The second empirical difference of degree between complexes is their wideness. Even if the artist's construction, or the dream, is fully objectivated, it remains isolated from the rest of reality, a rather limited complex—the latter more, the former less. Meanwhile, an objectivated part of the common-sense reality is by innumerable meanings connected with many other objects continually returning in actuality. Therefore, even if in my dream the objects and their connections are the same as a certain waking complex, after I awake they do not appear real to me because I do not find the expected connections between them and the rest of my usual environment. If I find myself unexpectedly in a new environment not connected with my usual environment, I have in a smaller degree exactly the same attitude toward my new experiences as toward a dream.

Of course both the fact that an object can belong to several different complexes and the differences of stability and wideness between these complexes themselves can be empirically ascertained only if our experience and reflection are not at every moment exclusively limited to the one more or less systematic, more or less stable and wide complex which we are actually producing or reproducing *here* and *now*. If our personality were always absorbed by the one complex which is actually reproduced, we would know nothing about the relativity and limitation of this complex and about the fact that an object which we are actually taking as part of this complex exists also within other complexes. This would be the case if our personalities were exclusively active, perfectly logical, and entirely isolated from other personalities.

But this is not the case.   It has been shown in the preceding chapter that a personality is both active and passive, that it not only objectivates reality in actual reflection but also subjectivates reality in actual experience.   And the actually objectivated domain of reflection is by no means identical with the actually subjectivated domain of experience.   While we are reproducing actively some complex, other complexes impose themselves upon our passive personality by becoming associations of data without entirely ceasing to be complexes, and an object which we have just incorporated into one complex may return at any moment as element of some other complex, preserving even as a passively experienced datum some of its original objectivity.   Our actuality is thus a ceaseless and chaotic alternation of active reproduction of some realities, or passive experiencing of others.   Further, even without this interference of passively accepted experiences our active reproduction of reality is far from being logically perfect: we seldom, and only by a special intentional effort, reproduce a pre-existing real complex fully and adequately with all its objects and connections, and we never reproduce a relatively wide complex continuously, but always in fragments, with interruptions during which other complexes occupy our active attention.   Finally, neither as passively experiencing nor as actively reproducing personalities are we entirely isolated, but our experience and reflection are at every step interfered with by the experience and reflection of others and vice versa.   The full, concrete sphere of experience and reflection of any individual taken within a certain period of duration presents from the purely empirical standpoint an irrational dynamic combination, fragmentarily experienced, fragmentarily reconstructed, intermingled, multiform, and changing.   And the total empirical, real world viewed in its full concreteness as a synthesis of all individual experiences and reflections is an enormous, wild, and rushing chaos of innumerable complexes, inextricably and irrationally combined, becoming and developing without any possible universal order whatever.

It is clear that under these conditions our conception of the concrete empirical object, and of the concrete empirical reality as composed of such objects, must be radically different from the traditional conceptions of realistic empiricism. The latter continually works under the assumption that reality is rationally one, even if we cannot reconstruct this unity a priori but must reach it step by step from experience, and that therefore each empirical object as element of this reality must be rationally determinable in one way, must possess one definite objective nature, be objectively similar to itself in spite of the manifold and often conflicting variations which it presents when reconstructed by different individuals and at different moments. The problem of realistic empiricism has always been therefore to reach this rationally one object from the varying and conflicting views of this object taken in different connections. And this is not an ontological, but a psychological problem. Treating reality as independent of both our experience and our reflection, realism entirely neglects the difference between a mere datum and an object as part of a complex actually constructed by reflective thought, ignores the empirical objectivity of the complex, and, instead of asking how the object is determined in its nature by the various empirical complexes in which it is taken, asks merely how can the object, which is supposed to be already completely determined in its nature, be known by human individuals with the help of their imperfect and varying experiences.

The usual and most popular attempt to reconcile the supposedly one real nature of the object with the multiple empirical views of this object is to assume that there is indeed a variety of individual "representations," but that these representations are not objects, but only refer to the one common object-as-such. The oldest and simplest criterion making it possible to distinguish what in individual representations belongs to this common object is the identity of content; that which is identically given to all individuals is supposed to belong to the object, that which is not is qualified as subjective, due to the personal peculiarities of the experiencing subjects.   But this criterion can work only when there is enough uniformity in a social group to make the variations of individual representations relatively insignificant, and when the problems concerning objects are simple enough to be solved with the help of such roughly approximate definitions of objects as are still preserved in popular language. For if we really compare, as far as can be done, individual representations of an object in many groups and at various periods, we find that their identical elements are relatively few, seldom sufficient to construct out of them even a very simple object, and dwindle to nothing when we pass from material reality to social, religious, aesthetic, moral, or scientific objects.   Moreover, we find more and more frequent cases in the evolution of culture where the representation of a single individual—for instance, a scientist—must be admitted to be more objective than the average of all the other representations put together, and yet differs from it very widely.

Realistic empiricism has thus to adopt necessarily a different criterion, which it expresses in the theory that the object, as distinguished from individual representations, contains of these representations all that can be rationally and without contradiction ascribed to it, all that is reconcilable with its objective nature as determined by the character of the reality to which it belongs and by the logical demands of the system of thoughts of which this reality is the object-matter.   This is to say, in other words, that the content of the object is determined by the system of objects of which it is a part; that there is one system in which its real content is entirely determined, and that, if various individuals try to incorporate it into other systems, these other systems either are merely components of that one system, or if they are not, then the divergent determinations which these individuals give to the content of the object do not belong to it objectively.

From whatever standpoint we look at this theory and its implications, it is philosophically impossible. We can understand how a scientist may delude himself that his science at the given moment is able to explain the content of a certain object entirely, because he is already dealing not with the full concrete object, but with the object as part of the specific real system which his science is then investigating; that is, an object from whose content all the variations which it possesses outside of this system have been excluded. But already in the past the same object was explained differently many times by the same science and will be explained differently in the future, and each of these successive explanations may be equally complete in its own sphere; for the problems which a science puts change with the evolution of this science, and none of its successive problematizations has the entire concrete object to deal with, but each takes the object only as determined by certain specific connections. Furthermore, the object is also being treated simultaneously in other sciences, where its content is again differently given; it is, perhaps, also the object-matter of technical activity, of religious worship, of hedonistic enjoyment, of economical exchange, of aesthetic reproduction, and in each of these systems its content differs. Only a metaphysical fanaticism can expect to reduce all these systems to one in which the objects are entirely determined in their content. And if, in spite of their plurality, the determination which each of these systems gives to the objects is, nevertheless, objective, where shall we put any limit to objectivity and how can we separate subjective representations from objective variations of content?

This much for the rational side of the question. But the theory of representations as distinct from objects and of objects constructed out of representations is also false empirically, because it does not correspond to anything in experience. There is certainly no distinction in empirical reality between the object and the representation or image of the object. When I see Lake Michigan, there is in my experience only one object, the lake, and not two, the lake and its representation. If someone else looks at the lake with me, I know that there is always one object, the lake, and not three—the lake, his and my representation—nor even two, his representation and mine. When sitting in my room in Chicago I remember the Notre Dame of Paris there is empirically again only one object, Notre Dame, and not two, Notre Dame and my representation. And again, if someone else, in my presence or not, is also at this moment remembering Notre Dame, there is still only one object, not two or three. The same is true of my or anybody else's actual realization of a myth, a mathematical proposition, an economic value, etc.; there is never any distinction or opposition in experience between the object and its image, but there is always only the object given as content in my experience and as object-matter of my thought.

If thus on the realistic assumptions it is impossible to reconstruct even the empirical content of the concrete object, the difficulties when its meaning is taken into account are still greater. The problem of the meaning as conditioning human activity is the central point of the theory of values, the chief stumbling-stone of both realism and idealism. Philosophy has always tried to simplify the question of the object by reducing either the meaning to the content or the content to the meaning. In the first case it assumes that the individual's activity in response to the object is naturally conditioned by the content of this object. In so far then as the content is supposed identical for everybody, the meaning should also be identical; in so far as the content is admitted to vary from individual to individual, the meaning should vary accordingly. The primary, naïve standpoint that contents are thoroughly common led thus, first of all, to a righteous indignation, typified in the first Greek thinkers, against the variation of individual reactions to them, rather than to an explanation of this variation; and when the explanation was attempted, it took the radical sophistic form of the assumption of a complete variety of individual contents. But the complete variety of contents explained too much, for a certain identity of meanings was undeniable, and it is from this partial identity of meanings as manifested in common valuations that Socratism took its start and concluded that contents must be also partially identical. The golden period of Greek philosophy is thus characterized with respect to this problem by an assumption of the community of the essential, conceptual part of contents and the community of the rational, perfect meanings corresponding to it and determined by it, while the varying individual meanings of objects corresponded to and were assumed to be determined by the individually differentiated, unessential, sensual part of contents. But the apparent harmony of this solution was soon disturbed by the circumstance that, on the one hand, the conceptual identity of content could not guarantee a rational identity of meaning, the most varying practical conclusions could be drawn, abstractly and in concrete behavior, from any theory of the world as world of contents, and on the other hand, a quite irrational set of religious and practical meanings became, in Christian dogmatics, the source of a common theoretic conception of the world. And thus, when after renaissance and reformation the problem was taken up again, it was put on a different ground, in view of the importance which individual conscious life with all its valuations had taken during the domination of faith. Contents and meanings were entirely separated from each other, the first as real, the second as ideal, and while on the one hand a unique objective system of reality was constructed as a system of natural things and relations, of absolute contents, on the other an equally

objective ideal system was attempted as a system of absolute values—of absolute meanings, more exactly.   The non-
common parts of contents and meanings both found their
refuge in individual consciousness.

Thus, the problem of the meaning has become much more
complicated and its solution depends essentially on the
question where individual consciousness, including both
contents and meanings, is supposed properly to belong.   If it
is conceived as a part of nature, then its meanings are supposed
to be reducible to contents, and their variations and identities
explicable by the variations and identities of the given contents
themselves and of human nature; men react to things in a way
that is conditioned both by these things and by their own
character as natural beings.   In this case the objectivity of
meanings and their identity for all become dissociated problems, for meanings may be identical without being objective, objective without being identical.   Objective meanings,
judged by the standards of natural objectivity, would be such
as would follow from the nature of the object to which they
are attached, whereas meanings identical for living beings
would have to follow from the uniformity of nature of the
beings and would change when this nature changed.   The
chief effort of naturalism in this line is therefore the harmonization of these two explanations by assuming that individual
meanings in so far as identically common to living beings
tend to adapt themselves to the objective relations of things.
The possibility of such an adaptation presupposes, first, that
individually given contents adapt themselves to the absolutely
determined contents of the things in nature, and secondly, that
individual meanings are exclusively conditioned by individual
contents.   The biological theory of knowledge tries to
demonstrate that by means of knowledge the individual
determination of contents subordinates itself to their objective
determination in nature.   But naturalism is unable to show
that individual meanings are exclusively conditioned by

individually determined contents, for this would imply that all individual activity is entirely conditioned by the rational organization in knowledge of the contents of individual experience, whereas the illogical character of emotion and will proves the opposite. Thence all the types of voluntaristic reaction against naturalistic rationalism. These take the opposite standpoint and emphasize that it is rather the meaning, as manifested in the intention, the feeling, the desire, etc., which determines the selection, qualification, and organization of contents in individual experience. But this reaction, in order to save this voluntaristic individual experience from the reproach of subjectivity, as against the theoretically determined objectivity of the world of natural things and relations, has either to deny the objectivity of the latter, which would lead to pure subjectivism, or to subordinate the objectivity of contents to the objectivity of meanings and thus lead logically to the philosophy of absolute meanings.

This philosophy begins by pointing out that in the world of meaningless existence, that is, nature, contents are in fact determined by meanings, by the meanings which the theorist gives them when treating them as objectively interrelated things, and that "the world of nature is valueless because it is valuable for us to conceive it as valueless." Then it goes on to demonstrate that the objectivity of the natural world is based on the objectivity of the meanings and that this demands absolutely objective meanings as supreme criteria. The scientific meanings are then considered only as part of the world of absolutely objective meanings, which includes also moral, aesthetic, religious, and perhaps other meanings as well. But even if we grant that in this theory the objective world of contents can be deduced from the objective world of absolute meanings, it is evident that the contents of individual experience always appear as simply given and are not deducible either from objective or from subjective meanings: they are, as we have seen, objectivated data whose source is in the trans-individual world of contents, and as data they come to the individual not only independently of his objective or subjective valuations, but often even against them. The philosophy of absolute meanings may subordinate the abstract world of nature to absolute valuations, acts of the absolute subject, but it cannot prevent the empirical subject with his empirical meanings from being in some way dependent, as to the contents of his experience, on the trans-actual empirical reality.

Moreover, the philosophy of absolute meanings meets for the first time, in its full significance as independent problem, the problem of opposition between subjective and objective meanings, entirely distinct from the problem of the opposition between subjective and objective contents, to be solved no longer, as in the past, in connection with the distinction of things and representations, but by entirely new methods. But it clearly fails to give any satisfactory solution. It is easy to say that, if individual moral, aesthetic, religious, valuations are not absolute, it is because the individual is not a pure subject of absolute valuations, but has also an existential character, as a part of the world of contents. But, even so, since the world of contents is supposed to be produced by the absolute subject, in so far as the individual is a subject, he should agree with the latter. The chief difficulty for the theory of absolute meanings, just as for the theory of absolute contents, comes not from the very personal, stupid, and egotistic appreciations, parallel to illusions in the sphere of contents, but from the numerous highly developed, but conflicting, valuations of morality, art, religion, etc., each of which imposes itself on different individuals with the same degree of objectivity and which it is impossible to reduce to one system, just as it is impossible to reduce to one the varying and partial systems based on the contents of things.

Thus the attempt to reconcile the principle of one reality with the empirical manifoldness of content and meaning which the same object possesses in different complexes is a complete and all-sided failure. However comfortable may be the common assumption that every object has one unique and self-consistent nature of its own, which does not vary though its subjective representations may differ and even contradict each other, it must be definitively classed with such beliefs as the "direct action" of magical causality and the existence of "faculties of the soul." The fact is that, viewed as to their contents exclusively, objects are determinable in innumerable ways according to the complexes in which they are included; these complexes cannot be reduced to one another because each constitutes a distinct objective whole, for between the most impersonal determination of a content in a physical theory and the most personal determination of this content in a dream the difference is merely one of degree. Viewed as to their meanings exclusively, objects can have innumerable meanings according to the systems to which they belong; there are no absolute unique meanings to which others could be reduced, and between the meaning given to an object by the wisest or holiest man in accordance with a deeply impersonal and highly moral view of the world, and the meaning given to it by an imbecile or a thief for his momentary personal needs, the difference is one of degree, not of essence.

Finally, between the objects viewed in their content and the objects viewed in their meaning there is a discrepancy impossible to overlook. Both the content and the meaning of an object are due to actual connections between this object and others, but to different connections, for, as we have seen, the actual connection is directed and one-sided and gives the meaning to one object and the determination of content to another, so that the connections which fix the meaning are necessarily different from those that determine the content. The same content may thus acquire the most various meanings; the same meaning may qualify the most various contents. Of course, certain meanings are, as a matter of fact, more often attached to certain contents than other meanings, but this does not constitute any logical ground for treating this fact as in any way objectively conditioned either by the character of the contents or by the character of these meanings. A stone is more often qualified as material object than as religious object, a bank note as economic value rather than as hedonistic or technical value, a picture as aesthetic rather than as scientific value. But it is no more essential for the content "stone" to be a material thing than an object of religious worship, not more essential that the content "bank note" be put into circulation than be immediately enjoyed by a miser or used by a spendthrift to light a cigar, not more essential for the content "picture" to be aesthetically admired than to serve as source for a study of the costumes of the epoch. On the other hand, though we more often ascribe material meaning to certain contents, economical meaning to other contents, aesthetic or religious meaning to still others, there is nothing in the character of these meanings which would exclude the possibility of their application to any other contents whatever. There is no content which could not acquire the character of a material thing, if it were only in a dream or a hallucination, no content which could not be treated as object of economical exchange, no content which could not become an object of aesthetic admiration, or religious worship, etc. This is no longer true when we have to deal with an object exclusively within a limited complex: there its content and its meaning do belong to each other, not because they depended on each other originally, but because the object has become defined in this complex with regard to both content and meaning. Thus the stone in the system of the mineralogist or of the stone-cutter is a material thing, but the stone Kaaba is an object of religious worship in the religious system of the Mohammedans of Arabia; the paper bill is an economic value in the system of the business man, a hedonistic value in the system of the miser, etc.

Within one limited complex the object is thus as rational in its content, its meaning, and in the coexistence of a certain content and a certain meaning as this complex by virtue of its own rational organization can make it.   But there is no rational connection whatever between the various aspects which one object presents in different complexes.   We have to separate definitively the problem of the object as rationally but only partially determined within a single system from that of the object as completely but irrationally determined in many more or less systematic and objective, but different and disconnected, complexes.   We must realize that the concrete, empirical object, taken in the totality of the content and meaning given to it in all the various empirical complexes to which it belongs, can satisfy neither the demands of traditional epistemology, which requires it to be the same for different individuals, nor the demands of traditional logic, which requires it to possess a self-identical, non-contradictory objective nature, nor those of traditional philosophy of values, which requires its meaning and its content to belong rationally together.

We call a concrete empirical object in its total content and meaning a *historical object.*   The choice of this term is justified by the fact that all the various more or less systematic empirical complexes of which a concrete object is a part are constructed or reconstructed in the course of historical becoming, and thus, as will be seen presently, the concrete object in its total content and meaning is not fully real at once, but realizes itself more and more in its entire historical existence, as simultaneously or successively produced or reproduced by various individuals at various moments.   The historical object includes thus all the determinations of content and all the meanings that it possesses in all the various complexes of which it is a part, with no distinction between subjective and objective characters. It is only the datum which is or rather becomes subjective in the course of its subjectivation; but the datum contains no characters which the object does not possess, it is not a subjective copy of the object, it is the object while becoming subjective, the same object which, in a subsequent objectivation, acquires a new meaning and a new variation of content. Every character which is ascribed to the historical object in the course of objectivation belongs to this object itself, because the fact that a character has been ascribed to an object in the course of objectivation means that this character has been added to it by connecting it with other objects, by making it a part of a complex. This principle is easily recognized in the case of many cultural objects. Thus, almost everybody will agree that a myth as such possesses all the content and meaning ascribed to it by the members of the group, that a word as philological object includes all the variations of pronunciation and of significance given to it when spoken, that a law as social value includes all the interpretations and applications given to it by the judges and by the people, etc. Though even here we find the marked practical tendency to limit the object to one system, to purify grammatically the use of the word, to prescribe exact limits to the interpretation of the law; but the scientist is able to distinguish the concrete social reality itself from these efforts of practical schematization. But it is much more difficult to get rid of the inveterate naturalistic presuppositions and to realize that not only a material product of human industry, but any natural object whatever, a tree, a lake, is in its concreteness a historical object, possesses all the variations of content and meaning which are given to it, not only by physics, chemistry, botany, geology, but also by ordinary human observation, by the aesthetic view of the painter, by the practical standpoint of the technician, even by the attitude of the tramp who searches for the shade of the tree or takes a bath in the lake. And yet we must be aware that if we once begin to qualify some of these contents and meanings as subjective and deny that they belong to the objects themselves, we cannot stop with the characters ascribed to the objects by the tramp or the painter, but must qualify as also subjective the properties which the physicist and geologist find in these objects. Then the whole discussion begins over again, for if everything is subjective, the problem how objects are constructed is not solved, but merely transported into the subject, expressed in terms of the subject; and this, as we shall see at a later point, makes its rational solution impossible.

Of course, the historical object is—must be—full of contradictions, precisely because it is not limited in its existence to a single rational system. These contradictions do not destroy its reality, for no one of these variations of content or meaning belongs to it absolutely, constitutes its essence. The ontological principle of contradiction has been worked out in application to the object within one limited system, and does not apply at all to the concrete historical reality. Whenever, therefore, we want to apply it to a certain object, we must first define with precision the limits within which the object is taken, the standpoint from which its content is determined and the objects with regard to which its meaning is fixed.

But, though the concept of subjective copies, of representations, as distinct from and opposed to the object must be entirely excluded from the theory of concrete empirical reality, there remains a very real problem: how far the variations which a historical object undergoes in various complexes affect the unity of this object, and on the other hand, how far a similarity of two objects in different complexes is a ground for considering these objects as one. The problem has evidently no direct connection with the variety of individual experiences, for the various systems may be realized either by different individuals or groups of individuals, or by the same individual or group.

objects must be actually experienced, the complex actually reproduced in order to exist at any *here* at all. It needs both a personal centralization of data around a *here* and an impersonal organization of objects in complexes because of which they can empirically exist at many *here*'s, in order to have objective extension.

We must clearly realize that the extension of reality is not deducible from the fact that spatial characters, that is lines, surfaces, three-dimensional bodies, and interstices between bodies, are included within some empirical data, together with other characters. For, as empirically given, the data possessing those characters are not parts of an objective extension but elements of the concrete course of personal experience and reflection, chaotically intermingled with other data which do not possess spatial characters, and following one another in actuality without any spatial order. If now such contents including spatial characters become incorporated into a complex in which they are reciprocally determined as spatial objects, such a spatial organization is empirically not a part of a general spatial extension, but a part of the concrete and chaotic historical plurality of complexes among which some may be spatially organized, others not, and all of which are parts of the same empirical extension only in so far as they are experienced and reproduced by the same group of individuals, belong to the same multiple spheres of individual experience and individual reflection. The spatial determination which an object may receive in a spatially organized complex is only one of many determinations which it may receive in other complexes; and thus, the same concrete historical object may be spatial and non-spatial at the same time, without its spatiality being any more essential to it than its non-spatiality; whereas, both as spatial and non-spatial it must be concretely extended, given at many *here*'s. We shall see later on how the conception of a general objective and rational space including reality is constructed. It is evidently only a rational unification and generalization of one particular type of rational determination which certain objects receive by being incorporated into one specific kind of complexes, the spatially organized complexes. And such a rational unification and generalization itself presupposes this primary, irrational, concrete extension of historical reality which we are discussing now. For it is possible to treat from a certain rational standpoint all the spatially organized complexes as parts of one spatial organization only because each and all of these complexes are concretely extended, because they exist in many individual spheres of experience and reflection, because the spatial organization of each of them and the spatial connection between them can be taken as independent of each individual's particular *here* separately. The substitution of a common space in which objects are supposed localized for the concrete extension over which objects actually spread is thus the substitution of a certain particular rational order of objects viewed with regard to certain particular determinations and taken within a special class of systems, for a universal empirical character which all objects possess in concrete experience, whatever determinations they may have and to whatever systems they may belong, a character, moreover, which pertains to all systems as well as to their elements. It was, therefore, one of the greatest errors ever committed in the history of philosophy for realism to identify spatiality with concrete empirical extension and conceive concrete objects as included within space, for this space is only one of many types of rational organization of the objects which are found in the concretely and irrationally extended historical world.

In the light of naturalistic prepossessions our theory must seem strange, though as a matter of fact, scientists when dealing with cultural reality do implicitly ascribe to many historical objects the character of extensiveness as herein described. They are forced to speak of myths and mores, of language and social institutions, of technical devices and economic forms as existing within a certain extensive domain of culture, as spreading out or becoming more limited, passing from one part of extension to another, etc. They are, indeed, under the influence of the naturalistic view, inclined to treat these expressions as mere figures of speech and if asked the exact meaning of them, to say that these objects are either spatial or absolutely inextensive and that by ascribing to them a certain cultural extension they mean only that they are recognized by the individuals who inhabit a certain geographical territory. This concession to naturalism not only forces a conception based upon the essential character of concrete reality to yield to a traditional and narrow view based on a certain special rational reconstruction of reality, but sacrifices the only methodical viewpoint which is adequate for dealing with cultural reality in its historical concreteness.

It is only this naturalistic tendency of thought which prevents historical and social sciences from realizing that the spatiality of the geographical territory inhabited by certain individuals cannot be the ground of the extension of cultural values as given to these individuals, because this spatiality is itself possible, can be itself empirically given only on the ground of the primary extensive character which conscious individuals give to the world of their experience, each by subjectivating around his personal *here* objects which are also given to others and by objectivating them from his personal *here* in various systems into which others also incorporate them from their personal *here*'s. The geographical territory with its spatial extension and limitation and with all the spatial things that it includes, among them the bodies of the individuals inhabiting it, the earth itself, the solar system, the entire astronomical "infinite" space, are empirically possible only in so far as actually given and empirically reconstructed by many individuals along with all other historical objects, with myths and mores, with language and social institutions, with technical devices and economical forms, with art and scientific ideas, as parts of the same general world of empirical reality. Concretely, from the standpoint of full empirical reality, they are included within the wider extension of the empirical world in general which abstractly, from the standpoint of naturalistic systematization, they seem to include. Their primary and fundamental concrete extension is not the absolutely objective and invariable spatial extension with which astronomy and geography are dealing, but the general, undetermined, and changing extension of empirical objects given in many *here*'s to many individuals; and they could not even acquire for us, experiencing individuals, the characters of spatiality, which from the naturalistic viewpoint appear as so important, if they did not possess the more primary character of empirical extensiveness resulting from the fact of their being given to many of us at once. We shall later investigate the problem of the relative validity of the naturalistic system with its conception of infinite objective space, an unlimited number of material bodies within this space, etc.; now, on the ground of the formal definition of historical reality, we simply state that the naturalistic conception of an objectively spatial world does not correspond to the form of the elementary concrete empirical world; it is valid within the material system, whatever be the sphere of validity of the material system itself, but valid nowhere else.

Of course, when we have once accepted the determination which objects possess within this system, we must also accept the form of spatiality which is involved in this determination and exclude all that disagrees with it as not belonging to reality materially defined. Thus, from the naturalistic standpoint the Notre Dame of Paris or the Rocky Mountains are material things, part of the material world, absolutely localized in the absolute space—though their localization is plus an aesthetic stylization, many particular things plus a general concept; there would be no objective unity either between each copy and other copies or between the copies and the model, no objective unity between each specimen of the natural flower and other specimens, or between the natural specimens and the artistic stylization. Objective absolute idealism, on the contrary, would sacrifice the plurality to unity and say there is only one essence of the instruments, one essence of the flowers, one essence of the particular things which science studies, and that this essence is identical in the model and the copies, in the natural flowers and the aesthetic stylization, in the particular things and the general concept: multiplicity would be treated as an illusion, or an accident, or a μὴ ὄν.

But neither unity can be sacrificed to multiplicity nor multiplicity to unity from the standpoint of concrete historical reality, because empirically we follow both the formation of many objects from one and the formation of one from many and see the continuity between the one and the many, and because unity and multiplicity exist for us empirically only so far as actually reconstructible. When one model of a table is objectively reproduced many times, this reproduction is an empirical development, which we see going on; we see how the same given content and meaning become embodied in many objects; and this objective reproduction is empirically real, has for us an actual objective character only because its primary ground is this one content and meaning developed in various complexes. A new object is produced only when a content is objectivated and determined in a new complex; thus, each new copy of a certain model table is a separate table, a new object distinct from other similar tables, only because in the course of its construction it becomes an element of a separate practical complex. The fact that when once constructed it has a separate history of its own, is incorporated into various complexes different from those of similar objects, is put into a different room, turned to a somewhat different use, belongs to different individuals, etc., increases its reality as a separate object, but without destroying the community of content and meaning with other similar objects which it originally possessed. Each new table is and remains a mere variation of the same model, so that all such tables can be treated as one concrete historical object existing in many increasingly real variations. When, now, many such specimens are taken together in one complex, as distinct objects, and determined with regard to one another as many, this determination is simply a new character added to this concrete historical object, the one table realizing itself in the many increasingly real variations, which in addition to its original historical unity and its gradually increasing historical diversity acquires also the characteristic of being objectively a physical multiplicity of similar things. This characteristic does not destroy its unity; on the contrary, it is possible only because the object is still one and all the physical things have therefore a common content and meaning; it is only superadded to the original unity. Nor does it create the multiplicity; on the contrary, the tables can be treated as many in one complex only because they have been already diversified in many different complexes. This diversity is itself objectivated in this one complex as an objective multiplicity of the objects incorporated into this complex. In this way the historical object, the table of a certain style, which was already objectively one in the aesthetic complex of the artist who produced the model, in the economic complex of the business man who paid for this model, and in the intellectual complex of the historian of applied art who studied it, becomes also objectively many in the technical or spatial complex in which the same content and meaning is characterized as inherent in many physical things. The same table, the same historical object, with its original content and meaning, with the variations of this content and meaning in many different complexes, is thus objectively characterized as one in some complexes, as many in other complexes. Therefore, from the empirical standpoint, this table, this historical object, is *both one and many*.

This is true likewise when it is the unity which is actually superadded to an original plurality. The gastronomer who qualifies the many bottles of wine as one value in his hedonistic complex, the artist who sees one aesthetic value in the many natural individuals of a species of flowers and from the standpoint of an aesthetic complex produces one stylization of the many flowers, the scientist who from the standpoint of a theoretic complex finds one essence in many particular things, each of them creates an objective unity on the ground of a similarity of content and meaning which existed originally in many more or less different objects. One object—the hedonistic value, the aesthetic stylization, the scientific idea—is the result of the incorporation by each of the many pre-existing objects into a new complex in which they are objectively determined not as many, but as one. From this moment the many historical objects are syncretized into one historical object, and this new object, the product of this syncretism, is both many and one: many in so far as each object of the original plurality is already qualified in some complex as a distinct thing—as a separate bottle of wine among other bottles in a cave, a separate flower among other flowers in a garden; one in so far as the new objective determination in the hedonistic, aesthetic, scientific complex qualifies the original plurality as one with regard to its common content and meaning.

This, however, does not imply, as Platonism presupposes, that in such cases it is an original unity of essence which becomes merely reconstructed by reflection. The fact that many objects have a more or less similar content and meaning does not necessarily imply that there was some one original object from which these objects have actually developed as its variations. In some cases there may have been such an original object, but we can know this only if we actually find this object in the cultural past.   When we find many industrial objects with a similar content and meaning we can usually discover or presuppose the technician's model which served as a common basis for the manufacture of all. The common content and meaning of some species of flowers can be traced back to a common origin, but the origin of most species of flowers as of most natural objects is lost in the pre-cultural past and we cannot be certain that they are all variations of a primary unit.   Whether they are or not is irrelevant from the standpoint of our present problem.   For, even when the multiple objects which the hedonist, the artist, the scientist, unifies by determining them as one, were actually produced by a differentiation of one primary object, the unity produced is from the hedonistic, aesthetic, or scientific standpoint a new unity, not the reproduction of the old unity, because the one object—the hedonistic value, the aesthetic stylization, the scientific idea—to which this new unity is due is not the same as the old original object which was diversified and multiplied. For instance, the concept "Louis XVI table," by which the historian of applied art gives a unity to the multiplicity of materially existing tables which have certain common aesthetic features developed under the reign of Louis XVI, is not the same object as the original model from which the various and materially multiple Louis XVI tables have developed.   On the other hand, even when the many given objects syncretized into one by an aesthetic stylization or a scientific idea were distinct objects from their very beginning, their newly acquired unity is nevertheless objective and real, though it does not destroy their plurality, and we can treat them, because of this syncretism, as a concrete historical object which is both one and many in its real nature.

THE EXTENSION OF HISTORICAL OBJECTS

The historical object can be defined, as we have seen, as a concrete irrational synthesis of all those special, more or less rational objects which constitute objective variations of it in various limited complexes. But this definition is still incomplete, for the historical object is not reducible to a mere sum of its objective variations. Indeed, the possibility of empirically ascertaining the existence of the historical object, as of something more than any particular rationally determined object, depends upon our being conscious that the given object, as determined within one limited complex, is not the full concrete object, that it belongs or may belong also to other complexes where it is differently determined. This consciousness is due, as we have seen, to the imperfect objectivity and rationality of our personalities, to the fact that actuality is not a systematic, objective development of a perfectly rational reality, but an active, progressive objectivation and rationalization of data accompanied by a passive subjectivation of rational objects, so that the same object may be given in the course of subjectivation with the determinations which it has received in one complex, and in the course of subsequent objectivation acquire different determinations by being incorporated into another complex; or vice versa, after having been objectivated in one complex, it may return and become subjectivated as an element of a different complex. The rational determination of an object within any one limited system is the one-sided static result of this two-sided dynamic development. And since the latter is essential in order to have a historical object empirically given as such, it is not enough to define the historical object from the standpoint of the objective results of actuality as determined in all the objective complexes to which it belongs: it is indispensable to supplement this definition by studying the historical object from the standpoint of actuality itself, by characterizing it with regard to this double process of subjectivation and objectivation, by virtue of which it is not a mere philosophical construction, but an empirical object.

By becoming a datum in the course of subjectivation, every empirical object, no matter what complexes it belongs to, becomes dynamically attracted, as we may say for the lack of any better term, toward the *here*. In the course of objectivation, on the other hand, whatever may be the complex into which the datum while becoming an object is being incorporated, this incorporation is progressing from the *here*. We shall call *the sphere of experience* of an individual the totality of objects which are, have been, or will be attracted toward this individual's *here*, and *the sphere of reflection* of an individual the totality of the objects which are, have been, or will be reconstructed from this individual's *here*.

If empirical contents were purely actual, they would be limited, both as data and as objects, to an individual's spheres of experience and of reflection. If, on the contrary, reality were purely trans-actual, it would transcend absolutely in its objectivity the individual's sphere of reflection, and only its subjective copies would come into the individual's sphere of experience. But concrete reality is both actual and trans-actual: actual in so far as actually subjectivated and objectivated, trans-actual in so far as belonging to more or less rationally organized complexes. As long as we treat an object as limited in its existence to one complex, we can neglect its dependence on individual spheres of experience and reflection, for in dealing with a ready objective complex we do not need to take into account the fact that this complex could not be a part of empirical reality, if it were not constructed and reconstructed in actual reflection, and that it could not be reconstructed in actual reflection if all its elements were not given in actual experience. But we must take this fact into account in dealing with the concrete historical object, for its existence can be ascertained only in the course of its objectivation and subjectivation in many complexes. The historical object therefore depends on the individual's spheres of experience and of reflection: its being attracted as datum toward the *here* and its being reconstructed as object from the *here* are features essential to its characterization as an actual object.

Since, however, the historical object at the same time belongs to objective complexes, as an element in these complexes it is trans-actual and thus transcends any particular individual's spheres of experience and of reflection. This transcendence can, of course, manifest itself empirically only in some actuality, which must be the actuality of some other individual. The historical object as actual must belong to some individual's sphere of experience and reflection, but as element of trans-actual complexes it enters, simultaneously or successively, into the spheres of experience of all the individuals who subjectivate it as a datum from any of these complexes, and into the spheres of reflection of all the individuals who reincorporate it as object into any of these complexes. In other words, though it is essential for the historical object as actual object to be an element of some individual's sphere of experience and sphere of reflection, it is equally essential for it not to be limited to the spheres of experience and of reflection of any individual, but to belong—or at least be able to belong—to the spheres of experience and reflection of all other individuals who have or will experience and reproduce it in any connection. It depends in some measure for its actual empirical existence on each personality which experiences and reconstructs it, but it does not depend exclusively on any particular personality or on any limited number of personalities.

Since each individual sphere of experience and sphere of reflection is centered around a unique personal *here*, the historical object, which can belong to many individual spheres of experience and reflection, can extend empirically and dynamically over many *here*'s, both in so far as it has been or will be actually subjectivated as a datum and in so far as it has been or will be actually objectivated as an element of empirical complexes. And because, on the other hand, it is not only an actual datum, but also a trans-actual object, its empirical and dynamic determination with regard to a *here* is not exclusively limited to the moment when it is actually experienced or reproduced by the individual; once reproduced as an object in an individual's spheres of experience and reflection, it belongs to them forever, because it has acquired an objective and empirical existence for this individual and can be indefinitely experienced by him and reproduced by him as part of his empirical world, conditioning thus more or less the future active and passive evolution of his personality.   From this it follows that the extension of the historical object over many *here*'s is not a mere passing of this object from one *here* to another, as it is experienced or reconstructed *now* by one individual or another, but a permanent extensive existence of this object, which permits it to become simultaneously given at any moment by approaching to many unique *here*'s, or to be simultaneously reproduced at any moment from many unique *here*'s, or to be at the same time given at some *here*'s as datum and reproduced from other *here*'s as object.

Since every real object or group of objects either is or can be experienced and reproduced by many individuals, every part of the empirical objective reality possesses in some degree this concrete dynamic extension, exists or can exist in many personal spheres of experience and reflection, extends over many *here*'s. Empirical objective reality is a multiplicity of extensive objects—extensive in this concrete and empirical sense of the term; and the extension of the historical world is the totality of the extensions of the historical objects of which it is composed. This concrete extension is the primary, the fundamental objective and empirical extension. The personal centralization of data around a unique individual *here* is evidently not sufficient to produce alone objective extension, though it is one of its essential conditions.   On the other hand, the rational order of objects in a complex is not alone sufficient to make these objects or the complex itself empirically extended, existing in many *here*'s, for these

It is clear that in concrete experience no absolute distinction between the one and the many can be established, that within wide limits the variations of a historical object in various complexes may be treated either as included in this object or as distinct, self-existing objects, and that the matter is merely one of degree of difference or similarity. Thus, take a word. In what measure can we treat the variations of content and meaning which the word undergoes by being pronounced or written many times in many different actual complexes, as constituting different words, and in what measure as being merely variations of one and the same word? This depends, first of all, on what we should consider to be different complexes instead of mere varying actualizations of one complex. We know that, because of the irrational character of concrete personalities, a complex is seldom, if ever, in fact exactly and fully reproduced, though it should be possible to reproduce it indefinitely by virtue of its own objective nature. Before we take into account the rational organization of a complex, which makes of it a system, we have no definite criteria permitting us to distinguish objectively and absolutely the reproduction of a complex from the production of a new complex, and in any particular case our distinction must be, viewed from the rational standpoint, arbitrary, though usually it has a partial empirical justification in the consciousness, more or less clear, which the individual or group has of producing a new or of reproducing an old complex. Thus, the mispronunciations, misspellings, or misunderstandings of a word by individuals who are learning how to use it in a certain formerly fixed, objective connection will normally not be considered as new determinations of this word in new complexes, but as inadequate reproductions of its determination in an old complex which from the standpoint of concrete experience are, of course, objectively real, but from the special philological standpoint are treated as half-subjective. In so far as the complex is thus one, though many times actualized, the word is evidently also one, both from the standpoint of this complex and from the historical standpoint; the problem of unity and multiplicity does not exist. Suppose now that the content of the word is widely and permanently differentiated by this word's being differently pronounced in different provincial dialects, or that its meaning is widely and permanently differentiated by being applied to different classes of contents, or that both its content and its meaning become modified by its passing into a different language. In the first two cases we shall probably, and certainly in the latter case, assume that the word has been differentiated objectively by being introduced into different complexes. How far, up to what limits, then, shall we treat the word as one? When shall we begin to consider it as many? Evidently, from the empirical standpoint, regarding this word as a historical object, we can assign it no limits whatever. The distinction is here not arbitrary, but free. We can treat the word as one in spite of the most far-reaching objective variations it has undergone, provided we then take these variations into account; we can treat each of these variations as a different word, provided we then take into account the fact that they do have a certain content and meaning in common and that they are thus variations of one and the same word; or we can divide the variations into several groups, according to the degrees of difference, and take the word as one within each such group only and as distinct from group to group, provided we then take into account not only the objective variations which each such word undergoes within its group, but also the common ground by which all these words together are characterized.

Similar examples are offered in the field of mythology. We exclude again as irrelevant those variations which we arbitrarily agree to treat as half-subjective, due to imperfect individual reproductions of a complex. When shall we treat

divinities which have more or less similar contents and meanings in different complexes produced by different groups or
within the same group, as the same or as different mythological
beings ?   Here again the choice is free and in each particular
case conditioned only by the question whether it is the common
or the varying contents and meanings which seem empirically
more important from the standpoint of the total concrete
historical domain with which we are dealing.   Thus, we shall
usually consider the Greek Zeus as one divinity in spite of
the variations of content and meaning which we find between
the Zeus of Dodona and the Zeus of Olympia, between the
Zeus of Homer and the one of Hesiod, whereas we shall
probably treat the Greek Zeus and the Roman Jupiter as two
divinities in spite of their possible common origin and of the
well-known later syncretism; but we are free in both cases to
take a different standpoint provided we always take into
account both the diversity included under the assumed unity
and the similarity existing above the assumed multiplicity.

Thus, in so far as determined within one complex as one
object, a historical object is certainly and indubitably one, in
spite of the various half-subjective reproductions of this
complex; but as variously determined in objectively different
complexes, it may be either one or many, we are free to treat
it either way.   There are, however, numerous cases in which
this freedom is limited and the problem complicated by the
fact that when we take a certain content and meaning as
object-matter of historical reflection, we may find that in
one complex it is explicitly and objectively qualified as one
object, whereas within some other complex it may be the
common ground of many objects.   Such is the case whenever
an object, determined as one in its content and meaning
within a certain complex, becomes within another complex
diversified by being materially multiplied in many physical
copies, or when, on the contrary, objects which within one
complex are determined as materially multiple and distinct

are taken within another complex with regard to their common content and meaning as one object. Examples of an objective multiplication within a new complex of an object originally one abound in the sphere of industry: an artist produces a model of a table or a technician a model of an instrument, and each of these viewed from the standpoint of applied art or of technical invention is and remains one object, however many copies are made; but from the standpoint of industrial production, of economical exchange, of spatial localization, in the complexes of the factory manager, of the dealer, of the casual observer who sees many similar tables or instruments side by side, each of these copies counts as a distinct object. Examples of an objective unification of objects originally many into one are frequent in hedonistic, aesthetic, scientific, and similar activities. Thus, many spatially and economically distinct bottles of wine of a certain vintage and year are for the gastronomer one hedonistic value in the sense that the distinct bottles do not count hedonistically as separately qualified values, but each and all are "the wine of this vintage and year." The artist who makes a flower the object-matter of aesthetic stylization is not concerned with the material multiplicity of flowers of this species; his stylization bears on each and all of them: *the* flower of this species is his aesthetic value. The scientific study of an object as typical representative of a class ignores the multiplicity of this object in the physical world; the object is one and not many with regard to its scientifically determinable essence.

The common-sense realistic solution of the problem would evidently consist in denying any real and objective community between the one object—the model of the instrument, the aesthetic stylization of the flower, the scientific concept— and the multiple objects—the copies of the model, natural flowers, particular things on which the concept bears. From this standpoint we would have simply many distinct objects, copies of the instrument, plus a model, many natural flowers astronomically relative, it is absolute geographically—and their presence outside of their position in space, in the *here* of an individual whose body is several thousand miles removed from them, has then to be interpreted not as their actual presence, but as the presence of their representations, which, as such, do not belong to the material world. But the empirical existence of the Notre Dame of Paris or of the Rocky Mountains is not limited to their existence as material things in space; they exist also in innumerable other complexes, hedonistic, aesthetic, economic, political, theoretic, religious, etc., and their contents and meanings are incomparably richer than those ascribed to them in naturalistic knowledge. They are material objects, but they are also much else besides. And as such full concrete historical objects, they are not localized in space; their spatial localization is just a certain particular feature added to the many other features, coexisting really though irrationally with non-spatial characters, even with such as would, if the concrete reality were rational, exclude spatiality, as for instance, the characters which they acquire by being analyzed into theoretic ideas, and becoming thus incorporated into various systems of knowledge. As historical objects, they exist at once and really wherever and however experienced; they spread with all their characters over all the *here*'s where they have been experienced and reconstructed, and will probably spread farther still, when new individuals introduce them into their spheres of experience and reflection. When the character of spatial localization is added to their other characters, it does not change at all the nature of their primary historical extension, for it must extend itself, it must spread over many individual *here*'s in order to be neither a mere personal datum nor a purely rational construction inaccessible to human experience, but an objective and yet empirical feature of these objects.

The problem is much simpler with regard to the immaterial objects to which naturalism, by contrast with material objects, has denied all extension.   The poem or the scientific theory are, of course, outside all extension in the rational determination which they possess as elements of an aesthetic or theoretic system; but they are not merely elements of those rational systems within which they have received their aesthetic or theoretic determination.   They are also empirical, actually accessible objects, and as such cannot be experienced by any individual otherwise than by being subjectivated as data with reference to his *here*, or reproduced by him otherwise than by being objectivated from his *here*: and they are incorporated into many real complexes, hedonistic and economic, political and religious, and are thus concrete historical objects like all others.   Their objective empirical existence in the cultural world depends, as much as the existence of any material or social object, on their belonging to the spheres of experience and reflection of many individuals, on their spreading over many *here*'s: they could have no historical importance whatever if they did not participate in the concrete extension of the historical reality, but were either exclusively and absolutely super-cultural or existed only within the closed receptacles of individual consciousnesses.   Their extension is, therefore, at the same time one of the factors and one of the results of their cultural influence.

THE DURATION OF HISTORICAL OBJECTS

We pass now to the problem of the existence of historical objects in time.   On grounds similar to those on which we have excluded absolute space, we can exclude in advance, from the definition of the concrete empirical world, the idea of the absolute pure time, without beginning or end, in which objects last and change and in which actuality itself develops. Absolute time, even as, at the opposite pole, absolute timelessness, is a specific rational, non-empirical form of reality, postulated within the logical limits of the naturalistic system of objects; what these limits are and what is the relative validity of the conception of absolute time, are later problems. But from the standpoint of concrete experience, it is clear that absolute time together with the naturalistic system itself must be constructed and reconstructed in actuality, and it presupposes a more primary and concrete objective duration, in the same way as absolute space presupposes a more primary and concrete objective extension. The starting-point of all duration is that relative and limited direction in time and of time with regard to the individual actual *now*, which characterizes the course of experience. Objective duration can be reached from this starting-point only in the form of an empirical unification and interpenetration of many such relative and limited dynamic arrangements of individual spheres of experience with regard to the *now*, as a synthesis of many particular durations into one general and complex duration with one future and one past, even as objective extension can be reached only in the form of a unification and interpenetration of many subjectively limited extensions organized with regard to the *here*. And the objectivity of duration, in the same way as the objectivity of extension, is a formally unavoidable consequence and condition of the existence of the concrete empirical objects themselves. Because, and in so far as, the object by being incorporated into a complex acquires an existence independent of any particular individual *now*, it must be able to be given at many successive *now*'s, and this is the only form in which the object, while transcending in duration the span of present individual experience, still remains an empirical object. Since historical objects become fully real by being incorporated into many complexes, and this incorporation goes on both simultaneously and successively, duration through many *now*'s, like extension over many *here*'s, is essential for the empirical reality of the historical object. The successive actualizations of the historical object are directed in time, are following one another objectively and irreversibly, and thus produce objective duration, precisely and only because they constitute a progressive empirical realization of one and the same object, because each of them influences the concrete reality of this object, leaves an objective trace after it.

Therefore it is not the duration of objects which is empirically dependent upon the duration of an individual personality, but on the contrary, the individual personality acquires objective empirical duration in the world of reality because of the objective duration of the objects which individual thought has raised to trans-actual existence. Indeed, if we leave aside the problem of the duration of active thought, which does not belong here, and take the individual only from the standpoint of the reality which he experiences and reconstructs, it is clear that the *now* at which objects are given as data and from which they are reconstructed as trans-actual realities is by itself not enough to qualify a personality as experiencing and acting continuously within a certain period of objective duration, during, before, or after the existence of certain real objects and of other personalities. The *now* by itself is unique, is not a part of duration; the successive *now*'s of an individual, viewed from the standpoint of reflectively analyzed experience, can be distinguished in themselves, but only by the different data and associations of data present at each of them; and if the *now* were not a ground of the duration of objective reality, we could assume that there is only one *now* for each individual filled out successively by varying data, just as there is only one *here* for each individual; the individual would be thus continuously and exclusively in a *now*, actual but timeless, like the God of Aristotle. If this is not so, if the successive *now*'s of an individual's actuality do objectively differ from each other and their series constitutes one continuous duration, it is because they are not only the *now*'s of the individual course of experience, but also the *now*'s of historical objects, because at each of them some object, whose existence is not limited to this individual's experience, acquires some additional real determination by being now incorporated or reincorporated into some complex. The same object has acquired some other real determination at a *now* of some other individual and will acquire new determinations at the *now*'s of others. Because each individual *now* is thus also the *now* of some trans-individual object, it is a moment of a trans-individual duration. And since all these objects constitute the chaos of concrete historical reality, the whole series of the successive *now*'s of an individual is a component of the total concrete duration of this reality. The individual's life is limited in duration from the standpoint of reality, has an objective beginning and end, because his participation in constructing the objective duration of historical reality is limited, because various concrete historical objects begin at a certain moment of their objective duration to acquire new real determinations at the *now*'s of this individual, and later, at another moment of their objective duration, cease to be experienced and reproduced at this individual's *now*'s.

On the other hand, it is evident that the duration of historical objects as empirical objects depends in turn entirely on their being experienced and reproduced at some *now*'s; it is logically impossible to think of the duration of a concrete empirical object before or after its being experienced and reproduced at some *now* by some individual. The formal character of the existence of historical objects as concrete objects in time can be thus most properly termed historical, as against the supposedly pure duration of the natural world in absolute time and independent of consciousness; the application of the latter conception outside the limits of the system of naturalism to concrete empirical reality is clearly self-contradictory, since concrete empirical reality involves actuality. The concrete object, element of the full empirical reality, while transcending in duration any particular actualization, is still dependent on the whole series of its actualizations for its existence. And every actual reconstruction adds something to its real constitution. Its duration is thus essentially its *becoming;* whatever it is at any *now*, it must have gradually become during the whole series of its preceding *now*'s, and every *now* is a moment, a stage of the process of its gradual creation. We have seen that at every *now* it is an extensive object and includes all the variations of content and all the variations of meaning ascribed to it by all the individuals who have ever reconstructed it. Therefore its duration must be conceived as a gradual becoming of its content and meaning; every actualization by incorporating it into a complex adds both a new variation of content and a new variation of meaning, and the totality of these actualizations up to a certain moment have constructed its total content and its total meaning as existing at this moment, that is, have created it entirely as a concrete empirical object.

Since this process is historical, the objects must have a beginning in historical time. It is not enough for us to have shown from the formal standpoint how a datum as object-matter of thought is a content, and a content by being connected with other contents becomes an object. This deduction of reality from experience would be sufficient if objectivation had, as was usually assumed in the past, a purely ideal significance, if it did not affect the objects themselves empirically in their extension and duration. Since it does affect them, since it leaves an empirical trace in reality, our logical explanation of reality must be supplemented. Every act of objectivation is an act which occurs in a certain part of empirical extension and at a certain moment of empirical duration, and we cannot, like the idealists or realists, neglect this point as immaterial, for these acts condition objects not only in their existence for any one of us at any moment, but also in their existence for themselves in their total objective extension and duration. In other words, the historical existence belongs to the essence of all real empirical objects as such. Therefore the phenomenological question, "How are objects in general empirically possible for us?" must be supplemented by the ontological question, "How is any particular empirical object historically possible for itself?"

Evidently there can be within the domain of historical experience no absolute beginning of an object in the sense of a pure and sudden creation of an entirely new content and its endowment with an entirely new meaning. Active thought must have data to turn into contents and objectivate in connection with other contents, and data can arise only out of the subjectivation of pre-existing reality. When we have an artificially isolated sphere of reality, we find indeed seemingly entirely new objects appearing within it, new works of art within the domain of aesthetic reality, new ideas within theoretic reality, new inventions within material reality, new myths within religious reality, etc. But in all these cases something pre-existed outside of this domain and the new object has been constructed from this pre-existing material; it may be absolutely new within the given system, but only relatively new on the ground of the full concrete reality. The concrete duration is indeed a continual becoming, but this becoming is possible only in the form of a continual appearance of new variations of pre-existing objects.

We find in the cultural world two distinct types of this becoming of historical objects. One is the intentional production of new objects on the ground of the rational organization of pre-existing materials and instruments. We shall study it in a later chapter. The other, more primary, is the unorganized evolution of new objects by a gradual differentiation of pre-existing objects. If a certain variation of content and meaning which may at first only be added to some existing historical object continues to develop by new actualizations, if within a certain part of the concrete empirical world it becomes more and more frequently actualized independently of the original object of which it is a variation, it acquires in this series of actualizations a growing fixity and objectivity and thus begins to be treated as a separate object rather than as a mere variation. As its content and meaning develop in new connections, it can indefinitely grow in extension. It is, of course, impossible to say when the new object is definitively constituted as independently existing, unless when we take it exclusively within the limits of some particular complex in which it is isolated and thus implicitly ignore any variations that remain outside of this complex. This evolution may be primarily founded either on a differentiation of content or on one of meaning; in the first case, evidently, a corresponding modification of meaning, in the second, a corresponding modification of content, has to follow before the new object acquires enough of an independent existence to be treated as a separate object.

Since the beginning of the historical existence of every single object is thus to be found always in pre-existing historical objects, the existence of the whole world of experience in time has a character of continuity. But this continuity is clearly not at all identical with the conception of causal continuity of the natural world, though the concept of causal continuity may have its origin in a special determination of this general continuity of concrete evolution in view of the specific problems raised by the necessity of adapting the closed naturalistic system to the temporal character of empirical reality. The fundamental differences between these two continuities are these: (*a*) while the natural phenomenon is conceived as effectively brought into existence by preceding phenomena, the new historical object is merely passively conditioned by pre-existing historical objects, needs them to appear in existence, but is produced not *by* them, only *from* them by active thought; (*b*) while the natural phenomenon is completely conditioned in its entire temporal existence by other phenomena, the new historical object is conditioned only in the very beginning, and even then not completely, by the content and meaning of the object, or objects, from which it evolves, and becomes less and less dependent on the character of this pre-existing historical object and more and more dependent on its own character as its evolution progresses. The continuity in duration of the concrete empirical world is thus historical, not natural; is a continuity of growth by the agency of creative thought, not a continuity of changes determining one another.

Examples like the evolution of a new word or of a new myth illustrate this gradual unorganized growth of historical objects. Every new actualization of a word brings with it a variation, however slight, of its content, due to the peculiarities of pronunciation determined in part by organic differences between individuals, in part by the conditions in which it is used which provoke special intonations, in part finally to the influence of other words in the phrase; and every such variation is added to its concrete content, which thus grows in complexity all the time. The philological fixation of this content in a dictionary or grammar is, of course, merely an abstract formula of its whole complexity, as is shown by the need to modify the formula when after a longer evolution of the word itself the old formula ceases to correspond to the prevalent characters of its content; the old prevalent characters have been, in the consciousness of the people, pushed into shadow by the gradually agglomerating new characters. But it may be also that the old and the new pronunciation coexist: we may have a word with two forms. A similar evolution goes on with respect to the meaning of the word, when the latter in different actualizations is applied either to different objects or to the same object viewed from different standpoints. Thus the complexity of the meaning may grow so that nothing but its general limits are outlined with a rough approximation in the formal scheme of a philological definition of the word, which must also change when a new and gradually agglomerated predominant meaning has pushed into the background the meaning that formerly predominated. But it may be that both the old and the new meaning coexist: we may have a word with two meanings. And if the evolution of content and the evolution of meaning go on side by side, the word splits definitely into two distinct words. The myth shows a very analogous process of growth, only here differentiation of content is more regularly followed by a differentiation of meaning and reciprocally.

As long as this conception of growth is applied to the reality traditionally called "cultural" in the narrower sense of the term, hardly any serious difficulties can arise, if we only remember that this spontaneous growth gives place more and more on higher stages of culture to voluntary organized production, which we shall study later. Historical and ethnological investigations have accustomed us to the idea of an incalculable development of historical objects, to the conception that the entire enormous complexity of cultural contents and meanings have appeared from exceedingly poor and simple beginnings as the product of active thought. But all our intellectual traditions revolt against the application of this formula to the duration of material objects, parts of nature—mountains, rivers, planets, etc. How is it possible to interpret the existence of these objects in time as the evolution of historical objects growing by the addition of new variations of content and meaning in a series of actualizations? And yet, it is not only by analogy that we are forced to extend our principle to cover natural objects as well.

By way of introduction, we may mention that the apparent theoretic difficulty of interpreting natural objects as historical objects becoming through actualization has been in a large measure due to the philosophical custom of first of all accepting the world of nature as ready with all its object and laws, as a perfectly closed, finished, and rational system, and only then trying to criticize its objectivity as a whole, instead of studying how this system has grown, step by step, and criticizing its

internal construction. Therefore, when naturalism introduced the idea of evolution into this system and attempted to
explain causally the origin of natural objects, idealistic
criticism willingly admitted that the origin of natural objects
as such could be explained causally from the standpoint of
the natural system in the same way as, for instance, particular
physical or biological changes: it saw no essential difference
between the explanation of a repeatable change by a cause
and the explanation of the origin of an object by a combination
of causes, and continued to criticize the naturalistic system
en bloc, as if all the principles assumed by the naturalistic
theory had the same validity within the system of nature.
Whereas the point is that, whatever may be the validity of
the causal explanations when applied to the natural reality as
already given, these explanations are inapplicable to the
genesis of this reality or of any of its parts; the naturalistic
system precludes the possibility of explaining not only the
origin of full historical objects, but even the origin of its own
objects, of objects as determined rationally within its own
limits. And therefore even some naturalistic theories of the
world which understand all the implications of the idea of
natural evolution see the necessity of appealing, as Bergson
does, to some mystical creative essence underlying empirical
nature. For the most striking feature about the evolution
of the natural world as material world is the gradual appearance of innumerable new contents, whereas the causal naturalistic explanation traces only the evolution of the mechanical
or energetic conditions under which these contents are
supposed to have appeared. The fact that they have actually
appeared in the empirical world is thus taken for granted.
But, if these contents are then considered objective, belonging
to the natural things in themselves, as pure naturalistic
realism presupposes, this is equivalent to an implicit assumption of a world of Platonic ideas existing besides the world of
nature and to an implicit admission that some of those ideas

come into materiality when the proper conditions are given; whereas, if these contents are considered, as in the conceptions of naturalistic dualism, as subjective, as occurring only in consciousness and constituting a reaction of conscious living beings to new conditions of their material environment in which these living beings are assumed to have appeared themselves as causal products of evolution, we have a theory to which we can apply the Schopenhauerian comparison with Baron Münchausen who pulled himself and his horse out of a quagmire by his own hair. But philosophy has had nothing to substitute for these pseudo-explanations because the individualistic limitation of subjective idealism did not permit it to trace the origin of objects beyond the duration of individual consciousness, and the timeless character of objective idealism prevented it from even stating adequately the full problem of the historical origin of objects. If, however, we now succeed in overcoming the subject-object dualism and the habit of looking upon nature as having become what it is without the participation of thought, all difficulties vanish.

We must first of all subdivide the problem. We neglect entirely that traditional part of it which concerns the existence of natural objects beyond the reach of our experience and reflection in general. We are concerned exclusively with empirical objects and it would be self-contradictory to ask whether these objects have any existence beyond all experience and reflection, for the concept of existence has no significance whatever unless used of empirical reality as empirically given object-matter of actual thought. Secondly, we exclude provisionally the problem of the determination of a natural object, for example, a mountain, a river, a planet, by the entire natural system of which it is a part, because the discussion of this problem would involve the question of the relative validity of the natural system as such, which we have already postponed. We are concerned here exclusively with the existence, in concrete empirical duration, of these objects as elements of the whole concrete world of our experience in general and not merely with their existence within the natural system as one of the specifically organized complexes which exist within concrete experience.

It is clear that in these cases a direct appeal to the testimony of experience cannot have the same conclusiveness as the one which we made in the case of words and myths, for the empirical evolution of a natural object through a series of actualizations can be scarcely observed; even on the basis of our theory, it takes thousands of years to produce a really important change in the sensual appearance of reality. Still, there are observations which may be termed suggestive at least. Probably no one has failed to notice the fact that the appearance of any material object changes after a long acquaintance with it. This change is, of course, put by common sense into the psychological subject; but there is no psychological subject. In any case, therefore, natural objects as empirical objects do evolve by being actualized, though it would be impossible to define exactly in any given example the character of the evolution. We have sufficiently demonstrated that in concrete reality any modifications are modifications of the objects themselves as historical objects, not of their representations. The question then is what is the relative importance for the objects of such modifications as compared with the more general content of these objects, and we can perhaps hope for some answer to this question from the history of culture, of aesthetic culture in particular.

However, this is not the central point of the problem. As long as we take only single observable changes in the sensual content of objects, we have no positive arguments to oppose to the assumption that such changes concern these objects only as subjective data and not as self-existing realities. But if we take into account the totality of modifications which an object undergoes during its empirical existence, the subjectivistic interpretation proves completely untenable. It is evident that any empirical object, and therefore also the mountain, the river, the planet, can have duration in concrete empirical time only by being given in a series of actualizations, so that the beginning of its empirical existence as real object cannot in any case go beyond the beginning of its actualizations, that is, beyond the beginning of individual experience and thought in general. The only problem which we must now boldly face is, whether it can be assumed that it began to exist as empirical object with all the content and meaning which it now possesses or whether its content and meaning were constructed gradually through an immeasurably long series of actualizations, even as the content and meaning of other concrete objects like the word or the myth whose origin we can trace historically. This alternative would hardly even be stated, if it were not for two arguments which seem to point toward the first solution.

The one is an argument by analogy, based upon the fact that when we find *now* a sensual object which seems to have never before been actually given to anybody—say a mountain in the polar region or a telescopic planetoid—it is given at once with all the characters of a mountain or a planetoid. From this it is concluded that when consciousness first began to exist it found nature at once possessing all the objective characters which it possesses now. But the fact is that, once given our present world of nature in general, whatever its origin, the content of any new natural object which we discover is a mere variation of some already existing contents of other natural objects, a variation whose highly developed form is now possible only because a long creative development of contents has preceded it and because it is itself a creative continuation of this development. It is evident that this content must be given as a natural object after its discovery, since the very process of "discovering an object in nature" involves the establishment in actuality of many connections between this content and various pre-existing natural objects, so that by assuming that we have "discovered it in nature" we have actually incorporated it into nature; we have made the content a part of the natural system, we have given it ourselves a meaning similar to those which other objects possess within the natural system, and thereby we have constructed it as a natural object. If somebody should presuppose that there is something, some trans-cultural reality underlying this empirical "mountain" or "planetoid," that this new object does not resolve itself into a content which is a creatively produced variation of other contents of already known mountains or planetoids, and an actually produced set of empirical connections, he would have to show what this underlying reality empirically consists in, otherwise his conception would be empirically meaningless, since an empirically inaccessible reality is nonsense. The only way he could show what there is behind this content and meaning which constitutes empirically the mountain or planetoid would be by historical analysis which, having excluded all that in mountains and planetoids is the product of the activities of conscious beings, might find something original and pre-conscious left in these objects. But we cannot tell whether any such discovered remnant really existed in fact before all activity or whether it is not a mere creation, a product of our own historical analysis, unless we have already demonstrated that nature did exist before consciousness, which is the very problem we are seeking to prove. From the fact that any particular object is given with all the properties of a natural object now when our world of nature in general is already given, it is evidently impossible to conclude that nature itself when first given was given at once with all the properties of our present nature. The situations are not at all analogous.

The other empirical argument consists in pointing out that, as far as our historical and ethnological researches reach now, the content and connection of natural objects do not seem to have changed except by natural causes. This is really the converse of the first argument and like it begs the question. The answer to the question whether natural objects have changed or not during evolution will depend, as we have already seen in our first chapter, on the philosophical standpoint taken toward this evolution. If we claim that all changes of the mechanical, physical, chemical properties and relations of objects as given to us are changes of our subjective views, are pure discoveries of previously existing properties and relations, then, of course, we shall say that objects have not changed; but this is precisely a matter of contention.

The irrelevancy of these two arguments leaves the problem open. The content and the meaning which natural objects, like all empirical objects, have for a certain individual depend on the spheres of experience and reflection of this individual. Whatever a reality may be in itself, for any concrete personality it is empirically only that which this individual experiences and reconstructs. Though at any particular moment an individual's passive experience and his active reconstruction do not coincide, because his subjectivation is concerned with different objects than his objectivation, the limits of his total sphere of experience tend to coincide with those of his total sphere of reflection, for he cannot reconstruct anything he has never approximately experienced and he cannot experience anything which he has never approximately reconstructed. We say approximately because in incorporating into a complex an object which he has passively experienced, he modifies it in some measure, and no object returns in his passive experience with exactly the same characters which it received when actively objectivated by him, since it is not a purely personal object but is modified also independently of this particular individual. Both the sphere of experience and the sphere of reflection are thus continually growing by new additions. But the growth of the sphere of experience is gradual and parallel to that of the sphere of reflection and vice versa, and these two spheres are dependent on each other: the individual widens his sphere of experience by widening his sphere of reflection and reciprocally. And the total field covered at any moment by both his experience and his reflection as developed up to this moment constitutes what we may call his "sphere of reality," that is, reality as existing for this individual at this moment of his evolution.

We do not need any particular intuition, any "feeling ourselves into" the consciousness of another individual in order to ascertain objectively how wide and complicated his sphere of reality is, because we find a perfectly adequate objective criterion in the range of his activity, in the widest sense of the term, as manifested in its real results. When measured by this criterion, the individual's sphere of reality not only increases during the development of his personality, but between the widest limits reached by various individuals, respectively, we find very great differences. If we compare the widest individual spheres of reality at different epochs of the cultural evolution, we find they have enormously increased even during the purely historical period of existence of the human race. A sociologist may affirm that a leading individual of five thousand years ago might have been capable of embracing by his activity as wide a domain of reality as a leading modern individual, but actually, as a matter of fact, he did not: the question of his potentialities may have some significance within the limits of race psychology, but is irrelevant for a philosophical theory of concrete reality. And, of course, the difference between the present and the past becomes much greater if we leave direct historical testimony and pass to an indirect reconstruction of the spheres of activity of the early representatives of the human race, with the help of paleontology and comparative ethnology; and it becomes quite incalculable if we go farther still and try to conjecture, not, indeed, about any particular "mental" properties, but about the domain or reality embraced by the activity of animal beings in the pre-human past.

Then, the next point which must be kept clearly in view, one which results, moreover, from our discussion in a previous section of the extensiveness of concrete reality, is that, whereas the empirical world at any given moment is not limited as objective world to the contents and meanings that its objects possess in the spheres of experience and reflection of any one individual, it evidently is identical with the total reality of all the individuals who live and act in it, with all their spheres of reality taken together. Therefore, at the present moment the empirical world includes all that is included in the spheres of reality of all the empirically living and active individuals, from the greatest scientist down to the protozoön. But it includes nothing more. The science of nature, from the standpoint and within the limits of the naturalistic system, claims that nature includes even now the things, properties, and relations which will be discovered in it a hundred years from now. But our standpoint here is that of concrete historical reality, not of any special ontological systematization of this reality. And from the standpoint of concrete reality the material reality does not include now the contents and meanings which will be given to it in the spheres of experience and reflection of some great scientist a hundred years from now, any more than art includes now the works which will be produced by some great artist a hundred years from now, or social life the forms of political organization which will be given to social groups a hundred years from now. We may try to foresee the direction of the future evolution of the concrete empirical material reality, even as we may try to foresee the direction of the future evolution of art or of political organization, that is as of an evolution dependent in a gradually decreasing measure both on the present character of reality and on the present direction of active thought;

we cannot foresee the future contents and meanings, because this would be producing them in advance.

The same considerations bear on every past stage of evolution. The concrete empirical real world contained at any past moment everything that was contained in the spheres of reality of all conscious individuals living and acting in it, and contained nothing more. At periods when in the empirical world there were no conscious beings higher than the mollusca, the empirical world was the totality of the spheres of reality of all conscious, that is, active, beings from the mollusca down.

It may be objected that this conclusion is absurd, for the mollusca needed a definite milieu to live in, so their world could not have been limited to their own spheres of reality but must have been such as we reconstruct it now, for only then it could have offered them the necessary conditions of existence. Let us again face the problem simply and squarely. Of course, the mollusca as the investigating scientist sees them now, with such bodies as they now have, can exist only in a milieu of the kind which the scientist reconstructs for them. But their bodies, like all bodies, are parts of our empirical reality, are objects of our concrete experience and reflection. As objects they determine other objects and are determined by them. Now, as parts of our present world of experience, they contain, like every other object, all the contents and meanings which they have ever possessed for all the individuals who have ever experienced and reproduced them as objects, and nothing more. Both the bodies of actually living mollusca and the shells found in old geological formations include all we ascribe to them as parts of our present nature, but the bodies of mollusca, when the latter were the highest conscious beings on earth, did not contain all they do now. As empirical objects they included only that which was practically experienced by their owners themselves and by other contemporary conscious beings.

They were "adapted to their milieu," even as the bodies of the present mollusca appear to us "adapted" to their present milieu. But their milieu was then adapted only to them, whereas now it is adapted to the bodies of all the innumerable superior conscious beings that live and act in this empirical world. Their bodies and their milieu were then both empirically all that and only that which they were as objects of their practical experience.

Whatever may now be the character of natural objects within the naturalistic system and whatever may be the range of validity of the naturalistic system, in so far as natural objects are historical objects, elements of concrete reality, we must conclude that their duration has the same form as the directly observable duration of cultural objects in the narrower sense of the term. All of them, the bodies of conscious beings included, are historical products, developed in content and meaning, like all historical objects, through a series of actualizations; only, in their case, the series has been incomparably longer and the development incomparably slower than in the case of those cultural objects whose origin we can historically follow.

If this evident conclusion has been usually avoided, even by those who have tried to reconcile objective idealism and historicism, it is simply because on the ground of the subject-object dualism, the active participation of thought in the evolution of objective reality could not be interpreted otherwise than by conceiving individual consciousnesses, each of which is evidently insufficient to explain alone the objective reality, as included in a general consciousness, a Super-Consciousness or an Absolute Life or whatever else it may be called. As a consequence, philosophers, even those who realized that the empirical world can be nothing more than what is given of it in experience and reflection, have still failed to see that in the early stages of development of experience and reflection, it could not have contained more than was given to and actively reproduced by all the individuals existing then, for they explicitly or implicitly thought of its being also given to that absolute all-embracing Super-Consciousness and therefore containing all that this Super-Consciousness was supposed to find in it. But this whole theory of Super-Consciousness is based on a misunderstanding. If reality exists empirically only as experienced and reconstructed by conscious beings, the latter exist empirically only as experiencing and reconstructing reality, that is, as active in it. We cannot assume any consciousness which does not manifest itself empirically in the modification of particular objects in their content and meaning by individual active thought, because consciousness is essentially actuality and actuality as we know it is exclusively the actuality of individuals, each with a limited sphere of experience and a relative reality as object-matter of his active and limited thought. To speak of an absolute consciousness is therefore either a self-contradiction, if by consciousness we mean what we empirically find within our world, or an empty combination of words, if we mean something else by it. The same is true of any conception of a conscious being which has not actively manifested itself within our reality. Our concrete empirical world as such—we do not speak here of the world as conceived in one or another rational system—could not have been present at its beginning as it now is, either for a Super-Ego, or for a Super-Consciousness, or for an inhabitant of Mars, for it is in its entire empirical concreteness what it is only for the conscious beings who live and act empirically in it and whose existence and activity leave traces which can be empirically found in it.

EXISTENCE AND REALITY

Having thus shown that the empirical world is entirely a world of historically evolved objects and can contain nothing but that which has been gradually added to it in actuality by the active thought of empirically manifested conscious individuals, we now meet a new difficulty. Does the world contain all that has been ever added to it, is the process of evolution only a process of creation, unaccompanied by destruction? And if there is destruction, as there certainly seems to be, how can we account for it? And supposing we do reconcile both creation and destruction, how shall we explain the prevalence of creation over destruction which is necessary to have produced this world?

Again we must subdivide the problem. We exclude the question of destruction and production conceived as brought about by natural causes. For, in a natural reality, by principle, there can be neither production nor destruction: there is only change, that is, production entirely balanced by destruction and reciprocally. This problem of change is connected with the general problem of the world of nature and will therefore be treated separately from the problem of concrete reality. Now, what does destruction mean for the latter?

When a house is burned, what is there destroyed empirically, what effect does the burning have on the empirical existence of the house? Does it destroy its content? No, for the content persists in memory, can be revived at any moment. Does it destroy the meaning? No, for the meaning established before can be revived, the acts suggested by it can be performed, and, though they can be performed only in imagination, still this does not make them unreal. And yet something has been certainly modified; the burned house is not the same as the standing house. From the standpoint of concrete reality, as object-matter of active thought, the difference between the new and the old conditions is clear; the house is no longer an object of certain activities. Its old content remains, but it is no longer enriched by being connected with other material objects; it may be developed still aesthetically, but not physically. Its old meaning remains, but no new material or hedonistic connections are established between it and other material objects or our own bodies. It has not ceased to exist, but it has been removed from the complex of present material reality.

Take another example. A speech has been made at a meeting. It is and remains an object with a definite content and meaning given to it by the speaker and all his listeners. But after a time many listeners forget it. It has not ceased to exist, for it can always be recalled by others and reconstructed; but it has been at least provisionally removed from the present spheres of reality of those individuals; it is no longer an object of active thought for them. Even those who remember it do not perform with regard to it many of the actions which were performed at the moment when it was made, do not reproduce it as element of the same complexes to which it then belonged.

Let us go farther. There existed an Egyptian civilization. It included technical products, economic values, political and social organizations, language, religion, art, science—in a word, everything a full civilization can contain. It disappeared with the ancient Egyptians, and for fifteen hundred years little was known about it. Does this mean that it has ceased to exist? No, because during the past century more and more of its objects have been gradually reproduced in their content and meaning, and they are still the same concrete historical objects, not different ones, in so far as the reconstruction is exact. Of course, not all their content and not all their meaning has been reproduced, but this is only a matter of degree. In fact, the reproduction of one or another object, of one or another variation of the content or meaning of an object, may be impracticable, but it can never be said to be absolutely impossible. And no historical object which can be actually revived has ceased to exist, however short or long the span of time between its successive actualizations, however small or great the variation of content and meaning which its new actualization brings

with it. Yet there is a fundamental difference between the
way these historical objects existed in ancient Egypt and
the way they exist for us now. They are not for us objects
of new actions of the same type as those performed by the
Egyptians; we do not take them as parts of similar complexes.
We do not use their technical products for practical purposes,
their exchange-values are not (or not in the same proportions)
exchange-values for us, we are little concerned with their
myths and ritual in our own religious systems, we do not speak
their language, their science is for us merely a historical datum,
not a source of our own truth; only their art, their morality,
their political and social organization, may have preserved
for us a slight vestige of their old vitality, may influence in a
minimal way our own art, our own morality, our own social
life. Their values have dropped out of those systems of
reality which are now within the limits of our vital interests.

These three examples, the burning of a house, forgetting
of an event by an individual, passing away of an old civilization, illustrate the same general principle, which we must now
take into consideration.

We postpone provisionally the question how it happens
that a certain historical object becomes excluded from a
certain complex of reality, and how it not only is not, but often
cannot be connected with other values of this complex. Such
an exclusion implies that the respective domain of reality is
rationally organized and excludes the given historical object
by virtue of its organization; and we shall speak of the rational
organization of reality later on. Here we are concerned with
the entire concrete existence of a historical object, independent of any special determination it may acquire and special
conditions to which it may be subjected within one or another
isolated system to which it may belong. From this general
standpoint the problem stated above demands that a distinction be made between the mere fact of the *existence* of a
historical object and the degree of its *realness*.

The concept of existence is, for the concrete historical world, retrospective. It bears on all that, and only on that which has been already evolved and as far as it has been evolved. To exist means simply to be in itself and for itself, not merely for actual thought. Of course empirically nothing exists which has not been produced by actual thought and which cannot become again an object-matter of actual thought, but as far as already existing it does not depend on actual thought for its further existence. The existence of concrete things is neither their pure actuality, nor a pure transcendence of all actuality, but a transcendence of any particular actuality and of any number of actualities. An object exists only as far as it has been actually created; an object that has yet to be created does not exist; possibility of being created is not equivalent to potential existence, and this differentiates the concrete historical reality from the abstractly determined physical reality in which the future may be said to exist in the present because it is supposed predetermined entirely by the present. However, all the objects which have been already created, with all their variations of content and meaning, exist if there is any possibility of their reappearing in actuality, because here the possibility is not an abstract and undetermined possibility of being created (which in the case of any particular object approaches zero, since the number of objects that can be created is, by the very definition of creation, unlimited), but a concrete and determined possibility of being revived, which for any particular object is theoretically a positive quantity, the number of objects that can be revived being always limited. Of course, like every other actualization, the revival itself is a creative act, for it always brings a new variation of the revived object, but it is not with the variation, only with the object which will include this variation, that we are here concerned. And as there is no historical object which, once created, could not possibly be reconstructed under some, however improbable, conditions, even without the explicit consciousness of its having been created before, there is no historical object which, once created, can ever cease to exist, even if as a matter of fact it never is revived after it once disappears from the domain of actual human interests.

There is a prepossession which has hindered this principle from becoming generally recognized, namely, that consciousness of the continuity of existence is necessary for the continuity of the existence of a historical object. This standpoint is almost always more or less clearly taken with regard to historical objects whose existence seems to depend prominently on human individuals or societies. It is imagined that a historical object can be simultaneously the same for several individuals only if they are conscious of its identity and have communicated it to each other, that when two individuals have simultaneously the same idea, concrete remembrance, or concept (for usually an exception is made for material objects), it is not one, but two ideas which become unified only when each individual knows about the other's having it and refers his own idea to the other's. In the same way also it is assumed that a historical object cannot be successively the same for two individuals unless the one to whom it has been given later knows that it was given before to the other individuals, and it is this knowledge which is implicitly supposed to create the continuity of existence, just as when two individuals have at a different moment of time the same idea without the first having expressed it and directly or indirectly communicated it to the second, it is not taken to be one, but two ideas. This double assumption is simply the product of an erroneous interpretation of a real empirical fact. The historical object, whatever it be, possesses always, as we know, a certain range of extension, spreads over the spheres of experience and reflection of a certain number of individuals. Its mere objective existence as element of a complex is not affected by the range of its empirical extension;

it exists as long as it can be reproduced with this complex, and it always can. But its actual influence on other objects, the rôle it plays in the concrete historical reality, does depend, of course, on its extension, and this rôle can decrease to approximately zero or increase indefinitely, depending on the decrease or growth of the extension of the object. Now, a historical object increases in extension by being introduced into new spheres of experience and reflection. This introduction may proceed empirically in various ways, but its fundamental mechanism is always the same. A certain object which belongs to the spheres of experience and reflection of some individuals living now, or which belonged to the spheres of experience and reflection of individuals who lived years or centuries ago, is objectively an element of a complex which has been partly experienced and reproduced by a certain individual, so that the latter is already acquainted with other elements of this complex, but not with this particular one. If, now, this individual reproduces this objective connection between the objects with which he is acquainted and the element which up to then did not belong to his sphere of experience and reflection, he introduces thereby this element into his actual sphere of reality as objectively the same. Of course, this object may have for him a somewhat different content and meaning than for others, if in their spheres of reality it was also an element in other complexes with which this individual is not yet acquainted. Thus, when an individual approaches a new locality, the material objects of this locality become gradually introduced into his sphere of experience and reflection and any material object which was ever given to others can be given to him because of its connections. By getting acquainted with the pictures on Egyptian walls he can reconstruct many of the values which were connected in the past with these pictures. By introducing into the spheres of his experience and reflection certain technical problems he may repeat, without knowing it, an invention which the same problems have suggested to others. And so on. The unknown historical object can be given whenever known and given objects, directly or indirectly, suggest it, owing to their pre-established connections. And since there are innumerable connections between an object and other objects of the historical reality, innumerable complexes more or less interfering with each other, there are for an individual many ways of reaching a certain unknown object and each known object may lead to the rediscovery of many others.

Now, the mechanism of social communication only makes this process more rapid and better organized: it permits an individual to suggest to others at once such definite objects as he wants to suggest among all the objects with which he is acquainted and others are not, and vice versa; it permits him to reproduce at once in his sphere such objects as are suggested to him among those with which others are acquainted and he is not. Thanks to social symbols, words, or signs, the extension of historical objects to new spheres of experience and reflection becomes intentional and selective, whereas without organized communication it is a matter of chance, depends on the question whether among the many suggestions which actually given objects offer to an individual he happens to follow the one which will lead him to the discovery of a certain personally unknown object. But the existence of this intentionally organized passage of objects from the sphere of experience and reflection of one individual to that of another presupposes the unintentional reproduction of objects as given to one individual by another individual; social communication, far from being the ground of the inter-individual community of objects, is entirely founded upon this community.

This is usually recognized with regard to material objects, since it is quite evident that symbols could not be the vehicle of social communication, if the community of their sensual content were not independent of social communication, if each individual could not, on the ground of his own sphere of reality, experience and reproduce them by himself; and it is equally evident that no social co-operation in the material world would be possible if this world were not at least in its essential features common to the co-operating individuals without their needing to construct this community for every common action with the help of social communication. Now, the same must be true of all objects; sensual contents are not privileged in this respect. In order to have a myth, an idea, an economic value, a political or moral rule, communicated to me, I must be able to reproduce them on the ground of my own experience and reflection; I must have within my own sphere of reality the possibility of reconstructing for myself the same cultural objects with which others are already acquainted, otherwise the help offered by social symbols would be lost for me; these symbols would not mean to me the same objects as they mean to others. Whether I reproduce these objects before or after their reproduction has been suggested to me by other individuals, whether in reproducing them I am conscious that others are already acquainted with them or not, has no importance whatever for the question of their being the same objects for all of us. They are the same whether I know it or not, if their contents and meanings in my experience are sufficiently similar to the contents and meanings they have in the experience of others. Social communication can, indeed, help me to make my view of the object more similar to that of others by suggesting to me how I should determine this object to make it similar; but this suggestion would be useless if I could not determine it like others in any case, if I did not possess in my spheres of experience and reflection all that is necessary to reconstruct the complex in which this new object will acquire a character similar to that which it possesses for others. The consciousness that this object as given to me and reproduced by me is the same as the object experienced and reproduced by others presupposes thus that the object can be the same without my being conscious of its identity in our respective experiences.

Further, cultural objects in the narrower sense of the term —scientific, aesthetic, religious, moral, political, economic— can be just as well the object-matter of social co-operation as natural reality; and though an intentional and organized co-operation requires in both cases that each individual be conscious of his reality's being the same as the reality of others, all co-operation, organized or not, would be impossible if the objects were not common independently of actual social communication, and if thus each individual could not find in objects as given to him the modifications which other individuals, with or without his knowledge, have produced in these objects, and if vice versa the modifications produced by him could not appear in the experience of others whether the latter knew or not who was the author. As a matter of fact, in the very beginning of social communication we do not even assume that there are differences between objects as given to other individuals and objects as given to us; we have to learn this, and we are still learning. The ground on which we begin to communicate is the general assumption of a universal and complete identity of objects for all conscious beings, and it is only gradually that we qualify it. The philosophical and sociological theories of social communication and of the continuity of culture as due to social tradition invert the original empirical situation, because they try to interpret it in the light of the supposition that human individuals are as many distinct, closed, and impenetrable minds within which all objects, or at least non-material objects, are supposed to be inclosed and whose communication becomes a fundamental, and in fact an insoluble, problem.

Existence, as the common character of all objects which have ever been given in the past and can therefore be given again with their once acquired content and meaning, applies equally to all of them, whether they happen or not to be within the sphere of present activities. But this is not so with respect to their "being real," their "realness," as we may call the character which an object possesses as a part of reality. The object is real, as we know, not because of the mere fact of its existence within the domain of actual or possible experience, but because of the significance which this existence has both for active thought and for other objects. What makes therefore a concrete object empirically real is not its having been produced by old activities, but its being now the starting-point for new activities. Realness is not the retrospective, but the prospective side of an object; it depends indeed on the past, on the connections already established between the object and other objects, but depends on them only with regard to the future, in so far as those connections are the ground for new acts. For it is clear that the more frequently an object appears in actuality and the wider grows the sphere of its extension, the greater becomes also the number and variety of new activities of which it is the object-matter, the greater its actual, not merely potential, significance for active thought and its influence on other objects. And thus, while existence admits no gradations, there are innumerable possible degrees of realness, though of course whatever exists has some degree of realness, however slight, however approaching zero, for there are no existing objects without any reference whatever, even though only distant and mediate, to the present sphere of reality of some conscious beings.

While existence, once acquired, is never lost, realness does not stay changeless, but either increases or decreases indefinitely. Its increase is the direct effect of the actual growth of an object in extension, of its introduction into new spheres of reality. When, on the contrary, an object ceases to enter into new connections, other objects take its place in the center of active interest, and not only it does not become the object-matter of new actions, but even old actions cease to be actually repeated, its importance for activity and its influence upon other objects decrease. This may be the effect either of that removal of the object from a certain system of reality which is destruction proper, or of simple oblivion, that is, of other objects and groups of objects actively taking the center of present experience and reflection. What is destroyed in both cases is neither the content nor the meaning of the object, but some of its realness.

It may happen also that an object which loses some realness in a certain domain continues to acquire some in another domain, that while a certain side of its content and meaning ceases to be the object-matter of new activities, another side develops even more intensely than before. Thus, an object that has lost some of its material realness by physical destruction may continue to exist chiefly as a mythological, or aesthetic, or scientific value. We know, for example, that in myths which have material realness as their basis the partial destruction of this realness is often a necessary condition of the development of the myth, and the time is not very remote when only happenings and personalities which had ceased to be materially real were considered the proper objects of poetry.

This possibility for an object to increase in realness in one line after the destruction of a part of its realness in another helps us to understand how it is that, while within any particular real complex creation may be balanced by destruction or the latter may prevail altogether, the whole concrete historical reality is ceaselessly and indefinitely growing. And the very rate of this growth increases in the measure in which organized, systematic, intentional creation of new objects becomes gradually superadded to the primary unorganized development of contents and meanings due to those innumerable, often insignificant, but continually agglomerating variations which all acts of thought add to the reality that is their object-matter.

CHAPTER IV

THE PRACTICAL ORGANIZATION OF REALITY

THE METHOD

The concrete historical reality, as it has been determined in the preceding sections, is evidently neither the reality of common-sense reflection nor that of science. The chief feature of both the common-sense reality and the scientific reality which we miss in concrete historical reality is rationality of objects and of happenings, for in concrete reality rationality is reduced to its minimum, that is, to the possibility of objectively reproducing by thought each particular determination of an object and each particular connection between objects within a complex, and even this only approximately, without any subordination of these determinations and connections to fundamental principles. The world of historical objects taken in its concrete totality or any concrete fragment of this world is an irrational chaos, and this chaotic character appears most clearly when contrasted with the perfect rational harmony of a world conceived as an Aristotelian system of timeless "essences" or a mechanistic system of eternal laws ruling all becoming with iron necessity. However exaggerated such conceptions may be, the fact that they have ever been constructed and accepted shows that there must be in empirical reality more rational organization than this minimal rationality of single determinations and connections which we have assumed. We have been forced by the demands of philosophical method abstractly to ignore in the first part of our investigation any rational order beyond that necessary minimum; now it is time to study the origin and character of any superior rationality which reality may possess. Admitting therefore that empirical reality is primarily and fundamentally a world of historical objects, we may now ask: "How did the common-sense reality and the scientific reality originate out of this concrete world, what part do they play in it, how much objectivity do they possess, and what are their essential characters as viewed from the standpoint of complete historical experience?"

Here we meet again, as in our last chapter, several problems of method. First of all, as against the realistic assumption of a perfect rational order originally inherent in reality, we find the idealistic claim that reality of itself, even if it has any existence independently of thought, has no rational order whatever except while and in so far as it is an actual object-matter of thought; the latter is then, in objective idealism, conceived as being a universally and timelessly actual, absolute reason, in order to account for the fact that individual thought finds some rational organization in reality independent of its own actual performances. The methodological problem implied in this opposition is evident. If all organization of reality is objectively inherent in it, we shall have to study only systems of reality in themselves without caring for thought, which can do nothing but copy the pre-existing order; if, on the contrary, all organization of reality exists only as actually produced by thought, we must investigate systems of thought to reach the essence of the real order.

However, neither of these methods would be adequate. For, on the one hand, our investigation of real objects and their connections has shown that, even when an objective real complex already exists before some particular activity which reproduces it *now* and *here*, this actual reproduction not only is necessary to have the complex actually given to the individual as objectively real, but influences in some, however small, measure the complex in its objective reality, and every empirical complex, however wide and stable, however real it may be now, has originated and grown because of the agglomerated results of past activities. This is true of any real complex in so far as empirical, independently of the degree of rational organization it may possess. On the other hand, any complex produced by actual thought exists afterward, as we have seen, beyond actuality and influences more or less future activities by the objective realness which it has acquired. Since there is no formal difference between active thought as producing a new real complex and active thought as reproducing a pre-existing complex, and the same organization of reality which has been once produced by thought can afterward impose itself on thought as existing in itself, a system of objects is thus, even when first produced, a system of reality, not a system of thought. Therefore our method of investigating the rational organization of reality can be neither realistic nor idealistic: in studying real systems we must take into account active thought which produces and reproduces them, but we must take it into account not in itself, but in its real results, not with regard to its own *logical* order to which it subjects itself in the course of its actual development, but with regard to the *rational* organization of reality which it leaves after its actual performance.

The second important methodological point concerns the relation between the rational organization of reality and the irrational chaos of the real world taken in its historical concreteness. Most of the philosophies which treat reality as originally unorganized, and rational organization as superimposed by logical thought upon the original chaos, assume explicitly or implicitly that reality in so far as already objectivated and distinguished from mere subjective data, that is, the reality with which our practical or theoretic reflection deals, is always perfectly and equally rational. The old realistic conception of one absolute reality is still alive, even in the most radical idealism. Irrationality is readily granted to subjective data, and idealism willingly assumes that the empirical matter of reality is entirely constituted by subjective data; but, in so far as objective reality has been built out of these data by giving them a rational form, it is supposed to possess a perfect rational order, and if irrationality slips into our empirical reproductions of this order, as it often does, it is assumed to have its source not in the imperfect rationality of the objects and systems of objects, but exclusively in the fact that we empirical individuals, because of the imperfections of our reasons, mix subjective data into this rational order of objects. How deeply this traditional prepossession is rooted is shown by the example of Bergson who, even while limiting the objective validity of traditional rationalism, still sees in the chaos of experience a problem to be solved, and attempts to solve it by assuming, just as the German idealists, a duality of orders which produce an appearance of disorder for us because we do not distinguish them sufficiently.

It is clear that under the assumption that reality must be either rationally perfect or not be reality at all, but subjective data, the distinction between the original irrationality of reality and its rational organization has no empirical significance, is a purely formal philosophical analysis of reality into two abstract components which necessarily and indissolubly belong together. All irrationality in experience is supposed completely overcome when we pass from experience to reality. The only task of philosophy, by which its method is determined, consists then in defining the one perfect order, or sometimes the two perfect orders, which constructs reality by overcoming the irrationality of experience.

But our investigation of empirical reality in the preceding chapter has led us to the conclusion that irrationality belongs to objective reality itself, not only to its subjective reproduction, because between subjectivity and objectivity, between irrationality and rationality, between chaos and order, the passage is continuous; absolute objectivity, absolute rationality, absolute order, represent the highest limit, absolute subjectivity, absolute irrationality, absolute chaos, the lowest limit, and it is between these limits that empirical reality fully exists as concrete reality, not as mere approximation to reality; and we have seen that to be reality, it needs only to be above the lowest, not on the highest, limit. Objective rational order may indeed increase for certain parts of the concrete reality in various proportions, and for a few parts it may even approach to the highest limit; but this growth of rationality remains within the total historical concreteness and leaves a wide margin or irrationality which may perhaps—we cannot tell now whether it does or not—diminish, but can never disappear. A rationally organized reality demands (1) a rational determination of each single object within a systematically organized complex; (2) a rational organization of each particular system; (3) a synthesis of many systems under one common rational order. But none of these demands can be ever fully realized in the empirical world, for each encounters a particular difficulty which it can never completely overcome.

First of all, we have seen that no concrete empirical object is entirely devoid of the character of subjective datum; it is indubitably objective, but it never can lose all dependence on subjective experience. And because it always still roots in subjectivity, it cannot as object ever rationally be exhausted in any system, however completely the latter seems to determine it; it will always be incorporated into many other, old or new, actually reconstructed or constructed complexes, and will be thus concretely an irrational historical object. Being composed of such objects, concrete reality cannot be fully rational, however perfectly organized and unified its systems may be.

Further, however rational may be the systematic organization of any particular complex of objects, this organization evidently cannot exhaust the complex in its empirical concreteness. For we know that each actual reproduction of the complex modifies the latter, even if in only a slight measure. As a part of concrete historical reality, the complex remains for us the same with all its modifications, as long as we want to treat it as the same, for all the personal variations added to it during its reproduction can belong to it without destroying its unity, since it does not need to be in any particular way self-consistent except in so far as it claims to be systematically organized. But such variations are necessarily excluded from its systematic organization, which by its rational nature must be absolutely self-identical. An empirical complex may be a rational system, even an almost perfectly organized one, but it will be also a concrete complex, transcending its systematic organization by its concreteness; it will include besides the objects and connections demanded by its systematic rationality other objects and connections which may not at all harmonize with these demands. Historically, this impossibility to cover any concrete empirical complex by a systematic organization manifests itself very well in the fact that no rational system can last empirically without special efforts to maintain its organization, for every one of them evolves as consequence of the additions which it undergoes in varying reproductions and after a time we find instead of the original system an empirical complex to which a completely different systematic organization must be given because the old one no longer corresponds to its empirical reality.

As to the synthesis of many empirical systems under a common rational order, it is evident that without such a synthesis reality would remain irrational, even though each particular system were perfectly rational; for the systems would be disconnected and incommensurable with each other; each would have an entirely different, unique rationality. But, as we shall see in detail later on, no rational synthesis of empirical systems can entirely overcome their variety; each system in so far as it is empirically distinct is in some measure different from others, has some exclusive rationality of its own, some peculiarity in the way in which it is organized, which is irreducible to any common order. Therefore, even if there should be one general order common to all reality, still within the limits of this order, reality would in some measure be a chaos of systems, besides being, as we have seen, a chaos of objects. This irrationality resulting from the variety of systems would be completely overcome only if the whole reality were one system of objects in which all empirically given systems were absorbed. But such an assumption, which is essentially that of Spinoza, evidently contradicts experience.

The rationality of the real world is thus not an absolute order, with logical necessity imposed at once by reason upon reality. It is an empirical, partial organization of concrete reality and must itself develop in duration and extension within the wider concrete development of the historical world; it tends continually to mold empirical reality in accordance with its own demands, but never succeeds in penetrating and ordering that chaos on the ground of which it has appeared and grown, cannot impose any of its demands, however small or great the latter may be, completely and unconditionally. Instead of speaking of the rationality of the real world, it would be more exact to speak of its progressive rationalization.

From this results the fact that in investigating the rational organization of reality we must follow the method of genetic construction. The passage from that minimum of rationality which we have assumed in the preceding chapter to the highest level of order which empirical reality can attain, must be made step by step, following the different stages of comprehensiveness and rational perfection which the real empirical systems and groups of systems found in our historical reality actually possess. We cannot, however, assume generally that the logical hierarchy of these different stages corresponds to the order of their historical development, that the entire reality which is being rationalized had to pass first through all lower stages of rational organization before a higher stage could appear at all. For if it is clear that in any continuous line of development a higher stage cannot be reached until the lower ones have been passed, still there may be in the evolution of reality many continuous lines of development independent of each other, and rational organization may be more highly developed in certain domains of reality than in others.

The third methodological problem is connected with the respective rôles of theoretic and non-theoretic activities in organizing concrete reality. This problem is important because of the old intellectualistic prepossession according to which all thought, in so far as bearing upon reality, is ultimately reducible to theoretic thought; that is, whenever our thought gets in touch with objective reality, there is some, however rudimentary, knowledge. We find this prepossession implied even in such philosophies as those which explicitly recognize the priority of "practical" activity, meaning by this term, activity which tends to modify its objects really. Thus, in Bergsonism practical activity is treated as fundamentally possessing the same kind of objective bearing as theoretic activity, so that any objective order which science or philosophy accepts is already involved in practical experience; in certain varieties of pragmatism, practical activity is supposed to use theoretic thought whenever it rises above personal data and associations of data and opposes reality to itself, so that whenever there is objective reality given as such there is knowledge.

But we have seen already that not only theoretic activity, but all activity bears upon objective reality as conscious thought upon its object-matter. Reality is accessible to our reflection even without being the object-matter of our knowledge, for reflection means not only theoretic reflection, but all actual thought which objectivates data as contents and incorporates them into complexes. It needs indeed logically organized thought in order to organize reality rationally; but we find logical thought wherever there is selection of objects and standards of validity, and there are other types of selection than those based on theoretic ideas, other standards of validity than those of theoretic logic. Non-theoretic activities are therefore perfectly able to create a rational organization of objects without the help of theoretic reflection, though, as we shall see later on, the latter greatly facilitates this task. The very fact that the practical importance of theoretic ideas is tested by practical activity proves that there is in the real world some rationality independent of theoretic reflection and which thus can be only the product of practical activity working alone. Whatever may be the part of knowledge in rationalizing the world, it certainly finds at every step some objective systematic order ready and constructed without its participation. On a high stage of culture we do see indeed the practical organization of reality mostly developing planfully, with the help of theoretic generalization and abstraction, but this development is preceded by and grafted upon a much slower and less critical development of rationality under the influence of activities which make little if any use of knowledge, and such activities are still continually going on all around us; theoretically controlled practice is still only a current in the sea of non-controlled practice.

It is this pre-scientific rationality which we must study first of all before we pass to the investigation of the rational order which science tends to impose upon the world, whether directly or through the intermediary of the practical activity which it controls. For even if historically knowledge had developed simultaneously with practice, which it evidently did not, there would be still two reasons for which the study of the practical organization of reality would be logically prior to that of its theoretic order. The first reason is implied in what we have just said, that knowledge in so far as applied in practice finds already some pre-existing rationality, and we cannot understand the part it plays in controlling practical activity without knowing what is this rationality with which theoretic control has to count. The second reason is contained in the very nature of knowledge as historical product:

whatever may be the order which knowledge when ready imposes upon its object-matter, knowledge itself is also a part of the historical reality, the ideas which constitute its body are also historical objects, and the activity of which these ideas are the results is not only a theoretic activity in so far as it knows other objects, but is also a practical activity in so far as it produces and modifies these particular objects called theoretic ideas. It is impossible to understand the theoretic order which systems of ideas give to the reality upon which they bear, which they "know," without having investigated first their own rational organization which, as a product of practical activity, must possess all the fundamental characters which practical activity gives to its object-matter independently of theoretic reflection. For systems of ideas, just as any practical systems, can be produced without a reflective theoretic control of the practical activity which produces them; this control, in the form of scientific self-criticism and philosophical reflection about methods, appears here as late or even later than in other practical fields.

We start therefore, in accordance with the methodical principles established above, by studying the practical organization of reality as a product of active organizing thought gradually developing from lower to higher, that is, from less to more comprehensive and rationally perfect forms.

THE SYSTEM OF OBJECTS IN THE COURSE OF ITS ACTUAL CONSTRUCTION

It should be remembered that whatever rational organization there may be in reality, whether narrow or comprehensive, imperfect or perfect, the organization which we empirically find is always the one given by us to the systems which we are constructing in actuality from actually experienced objects and by actual reflection. We may be able to transcend this actually realized rationality by extending it, also through actual reflection, beyond the limits of the system which we are constructing, by practically postulating the possibility of its application to other empirical complexes and realizing this postulate. We may be also able to turn other ready systems into objects, to treat them as actually given contents with actually suggested meanings, and thus construct in actuality a system of systems, a system of which other systems are mere elements within the limit of present activity. But we have no means of ever discovering any rational organization which we could not actually construct ourselves, directly or indirectly, nor even of ascertaining whether there is any such rationality transcending the possibilities of our constructive activity. Of course, this construction is usually the reproduction of an organization which preceded our present activity, and we know this because a certain way of systematizing given objects often suggests itself to us with an almost invincible authority; but our reproduction is always active for the very reason that it is actual; it always implies some possibilities, however slight, of not exactly following the suggestion, of modifying or supplementing the system which we reproduce. Between reproducing and producing there is only a difference of degree of creativeness; but reproduction and production both equally involve actual construction. Construction being the only way of bringing systematic organization into experience, constructive activity, more or less creative, is the only possible source of all empirical rationality. The only systems which I can experience are the systems which I can actually construct, and the systems which I can construct are either created now or have been already actually created. If we want therefore to understand the rational organization of reality, we must study the way in which rationality is created by the activity which constructs systems of objects.

We have seen in studying the object that any connection whatever actually established between two given objects implies an actual modification of these objects, a new variation of meaning given to the first of them and a new variation of content given to the second. In a word, every actual connection between objects is practical, meaning by this term, productive of some reality. The actual construction or reconstruction of a complex of objects is merely a series of such elementary practical connections. Since a system of objects in so far as empirical is a rationally organized complex, the actual organization of a system must thus be also practical in its essential features. The difference between an unorganized complex and a rationally organized system can manifest itself empirically, in the course of their actual construction, only by a practical unity, a practical order which the system possesses and the complex lacks. The practical modifications of the objects composing the system must be subordinated to some fundamental modification of reality produced in the course of actual experience and reflection, and this subordination must be the source of all rational organization of the system.

Now, there is only one way in which such a subordination can be effected: it is the conscious creation of a new object with the help and on the ground of pre-existing objects, which constitutes the task of every *intentional* activity. For the essential feature of the latter is that it tends to introduce, with the help of a single, more or less multiform but unified, series of activities, some empirically ascertainable real modification into a certain sphere of the empirical reality; that it tends to produce a status empirically different from but as real as the status which constituted its starting-point. This new status must include a new content—otherwise it would not be empirically given; and a new meaning connecting this content with others—otherwise it could not be real. This is enough to characterize it, within the limits and from the standpoint of the actual organized and intentional activity, as a new object, though if we look at it from the standpoint of the whole concrete empirical reality beyond the limits of the actual intentional activity, it may be either a mere insignificant variation of some already existing historical object or a whole system of objects which for the present purpose is treated as one object; and the creation of a new object requires the use of several pre-existing objects as concrete real ground, whose partial modifications are made to co-operate in producing the content and the meaning of this new object. Intentional creation requires thus a selection of certain particular objects and an organization of actual practical connections between these objects in view of a certain common result; it requires, in a word, the actual formation of an *organization of objects.*

For instance, even such an elementary intentional activity as the consumption of food creates a content which within the limits of this activity is new—the set of experiences which constitute this particular "experience of satisfied hunger." This content receives a definite meaning by being actually connected with the body as given to the acting individual, a meaning which characterizes it as organically real and distinguishes it from a merely imagined experience of satisfied hunger. This activity clearly needs for the realization of its intention, for the production of this relatively new object, that several pre-existing objects be selected, for instance, various parts of the body involved in the perception, apprehension, preparation, and consumption of food, the food itself, and probably also some other objects within the individual's sphere of experience; and it needs also that these values be so connected and their actual modifications so combined as to produce together this one particular result. Or take an example where the whole question appears still clearer, the production of a piece of furniture by a carpenter. Here the new content, the size, shape, color, resistance, weight, etc., of the piece of furniture, has to be determined on the ground of definite previous experiences, by analogy or contrast with definite existing contents, such as models, properties of the raw stuff from which the piece of furniture is to be composed, etc. This content acquires the meaning of a physical object by all the connections with the carpenter's body, his instruments, his materials, his environment, etc. All these objects necessary to give the new object its sensual content and its physical reality have to be intentionally selected out of the whole complexity of the carpenter's experience and actually organized with the special view of creating this one particular object; their interconnection for the given practical result is superadded to all other connections which existed between each of them and the rest of empirical reality, and thus without ceasing to be concrete historical objects, they become elements of a specific organization within which they are really ordered in a special way.

This practical actual organization of objects for the creation of a new object evidently does not mean that active thought, ignoring the concrete chaos of empirical reality, follows a pre-existing and ready rational system, but that it gradually evolves a rational system out of the more or less chaotic complex or group of complexes empirically given to it. At any stage of this evolution we find a vague empirical complex within which some rational order is more or less definitively outlined, but in which there is much which does not belong to this rational order, many objects that are not needed for the production of this particular new object as already determined, many connections that do not co-operate for the particular result which is intended. Only when a certain result has already been achieved, when the activity has been finished, we can say in looking retrospectively upon the past evolution of this activity that it has selected the very objects and all the objects necessary to produce this particular result; that it has organized them rationally in the only way by which this result could be obtained. But as long as we are actually constructing this organization, it does not exist for us in any form as an order of pure reality objectively ready and independent of our experience and reflection: it has to be actively produced from the chaos of our present sphere of concrete empirical reality. This holds true even when the organization which we are actually constructing is merely a reproduction of some pre-existing and fixed system; the latter can actually exist for us as a system only by being gradually built within that part of the concrete historical world which is actually accessible to us, thanks to an active selection of objects and an active systematization of these objects, and this selection and systematization are always practical, have always some actual modification of our reality in view. And since a system, however perfect, however objective and impersonal it may be when taken abstractly and exclusively in its objective rational order, is also always an empirical complex; it is dependent on its actual reproductions for the empirical preservation of its rationality in the concrete evolution of the historical world. In other words, any rational system of objects, just as any particular object, can be historically real, can remain within the domain of actual interests only by being actually reproduced; otherwise, though having once been constructed it always possesses existence, it gradually loses realness. The practical organization of objects in actuality is thus both the source of new systems and the ground of the realness of old systems. We shall take it here in its first rôle with regard to the new systems which originate in it; but we must remember that it remains always the empirical background of every one of those stabilized and more or less perfect existing systems whose internal rationality we are going to investigate.

The essential feature of all actual organization of objects is thus evidently its dynamic character. The system which activity gradually constructs for the creation of a new object, including this new object itself, is evolving in its totality during the whole period of its actual formation. In so far as thus evolving, it cannot be exactly assimilated to any pre-existing rational organization of the real world; it is not a part of an objective rational reality. On the contrary, in order to be incorporated into it, objects must be taken out of all pre-existing complexes, rational or not, to which they belong; all their pre-existing connections must be ignored except those by which they are fit to become the elements of the actual dynamic organization, and which ones among their connections may be thus utilized for the present purpose can be discovered only by actually reproducing them. We must therefore, in studying the actual dynamic organization of objects, carefully avoid the error of ascribing to it such characters as only ready systems can possess.

Thus, first of all, it must be realized that, though the actually established organization of objects implies *intentionality*, it does not imply *finality*. The latter develops indeed by degrees, and we shall follow its development; but it develops on the ground of the former under certain special conditions. All we mean by calling a certain activity intentional is that it makes such a selection among the objects which are its object-matter and gives to the selected objects such modifications as to have these modifications combine in producing a new object, which, in the measure it is produced, takes its place in the set of the selected objects as part of the same sphere of reality. But this does not imply yet the existence of a conscious aim; that is, the determination in advance of the object which is going to be produced. The conception of the aim has arisen on the ground of the dualism of object and subject, of real things and subjective unreal representations. The aim is taken as the future real thing represented before being realized, and activity is conceived as the realization of this unreal representation, so that the aim is supposed to be ready before activity begins and to determine the latter. In fact, however, at the moment when the aim is "represented," activity has been already going on for some time and this "representation" is its result in so far as achieved at that moment; the further realization of this representation is the continuation of the same activity, its second part which would be impossible if it had not been preceded by the first part.

We shall see later in detail why and how does the continuous empirical activity become thus divided into two parts, and how the first part, the creation of the "representation," becomes qualified as "subjective," "unreal," and not belonging to the activity proper. The general reason for this division lies in the very progress of practical organization of concrete reality, and the division is justified from the standpoint of practice and of science in so far as subservient to practice; but this division can be understood only if taken on the more primary ground of concrete empirical reality and thought. From this more fundamental standpoint, it is clear that although the "represented" aim has less realness than the "realized" aim, the difference is only one of degree. Only nothingness is unreal. The active development by which the aim becomes defined and its content and meaning partly determined, is in its nature, even if not always to the same degree, a development as creative as the further realization of this aim by which it will become a material or social object. Some reality is produced which was not there before; but it is produced step by step, from non-existence to the less real existence of the "representation," from that to the more real existence of a materialized technical product, of an accomplished work of art, of an established social institution, etc. We may divide, practically or theoretically, this production into sections and the division may be very real, but there always remains a continuous undercurrent uniting the separated sections. Fundamentally, in view of this essential continuity of the action, the "represented" product is the same concrete object as the fully realized product, only taken at a lower stage of its realization. The picture which the artist has drawn in his imagination and the picture which afterward appears upon the canvas are one and the same picture; the conception of a political institution germinating in the consciousness of a statesman and the ready political institution realized in the state are objectively one and the same historical object, *the* political institution at different stages of its becoming.

Thus, to say that the future result can be in some way *given* before being *realized* is from the standpoint of concrete reality equivalent to the proposition that something can exist before existing. The future result is given only in the very measure in which it is realized. The aim cannot pre-exist in consciousness at a moment when it has not yet begun to be realized, for its appearance in consciousness is precisely a part of its realization. The provisional determination of the content and meaning of the aim to be attained is already a partial attainment of this aim, for this attainment from the beginning to the end is precisely nothing else but a progressive determination of the content and meaning of the new object. If the future object is at a certain moment represented by analogy with some pre-existing, formerly experienced object, this means that this pre-existing object with some of its content and meaning is introduced into the actually constructed organization as a material for the creation of the new object; that the content and meaning of the latter are by this very introduction determined in certain respects on the ground of pre-existing reality and are already in some measure realized. The determination is not definitive; we do not know yet what use subsequent acts will make of this material, precisely because the mere introduction of some pre-existing object as a model for the new object is not enough to determine the whole content and meaning of the latter; it gives only a provisional and partial determination, which will become definitive and complete only after a more or less long series of creative acts, and only the totality of these acts will determine the new object as more or less similar or dissimilar to the pre-existing object taken as a model; that is, as material which, together with many other materials, will contribute to make the new object.

Another serious mistake which must be avoided in characterizing the practical organization of objects in actuality is stating the problem in terms of an ideal or real *adaptation* between the active being and the pre-existing reality. The conception of ideal adaptation is inherent in the current belief that the active subject consciously selects in advance, from among pre-existing objects, those which, by their nature as determined independently of the present activity, are apt in themselves to be the *means* for the realization of the *end* which, though set freely, must be set so as to be attainable with such means as reality puts at the subject's disposal. The theory of real adaptation treats activity as causally determined by the given conditions, objective and subjective; the organization of objects in activity is a product of the reciprocal adaptation between the subjective and objective conditions, the individual and his environment.

Each of these conceptions is based on a misunderstanding. If we take the active being in the idealistic sense as the conscious subject, the source or the synthetic unity of actions, then it does not adapt itself to any reality; nor does it adapt any reality to itself, because it is the very activity which takes the existing reality for its object-matter, and the concept of adaptation cannot be applied at all to the relation between activity and its object-matter. By taking reality as its object-matter, the active subject modifies it, and if in a certain case a certain object appears in his present activity with the character of an ·end and other objects with the characters of means, it is because by modifying them he has actively given both these characters to the respective objects simultaneously and with reference to each other, because by determining an object as something which actually is being reached by him with certain means he has made it an end, and by determining, vice versa, some objects as something with the help of which a certain end is being actually reached by him, he has made them means. We cannot speak even of an adaptation of both the end and means to the pre-existing rational organization of reality. For, if we take the standpoint of the total empirical reality, the determination of an end and of the means for its attainment is simply an *addition* made to this reality, a creation of some new contents and meanings, not an adaptation to anything. If, on the other hand, we take into consideration the specific organization which is expressed in the subordination of means to the end and the combination of the means, this order is not a result of any adaptation to the pre-existing organization of reality, for it is, on the contrary, a creation of a new organization outside and in some measure in spite of the pre-existing one. Objects are not ends or means before being used as such actually. We shall see later under what special circumstances activity does create an approximately teleological systematic organization, an ideal combination of definite means for the attainment of a definite end; but whenever it does this, it must first of all isolate objects from the rest of reality; it must ignore the systems in which they participate so as to incorporate them into the new actual system.

If we pass now to the modern realistic concept of adaptation, it is clear that the active individual as biological or psychological being may be distinguished by the observer from his material or social environment when we take him merely as element of a reality given to our scientific reflection. But for "his own" activity, that is, for the activity which has its source in his actuality, "he," his body or his social personality, is a part of the reality given to his active thought as an object-matter. He does not adapt his body or his social personality to his environment or his environment to them, because his body or his social personality—or, more exactly, certain parts of his body or of his social personality—are for the present activity elements of the system which this activity organizes, and of which other elements are drawn from among the material objects surrounding his body or the social values constituting the cultural reality of his group. The practical significance which all these objects, the individual's own person included, have for his activity as pre-existing conditions, as possible object-matter of his active thought, does not depend on what they are assumed to be by the scientific observer who takes them as elements of an absolute, objective, rational reality, but on what they empirically are for the acting individual himself to whom they are given as components of that section of the concrete historical world which constitutes this individual's particular sphere of reality. The practical significance which these objects assume when already used by present activity depends on the latter, which thus, far from being determined by the pre-existing conditions, either as reconstructed by the observing scientist or as given to the individual himself, determines itself these conditions in its own particular way, ignores most of them, and shapes those which it has selected as its object-matter into a new systematic organization.

There is indeed adaptation in intentional activity, but it is not adaptation between the active being and reality, only between pre-existing reality and the new object which is being created. On the one hand, the new object must be adapted to the pre-existing reality in order to become real itself; since there is no absolute creation possible, since every creation needs some material, the new must adapt itself to the conditions imposed by the old in the measure inversely proportionate to the creative power and originality of the activity which produces it. On the other hand, the pre-existing reality must be adapted to the new object in order to be able to include the latter; since every activity is relatively creative, brings something new, the old must adapt itself to the new in a measure directly proportionate to the creative power and originality of the activity which modifies it. In unorganized creation this reciprocal adaptation becomes immediately realized by each act, since each act is independent and does not have to combine with others; in organized activity, reciprocal adaptation between the old and the new becomes a complicated task whose importance grows with the importance of the total modification of empirical reality which has to be realized by one organization of co-operating acts.

But the task is not imposed upon activity from the outside and in advance; it is undertaken and fulfilled by activity itself and within its own limits. The measure and the manner in which the new object has to be adapted to pre-existing reality depends on the choice which we have already made among pre-existing objects in order to determine the content and meaning of the new object from the standpoint of past experience; the measure and the manner in which pre-existing reality has to be adapted to the new object depends on the content and meaning which we have already given to the latter. The task is undertaken and fulfilled gradually and continuously in the very course of activity.

Every new determination of the new object with the help of that set of pre-existing objects which we have already selected from the concrete empirical reality as the particular field of our action forces us to modify this field, to introduce some more objects into it and to establish some new connections; and this modification of the already given field of action forces us to determine in some new way our new object. The latter is a dynamic, gradually constructed center of a dynamic, gradually effected, partial systematization of pre-existing reality, a center whose own determination in content and meaning continually increases with the growth of the sphere organized around it and which reciprocally, with the growth of its own determination, becomes more and more important as a basis for the selection and determination of the objects constituting this sphere. Whether this systematization of pre-existing reality constitutes an important new addition to the rational organization which already existed within the historical world before the action started, or whether it only reproduces with slight variations a fragment of this organization, depends on the relative concrete novelty of the object which is being created; and vice versa, the degree of novelty of the new object when viewed from the standpoint of the total historical reality depends on the degree of novelty of the organization of old objects developed during its creation. The ultimate reason of the relative novelty of both is the relative originality of the action.

Examples of such a gradual reciprocal adaptation between the old and the new are particularly clear in all those activities in which the creative effort is not chiefly concentrated in the first, inventive and organizing, part of the action, as it is in certain industrial activities, but has to be continued up to the end. Thus, a social reformer who wants to create a new institution must continually adapt the content and meaning of this institution to the existing social reality, and continually modify social reality in adaptation to the institution as already formed. The institution becomes the center around which and with regard to which he organizes social objects as they gradually become utilized for the realization of his intention. In the beginning the new social value is mostly determined in its content from the standpoint of the meaning given in the course of this activity to certain pre-existing social values: it has to satisfy certain needs which the social reformer has observed in society; it has to be similar to or different from certain other institutions which he knows; it has to possess certain characters which make it realizable with the help or in spite of the hindrance of some existing beliefs, laws, customs, traditions, economic values, social personalities, etc. Gradually, as the content of the new institution becomes realized, it imposes more and more definite demands on the pre-existing reality; the social reformer, in order to give the new value its full social meaning, has to modify the content of other social values, arouse new needs in society, supplementing those which the institution was at first meant to satisfy, modify in some measure old beliefs, customs, traditions, and laws, raise funds, publish articles, obtain the co-operation of influential personalities, train social workers, etc. Similarly, for a literary man who writes a novel, the novel becomes both an expression of reality and a basis of reinterpretation of reality. In the beginning it is mostly the content of the novel which is determined on the ground of the observations which the writer selects and to which he gives an aesthetic meaning as material for his work; in the measure that the new content grows in concreteness, it acquires in turn an aesthetic meaning by forcing the writer and later his readers to look upon reality in a new way, to see in it such contents as nobody saw before.

The difference which we find in the foregoing examples between a first period of activity during which the content of the new object is determined to fit pre-existing objects and a second period in which the content of pre-existing objects is modified to fit the new object, evidently does not mean that the new is at first exclusively adapted to the old, and afterward the old exclusively adapted to the new. For when, in the first period, old objects are given new meanings by being used to create the content of the new object, this is already a modification of pre-existing reality just as much as if these old objects were given new contents; and when, in the second period, the new object is given a new meaning by having the content of old objects modified for its sake, this is still a continuation of the creative activity as important for the new object as a determination of its content. The fact is that in every creation of a new object a determination of content must always precede a corresponding determination of meaning, since meaning cannot exist without content; and the more complex and rationally organized empirical activity becomes, the more it tends to separate these two tasks, to create first the whole content of the new object and afterward only to realize it as an object in giving it a meaning with reference to other pre-existing objects. The separation is never complete; from the very beginning the new object acquires some meaning and up to the end its content continues to grow. And yet, though the difference between the first period and the second is only a matter of degree, there is a relative prevalence of the creation of content in the first and of the creation of meaning in the second period; and, although the gradation between these periods is continuous, this difference may lead to a partial but distinct division under the influence of a factor which we shall investigate at once. In so far as the division is performed, activity assumes the subjectively finalistic character which originally it did not possess. The first period, that during which the content of the new historical object is created, is then characterized as the determination of an *aim;* the second period, when this content acquires reality with reference to pre-existing objects, is the *realization* of this aim.

THE SITUATION

The factor which leads to this distinction between the determination of an aim and the realization of this aim is the use of *instruments*.

We remember that the power of direct creation which an individual act of thought possesses by itself with regard to those historical objects whose content and meaning have been developed and fixed by innumerable past activities, is very limited. The modification which an act by its own creative influence alone can introduce into an old and rich reality is relatively small; it may indeed modify in a marked way that particular variation of a historical object which is given to the individual in his actual sphere of reality, but since this variation itself is only an insignificant part of the total content and meaning of this object, which extends over many individual *here*'s and lasts through many individual *now*'s, the modification will be almost lost in the total evolution of the concrete historical object. There are indeed objects which are less real and with regard to which the direct creative power of the act manifests itself more clearly. Such are, for instance, new intellectual and aesthetic objects. But even there the individual cannot give to the product of his act the full degree of realness which other, already existing objects of this kind possess without at least the help of words, spoken or written, or some other sensual symbols.

The instrument is an object which permits us to overcome this limitation. Its essential rôle is to intensify the degree of realness of the modification which active thought produces by putting at the disposal of the latter the accumulated results of innumerable past activities; it is an object intermediary between thought and other objects. This rôle would be impossible if it were not for two characters of the empirical world: first, that the concrete object has both content and meaning and its content is the product of activities different from those which produce its meaning, it is the expression of different connections; secondly, that the world of objects is not an absolute reality, that objects and connections are not all on the same level, but present innumerable gradations as to their realness, all the way from a momentary personal "illusion" to the oldest and most fixed "material thing." Thanks to the first character of the object, a modification of the content of an object may prepare the ground for a completely different modification of its meaning by which the content of another object will be affected, and thus the first object may become the medium of an indirect influence upon other objects. As a result of the second character of the empirical world of historical objects, the content of an object may be not only the expression of different connections, but of connections less real than its meaning; it may possess a smaller degree of realness, so that a relatively small and therefore easy modification of the former may open the way for a modification of the latter, which is much more important from the standpoint of the historical reality in general, has a wide influence upon other objects, and thus helps produce at once some deep and very real modification in the content of these other objects. An activity which uses instruments can reach a more real effect with less creative power than if it had no instrument at its disposal, for it profits by the fact of the coexistence in the instrument of a relatively easily modifiable content with a highly extensive and fixed meaning, and it thus obtains, by using the modification of the former as a basis for the modification of the latter, an increase of the realness of its results. Moreover, it can use a whole series of instruments so arranged that a relatively smaller modification of each preceding instrument leads to a more important modification of each succeeding instrument, and the degree of realness of the modifications thus produced may grow indefinitely from the minimum found in a modification of the present personal "image of an object" up to the widest and most important material or social changes.

Examples illustrating this effect of instruments of various degrees of complexity are easily found in all spheres of activity. Take, for instance, a political institution. Its content is constituted by a small number of social personalities whose political character is defined by the constitution; its meaning consists in all its national prestige and legal influence, in the suggestion of all the acts performed by all the members of the nation in accordance with the demands which the institution puts upon them. By influencing this small group of political personalities, we can give to a social act which we want to perform the whole social realness of the institution as real background and produce through its intermediary an effect upon the social and political life of the country greater than the effect which we could produce by acting on the social group directly, in the very proportion in which it is easier to influence a few political leaders than to change the meaning which the political institution has in the eyes of the nation.

The human body is a system of instruments—central and peripheral nervous systems, muscles, bones, etc.—which by a series of gradations increase the real efficiency of active thought from the minimum of an actual connection of personal data to the high degree of a material movement. Systems, somewhat different in their construction and starting at the point where the organic system ends, that is, with an act manifested by a movement of the body, are found in technique where a proper synthesis of a series of instruments permits us to put a train into motion or to light thousands of street lamps by merely pressing an electric button with a finger. Here we see with particular clearness how an insignificant and therefore not very real modification of an instrument, because of an agglomeration of results, leads to a modification possessing an incomparably higher degree of realness. Different again in its secondary characters but similar in its essential significance is the part played by the mathematical symbol in which the idea of some physical law is formulated; the concept of the law, by being symbolically expressed, exercises through the intermediacy of its formula an influence upon the entire system of physics which its creator could never give it directly by acts of theoretic thought alone.

In interpreting these examples on the ground of concrete experience, we must, of course, put provisionally aside all the explanations which the sociologist, the biologist, the physicist, the logician, may give from the standpoint of his conception of reality about the way in which the instrument acts. Thus, from the physical standpoint there is no growth of reality occurring between the pressure of a button and the movement of a train or the appearance of street lights in a city; there is only a process of transformation of energy started by the pressure, during which the total quantity of energy in the world remains the same. But this explanation is already the product of a long evolution, first of practical systems, secondly of systems of theoretic ideas drawn from the practically systematized reality. The rejection of creation is the essential principle of physical explanations, whereas creative growth is the essential feature of the empirical world. From the standpoint of present empirical activity, the modification produced in the instrument with the help of a movement of the human body is incomparably less real than the modification produced in other objects with the help of this instrument, and a naïve observer who does not yet know anything about the principle of conservation of energy and is not accustomed to see such an accumulation of results will invariably express his astonishment at this accumulation in searching for *more* original activity than that actually performed. In fact, *within the limits* of the present action the instrument cannot possibly be defined as a mere medium transferring modifications; it must be conceived as increasing the realness of the modification.

Even physical science cannot deny that it does perform this rôle, only it tries to explain it away by assuming that the accumulation of reality noticeable between the beginning and the end of the instrumental action is due to the fact that action draws into the system of objects which it uses to attain its result some pre-existing real power stored in the outside world, which is interpreted as utilizing ready energy. But this presupposes that activity finds its means ready in pre-existing reality which, as we have seen in the preceding section, is false. "Utilizing the energy" of an outside object is precisely using this object already as instrument within the action to obtain an increase of reality. The object has acquired the character of an instrument only by being incorporated into a dynamic practical organization of objects; it is not used as instrument because it possesses utilizable energy but is characterized as possessing utilizable energy because it can be used as instrument.

Another scientific assumption concerning the instrument must be also excluded from the fundamental empirical definition of the latter: it is the principle that the modification produced *in* the instrument must be of the same order as the modification produced *with its help* in other objects; that to produce physical change with the instrument it is absolutely and always necessary to act physically upon the instrument; that a social effect must have necessarily a social cause (Durkheim); that an influence which is psychological in its consequences must be psychological in its nature; that scientific ideas can be affected only by logical reasoning, etc. As a matter of fact, the modification produced with the help of the instrument is always different from that produced in the instrument, since it is based on different connections. The range of the differences is quite indefinitely wide. Empirically, the pressure of a button is probably as much different from the appearance of electric light as is the "desire to walk" from walking, or the plan of battle constructed by a general from the attack performed by his soldiers, or the modification of symbols in a mathematical formula from the modification of scientific ideas to which it indirectly leads.

In concrete experience objects are not absolutely divided into physical and psychical, social and ideal. This division of reality into different orders is a product of rational systematization, and we shall study it presently. But it is only superimposed upon concrete reality; it only partially determines concrete objects; any concrete object can belong to all these orders. Since from the standpoint of concrete experience the modification of an instrument may be indefinitely different from the modification of another object which is produced with the help of this instrument, it is contrary to all fundamental characters of empirical reality to assume that an action may not, by using instruments, pass from one order of reality to another. The consequence of this assumption is well known: it is the introduction of impassable gulfs between the "physical" and the "psychical," between either the physical or the psychical and the "social," between the physical, the psychical or the social, and the "ideal" domain. But activity crosses these gulfs all the time and this fact can be understood only if we realize that it is precisely the instrument which permits it to do so, because every instrument as real object is real in several domains at once. Thus, the influence exercised by the psychical upon the physical and vice versa is possible only because our oldest and primary instrument, our body, is originally, as a part of concrete reality, neither psychical nor physical, and thus can become in a rationalized reality a part of both the psychical and the physical orders and serve as intermediary to any activity which passes from one of these orders to the other. The influence of the physical or psychical upon the social, and reciprocally also, presupposes that the chief instruments of all social activities—other human personalities—are originally neither physical nor psychical nor social, but can belong to all three orders by various connections and thus an activity which uses them can pass freely from the social order into the physical or psychical order or vice versa. Finally, the influence which physical, psychical, social activities have upon the order of theoretic ideas and vice versa is possible only because the primary instrument of theoretic activities—the symbol—is neither physical nor psychical nor social nor ideal originally, but can by its various sides belong to any one of these orders and thus serves as intermediary between the ideal and the social, the psychical, or the physical creation.

Before we pass to the investigation of the part played by the instrument in the practical rationalization of reality, we must take into consideration the point that the use of an instrument is not determined in advance by its concrete nature alone. There is, as we know, no rational connection whatever between the content of an object and its meaning, and no way of telling in advance how its meaning will be affected by a certain modification of its content. Two instruments, or the same instrument at different moments, may lead to completely different results when directly modified in a similar way, and, on the contrary, may lead to similar results while being modified each in a different way. It must be realized also that a modification of the content of an instrument does not bring automatically any modification in those objects upon which we want to act through this instrument; it only creates in the instrument a basis for a new act which on account of this basis will be able to produce a more important modification in some other object than it could do without it. We shall see later under what special circumstances a causal sequence of changes develops, so that a change of one object leads to a change in another object without— or, more exactly, *almost* without—the help of a new act. But this is not the original condition. The introduction of an instrument does not diminish the amount of activity; on the contrary, where only one act was necessary, the instrument requires two at least; only it increases the importance of the results in a much higher proportion. Once introduced the instrument may be perfected, and it is this perfecting which has the effect of diminishing the amount of activity necessary to have the instrument work. Originally activity must rationalize the instrument along with the rationalization of the reality for which the instrument has to serve. It must establish a fixed correspondence between a certain change of the content and a certain change of the meaning of the instrument by determining both of them with reference to each other; it must direct the change of the meaning by turning the instrument to a specific use, by taking it as intermediary for the production of specific changes in specific objects; in a word, it must make it a definite instrument by introducing it, together with other objects, into the dynamic organization constructed for the creation of a new object.

There is one fundamental difference between the instrument and all other objects which activity uses in organized creation. While active thought is perfectly free in dealing with any empirical objects, can give them any determination, and connect them in any way whatever, its possibilities become limited when it begins to use instruments. It puts upon the instrument a demand whose realization no longer depends on actual thought alone, but on the pre-existing real nature of the instrument, for it is a demand to have certain specific characteristics of a real object, the agglomerated results of past creation, help actual thought produce at once new results which would require otherwise a series of innumerable acts lasting for a very long period of time. It is clear that only a few objects possess the required characteristics; the higher the demand which thought here puts upon reality, the more difficult its satisfaction and the more limited the possibilities of the activity which has made its results dependent upon this satisfaction.

Thus, in the organized plurality of acts producing a certain new object, there is a marked difference between acts which use instruments and those which do not. The latter, though some are more original and others more influenced by the past, are nevertheless entirely free; they may select any objects as ground for the construction of the new object and establish between them any connections whatever; each following act is only required to co-operate with the preceding acts so as to reach a common result; but neither the result nor the manner of this co-operation is in any way determined in advance or conditioned by pre-existing reality. Whereas the acts which use instruments to attain their results become bound by their own claims. They are not bound absolutely, for the use of the instrument is, as we have just seen, not absolutely determined in advance and a certain range of possibilities left; but this range is no longer unlimited. An instrumental act is also required only to co-operate with other acts in producing a common result; but the nature of this result and the way in which it shall be reached are in some measure at least conditioned by the pre-existing nature of the instrument. A given instrument can reach a certain result only with a limited variety of material, and, having at its disposal a given kind of material, it can reach only a limited variety of results. And vice versa, if we want to realize by instrumental activity a certain result on the ground of a given material, we must use a certain specific variety of instruments. The partial result obtained by one act with the help of a certain instrument and on the ground of certain materials imposes a definite condition on other acts which can co-operate with it only if they supplement it and do not destroy its work. Thus, with every step, even that range of possibilities which each instrumental act originally possesses when performed independently of other similar acts, becomes more and more narrowed, until finally toward the end of a complicated instrumental action, everything, materials, instruments, and results, is quite unconditionally determined.

This differentiation between non-instrumental and instrumental acts largely coincides with that between acts constructing the content of the new object and those which give it a meaning with reference to other objects by modifying the content of the latter. Though the content of the new object becomes in some measure enriched even by acts whose chief intention is merely to make this object, with its content once given, fully real by incorporating it with the help of instruments into pre-existing reality, still it is possible to construct most of this content without the help of instruments. Thus, the content of the new piece of furniture which the carpenter makes acquires some additional characters in the course of these acts which, without trying to determine its shape, color, size, etc., tend only to materialize physically the determination reached before. We can in a large measure "represent" what a house which we want looks like before having started to build it, we can outline mentally the organization of an institution and make the choice of its leaders without having yet tried to realize it socially, we can imagine the content of an emotion before having produced the conditions which will make it psychologically real, etc. On the other hand, though the meaning which we give to this content by connecting it mentally with pre-existing objects, by representing the house built in a certain place with certain materials and tools and by certain workers, by reflecting how the institution can be socially realized in the existing social, political, economic conditions, is already a beginning of its realization, still this realization can be fully achieved only by producing such real modifications in pre-existing objects as actual thought cannot create directly by the mere power of its acts, and therefore most of the activities by which the meaning of the new object is created and this object incorporated into pre-existing reality as a part of it are instrumental activities. Thus a difference of nature is superimposed upon the difference of degree which distinguished the two periods of organized activity: creation of the new content and its realization in the objective world.

The separation of these two periods becomes deepened with every repeated use of the same instruments which fixes the practical significance of each of them and determines more and more definitely the ways in which their influences can be combined so as to reach a common result. Of course, their repetition is not absolute. The efficiency of an instrument depends on the stability of that old and fixed meaning on which its use is based, and this meaning has to be modified in some measure every time the instrument is actually utilized since this is precisely how new results can be produced with its help. Every given instrument must therefore gradually lose this original meaning; it becomes used up, destroyed. But the new and specific meaning which it has acquired in the course of the very activity which has been using it as an instrument, the meaning of being a certain particular instrument

with which definite results can be obtained, may become
attached to other similar objects—a phenomenon which is
particularly clear in the case when many copies of an artificial
instrument are especially made with the help of other instruments, but which is found also when a certain class of natural
objects, such as stones for example, on the ground of their
similarity become permanently qualified as instruments to be
used for certain purposes. However fixed may become a
certain way of using an instrument, other ways are of course
always possible. A technical tool may serve in emergency as
a weapon; a weapon, as a technical tool. But when a certain
kind of practical activity requires a combination of several
instruments, with the growing fixation of the use of each of
them, the number of possible combinations may become very
small. When thus, into a certain dynamic system several
definite instruments are introduced, the further development
of this system becomes at once very limited; the content of
the new object which can be realized by this combination of
instruments, the nature of the old objects which will serve as
material for this realization, are no longer left to the free
determination of active thought but are settled with reference
to the possibilities of realization implied by the choice of the
instruments.

The status of the dynamic practical organization of objects
at the moment when instruments have been chosen, the realizable content of the new object settled, and the ground upon
which its realization will go on defined with reference to the
given combination of instruments is what we call the *situation*.
The situation separates the period during which the content of
the new object is constructed from that which is filled chiefly
by the realization of this content; it corresponds more or less
exactly to that stage when activity ceases to be limited to the
sphere of experience of the agent and by beginning to use
instruments enters at once into the full objective reality. All
the elements of the practical system are, or are supposed to be,

already there and interconnected, but the more difficult part of activity, that in which the latter makes itself dependent on reality, is still to be performed. Only because all the objects necessary for this part of activity are supposed to have been already selected, already incorporated into the practical organization, the many partial practical problems concerning the adaptation of the old to the new which activity was to put and solve in succession during its second period, are now put all at once with reference to one another and constitute one complex problem: how to realize this definite new content with these definite instruments and materials which are actually at our disposal. The whole subsequent activity is expected to give the solution of this problem.

The situation is thus both personal—"mental," and supra-personal—physical, social, objectively psychological, ideal. It is the product of non-instrumental acts of thought selecting and connecting pre-existing objects and creating the content of the new object, and at the same time it is the foundation of instrumental acts which will use these selected and connected pre-existing objects and construct the meaning of the new object. Because the complex problem facing activity in the given situation appears essentially as a problem of realization, from the standpoint of this problem a natural distinction develops. All those elements of the situation which are given as real ground for the solution of the problem, first of all the instruments and materials whose pre-existing realness is expected to serve as a basis for the task of realization which activity is going to undertake, appear as real and supra-personal *par excellence;* the fact that they had to be selected out of the whole concrete reality and especially determined for the present use by active thought is ignored as irrelevant for the problem of realization as already defined. On the other hand, those elements whose complete realization is expected to come only as the result of instrumental activity, first of all the new object, are treated as still unreal and subjective; the fact that they have been realized in some measure by active thought while the situation was constructed and that there would be no situation at all without this partial realization, does not count from the standpoint of the actual problem, since it is precisely the insufficiency of this realization which calls for instrumental activity. We have thus a distinction and opposition appearing on the ground of the situation: objective reality, constituted fundamentally by the instruments and the materials as determined with regard to the instruments, is opposed to subjective representation, whose nucleus is the content of the new object. In so far, however, as the realization of this representation is precisely the expected solution of the actual problem from the standpoint of which the distinction is made, the representation appears as a future reality to be brought into existence by action, as the *aim* imposed upon instrumental activity.

From this standpoint of the problem involved in the situation, which is the usual standpoint taken by common-sense reflection about activity, it does not matter at all how the situation has been reached. The whole first period of activity, creation of the aim and organization of the situation, is left outside; the situation, which is both a result and a starting-point, is taken only as a starting-point, is defined exclusively with regard to the future, not with regard to the past. Its imperfectly realized elements being excluded as subjective, its fully real elements, those which will constitute a basis for the solution of the problem, acquire a type of rational determination which in its essential characters becomes the most important constitutive part of our common-sense view of reality and if not the only, at least the primary, real foundation of our scientific conceptions.

It is evident on the ground of the preceding discussion that the more definitively is the organization of the situation conditioned by the nature of the instruments and of the materials upon which these instruments are going to be used, the less are these instruments and materials and their connections dependent upon the present course of experience and reflection. The whole situation at the moment when it is ready and is going to be solved appears as self-existing and self-determined, with all its objects objectively present at once and all their connections settled. Since for the co-operation of instrumental activities which are to realize the given aim it is indispensable that the character of every object, instrument or material be fixed with reference to all other objects, the determination of the objects in the situation is completely reciprocal and, the situation being ready, simultaneous. Under these circumstances, the way in which objects and their connections are given is quite different from what it is in the course of the development of activity. The object, when introduced into the dynamic actual organization which activity produces step by step, becomes indeed determined in its content specifically with reference to all other objects with which it serves to realize a common result, but as this determination is gradually achieved in the course of activity, the evolution which the content undergoes appears as an actual, more or less intentional, modification by which a certain side of the content is pushed forward, experienced more and more consciously, whereas other sides are neglected, drop into the background. For instance, when a painter begins to paint a landscape, each of the objects included in this landscape acquires its aesthetic significance step by step in the very course of the artist's activity, and it is a special and usually consciously fulfilled task of the artist to bring forward such features only as will permit it to contribute in combination with other, also selectively determined, objects to the production of a harmonious aesthetic work of a certain style. This analysis of the content, this distinction of those particular characters which are important from the standpoint of the practical system, appears as achieved when the situation is settled. These particular characters, which in concrete experience were rather one-sided determinations of the content as a whole than distinct components of the content, which were merely different, more or less special aspects which the concrete object was given in different connections, now in a definitely fixed situation become separate constituent parts of the content, *properties* of the object. The more definite the situation is, the more the objects included in it lose within its limits that indefinite and evolving complexity of content which belongs to concrete historical reality, and become, of course, only within the limits of the situation, stabilized *things* with a limited number and variety of uniformly determined properties which are objectively inherent in them and exhaust the reality of the things as elements of this situation.

A similar evolution is undergone by the connections between the objects included in the situation. During the actual dynamic organization of a practical system, of all the possible connections which the meaning of an object suggests, a few acquire a predominant importance. They are those which have to be modified for the present purpose. Certain suggestions become analyzed out of the complex meaning of the object. But this analysis is active and conscious; the connections become isolated in the course of the very acts which are using them. Thus, in pursuing the realization of a new social value, out of the whole complexity of connections existing between the personalities and the institutions which we are using, we pay no attention to most and take only those which we need; we qualify the total social meaning of these personalities and institutions in a special way for the present purpose. This analysis, which is still rather a qualification of the total meaning of the given object than a clear separation of isolated connections from others, appears as pushed to the end in a situation. Here the meaning of each object is reduced to a definite number of specific suggested connections and the rest is left out of the situation; and in the very measure in which the situation is ready and objective, these connections no longer seem dependent on actuality. Being the only ones possible within the limits of the situation and, from the standpoint of the practical problem, each of them fully determined, they appear as rooted in the reality itself, as existing in fact between the objects, as completely real conditions which active thought has simply to accept. A connection which is supposed to exist fully between the objects and does not need to be reproduced in actuality is a *relation*. Thus, in the definite situation objects no longer *become interconnected* but *are interrelated*. The specifically determined meaning of each object by which it actually leads us to other objects has no longer the character of a suggestion for creative activity; it is no longer a meaning, but appears merely as the consciousness of the existing relation; it is a subjective possibility of recognizing a relation, not an objective possibility of reproducing a connection. For instance, the spatial arrangement of material objects which for concrete activity is a suggestion and a possibility of organic movements, of passing from one object to another, in a stabilized situation acquires the character of a system of spatial relations; the possibility of exchanging socially a value against other values, which is originally merely a suggestion of social action, in economic situations becomes an objective economic relation between these values and is symbolically expressed in their relative price.

In the situation a foundation is thus laid for this rational determination of reality which the Aristotelian logic assumes—thing, property (quality, quantity, or state), and relation being the three fundamental categories to which the Aristotelian ten categories can be reduced. The particular form which this determination assumes with regard to various objects depends on the character of the situation, on the nature of the instruments, materials, and aim. The things may be physical bodies with physical properties and relations, or social personalities with political properties and relations, or economically determined values, or psychological entities (emotions, volitions, perceptions, remembrances, etc.) qualified by specific properties which make their various classifications possible and interrelated as elements of a consciousness; or they may be theoretic concepts in which the elementary ideas composing them play a part similar to that of physical properties in physical objects, and whose relations are those of subordination and subsumption, etc. We shall see later how various types of this rational determination become standardized. But their fundamental character is always the same, because it results from the general practical origin of every rational organization and from the particular conditions which organized creation imposes upon itself whenever, in order to shorten its duration and to increase its real efficiency, it makes use of instruments.

Every situation is apt to be approximately reproduced. The reproduction, unless specially aimed at and regulated, a question which we shall discuss presently, is dependent on the reappearance of similar real conditions in concrete reality, and since the latter is continually evolving, the similarity of conditions and therefore also the reproduction of the situation is always only approximate. The dynamic practical organization in which the situation, as a fixed and completely objectified status, has its origin can never spontaneously repeat itself, for either some of the objects which enter into its composition or some of the connections actually established between these objects differ from case to case; and when neither the aim nor the way to realize it are fixed in advance, any variation appearing in the course of concrete activity leads to new variations, which accumulate and grow with every step. Therefore in the activity which has perhaps preserved most of the original concrete character—in artistic creation— there is the least uniformity, as long as this activity is not subjected, like other activities, to minute technical demands connected with the use of specific and highly determined instruments. Indeed, it is the use of instruments which not only stabilizes the dynamic system into a situation, a static problem to be solved, but also increases the chances of repetition. This is, of course, again only a matter of degree. Neither does each instrument in particular remain exactly the same, nor is a given combination of instruments which necessitates a stabilized situation ever reproduced in experience without special regulative measures. It is easier to have a certain combination—one of the few possible combinations— of a limited number of instruments reappear approximately similar in concrete activity, than one of the unlimited possible combinations of an indefinite number of concrete objects which are not instruments. When once a combination of instruments is approximately reproduced, the situation reappears in its fundamental outline. There may be wide differences of detail in the content of the aim, in the selection of the materials, but the problem of realization of the aim is put in a similar way and with regard to this problem the aim and the materials undergo a similar determination.

An interesting example is furnished by the activity of nourishment. In so far as in this activity the organism, or rather certain parts of it, plays the rôle of a set of instruments, this set being very definitely fixed, every food situation is similar to all past situations; its aim, neither physical nor psychical, is the organic status of satiety; its materials are the objects which, however different from one another, are similarly determined as food. But on a certain level of hedonistic development a new type of activity evolves, in which the body is no longer a mere set of instruments for the absorption of food, but material for pleasant sensations, and food in turn becomes instrumental to the production of these sensations. The varieties of food which can be used to realize the aim of gastronomic satisfaction and the number of possible combinations of these varieties are such that for a refined gastronomer there can be no repeatable hedonistic situations;

all repetition there is comes from the fact that the food as hedonistic instrument is an instrument of a secondary and derived character; its use always presupposes the use of the primary instrument, the body; the hedonistic gastronomic activity, being grafted upon the organic activity of nourishment, can develop its variety of hedonistic situations only on the uniform foundation of organic situations.

The approximate reproduction of situations has a double consequence. In so far as the repeated situations have a common organization, this organization grows in stability with every repetition, appears more and more independent of active thought, more and more objectively inherent in reality itself. At the same time the fact that the materials with which the same instruments deal vary in some measure from situation to situation and yet can be determined every time in a similar way, that, in other words, the organization of the situation can be extended to new objects, makes this organization appear as not limited to the actually given set of objects, but as indefinitely applicable to a vague class of future experiences. It should be remembered that actuality never limits itself to the present and given, whatever this present and given may be; that actual thought transcends actual experience and prepares other experiences. At every step, objective reality proves dependent on actual thought. It was dependent on it both for the character of its concrete objects and their trans-actual extension and duration; similarly, it is actual thought which constructs the elementary rational systematization of objects and then extends this systematization beyond the actual limited system. Since this system itself, once constructed, appears as independent of active thought, this tendency of actual thought to apply the organization of the situation to new objects has no longer the character of a tendency to *create*, but of a tendency to *find*, certain objects and connections. Once let it be assumed that the determination of objects in the situation is fully real and self-existing and it results that the introduction of a new object into the situation seems dependent not merely on the possibility of actually determining this object in a similar way, but on the objective possession of such a determination by the object itself. For instance, when the painter thinks of painting a landscape somewhat different from those he has painted before, his problem is chiefly one of creating, not of finding; he does not ask himself: "Are these new objects fit to be painted?" but: "Can I give these new objects as my models an aesthetic meaning?" On the contrary, when a handworker is going to use a new material to produce a technical object, his problem is chiefly, if not exclusively, one of finding and must be formulated: "Is this material fit for the production of an object of the desired kind with the given kind of instruments?"

But such an extension of the systematic organization produced in the situation to new objects makes this organization appear as applicable beyond the limits of the one actually constructed situation only in so far as it is *successful*, that is, as the new objects do possess the required real characters in a degree sufficient for the intended instrumental activity. In the contrary case, the situation evidently cannot be reproduced; the attempt of its reproduction is a *failure*. The failure can be remedied only by producing in the object the expected characters practically, that is, by making from it a different object. Since the required object must possess a degree of realness fitting it to be an element of an instrumental situation, it can be itself created only with the help of instruments; and since its required character is determined in advance, a new situation must be constructed on the ground of which the production of the required character will be at least approximately assured. This is a practical problem which leads to a further step in the rational organization of reality.

THE SCHEME

The question of failure and success in the sense in which it is commonly understood, that is, as failure or success in attaining a certain result by actually performed acts, does not exist in non-organized activity, in which each act, being independent, bears the standard of its success in itself, is always successful when performed and because performed. In organized concrete activity, in so far as it is continuous and not divided by a situation into a period of setting and a period of realizing the aim, there is already an alternative of failure or success in performing an act, because the results of this act are intended to be such as will co-operate with the results of other acts in creating a new object. But as neither the latter, nor the conditions in which it has to be created, is determined in advance but becomes determined in the very course of activity, the standard of success changes with every act, for every act by bringing something new to the determination of the content or meaning of the new object and correspondingly to the meaning or content of pre-existing objects, modifies the total result with which the results of the following acts are expected to harmonize. Moreover, the possibility of failure or success does not precede the actual course of creation but appears and develops during it. The standards of success are produced by activity itself and, while changing in nature, grow in definiteness together with the growing determination of the new object and of the ground upon which it is created.

The creation of a work of art shows this very distinctly. For instance, when a novelist has only begun to reflect about his subject, there is very little limitation imposed upon his following acts; it is already clear that those acts will have to be of a certain general type, acts of aesthetic idealization whose results are to be expressed in words; but within this wide field almost any act is permitted, for preceding activity has not yet produced anything definite that would impose upon the following acts clear conditions with which they have to count. But in the measure in which the content of the work and the domain of human life from which its materials are drawn become determined, the range of liberty left for each subsequent act decreases; the standards of success become more definite. The introduction of some aesthetic element weakening the unity of the work in so far as already produced is a failure in so far as it is not in accordance with the claim inherent in every intentional activity, that of having all the acts of a series co-operate in producing a common result. Failure and success are not yet definitely opposed; there is between them only a difference of degree. For every new act in so far as original and spontaneous has an influence on the total result of preceding acts and modifies it in some, however slight, measure. The question is only whether the new object has already so much unity and definiteness that it excludes too far-reaching modifications, can accept only a more or less definite kind of additions to its content and meaning. Certainly, the unity of the concrete historical object is, as we know, also a matter of degree; but the new object in the course and within the limits of its organized creation is not yet a concrete historical object; it is determined only with regard to the system which is being dynamically constructed for its creation, and this system, in the measure in which it progresses in definiteness, imposes on the new object growing demands of unity. Thus, there comes a moment when only very definite new acts are expected, and an act whose result does not agree with the total results of preceding acts is a failure. We could also say in this case, strictly speaking, that the whole preceding activity is a failure if judged from the standpoint of the result of the new act; but it is clear that usually it is the standpoint of the total result of preceding acts which is taken as a criterion of the success or failure of each new act and not vice versa. An artist whose work is near its fulfilment will rather reject a new aesthetic idea which does not fit into the work than the work itself; he will prefer to perform one new act instead of that which failed to harmonize with the preceding ones rather than recon-struct the entire organization and reshape his whole work,

giving thus a character of failure to a long series of organized acts.

When a situation is determined, the standard of success
evidently becomes more definite.   Since the aim is settled and
the instruments and materials selected and determined, the
choice of actions which can with the given instruments and
materials realize the given content is relatively small.   It is
not, of course, absolutely limited: the situation in concrete
activity is never entirely fixed; the determination of the aim
in some measure evolves during its realization, and thus there
is more than one possible way of solving a practical problem
on the given ground.   But already the situation constitutes a
criterion not for each separate act alone, but for the whole
combination of acts by which the problem will be solved.   In
so far as the activity which is meant only to realize the aim
still preserves some characters of the primary concrete action,
it still remains true that each particular act succeeds if its
result fits with the total result of preceding acts and fails in
the contrary case; but upon this original fluid standardization
of particular acts is superimposed a new and more fixed
standard, bearing on the whole combination of acts composing
the second, realizing period of the concrete action.   This total
combination of acts is either a failure or a success from the
standpoint of the situation.   Neither failure nor success is
complete: the instrumental activity always realizes something, and this something never exactly corresponds to its
aim.   But in the gradation of partial failures or successes
the two ideal limits of complete failure or complete success
are very definitely opposed, and an action can be judged
clearly in the measure in which it approaches either of these
limits.

It is manifest that a particular unique situation gives us
no foundation by which we can judge the success or failure
of the activity which led to its formation, of the first, non-
instrumental period of action.   There can be no failure, no

"error," in practically determining a situation, for every situation, such as it is determined, is soluble. It is always possible to realize the given aim with the given materials, for the aim has been determined in its content with regard to the conditions of its realization; it is always possible to use the given materials for the realization of the aim, for the materials have been selected and determined for the sake of this realization; and the instruments necessary are there, for it is precisely their presence in the situation which has led to this particular determination of the aim and of the materials. The situation is ready only when all this reciprocal determination has been reached; once ready, it does not matter how it has been reached.

The activity which constructs a situation becomes subjected to the criterion of success only when the situation which is being constructed has to be similar to some past situation in spite of the more or less changed circumstances. Success and failure then depend on the existence, within the sphere of reality in which the situation has to be reconstructed, of objects whose contents and connections present the characters required by the situation. If these conditions are not fulfilled, the situation cannot be reconstructed until an auxiliary action has modified reality in such a way as the situation needs. But, since this auxiliary action has to satisfy certain definite requirements as to its result, since it has to produce an object determined in advance, it can fulfil this demand of the original situation and be successful only if it can construct for itself a situation whose solution will lead to the required result, and this is possible only if it reproduces in turn an already defined situation whose solution has proved in the past to be the needed one. Thus, with regard to this auxiliary action a problem arises similar to that regarding the original action—how to reproduce a situation. Again sub-auxiliary actions are required, and thus the original action may necessitate a large complex of subordinate actions; the original situation becomes a center to which, directly or indirectly, many other situations converge.

It is hardly necessary to quote particular examples of such an expansion of the practical organization of reality. Every more or less complicated political activity, every business enterprise, involves a system of situations in which the main practical problem can be put and solved in accordance with past experience and reflection only by putting and solving a number of subordinate practical problems whose solution prepares the necessary materials and instruments. It is, however, clear that if this system of situations is not organized in advance, but has to be organized in the very course of activity, the result cannot be exactly the required one, for the exact reconstruction of the main situation depends on the exact reconstruction of the subordinate situations, which in turn cannot be exactly reconstructed without the help of still other situations, etc. It is not only practically impossible to follow this development too far into detail, but by attempting a too perfect result we increase the chances of failure, for the wider the field embraced by activity the more concrete changes of empirical reality it has to face, the more unexpected and new problems it must put and solve, and the more numerous its difficulties. Therefore all activity which has to construct such systems of situations spontaneously during its development must be satisfied with approximate success and be able to redefine its main aim and its main situation from moment to moment, so as to be able to meet the unexpected and undesired, to proceed in spite of the partial failures of subordinate activities. Every politician and business man knows this. The point is that the situation could be perfectly reproduced only if during its reproduction it could be practically isolated from concrete reality and made independent of concrete historical becoming. By creating auxiliary situations when needed in the course of the reproduction of the main situation, we remove indeed from case to case the chief hindrances which reality opposes at that particular moment and at that particular place to this reproduction; but since we have to extend the sphere of our activity, we open an ever-wider field for future new and unexpected hindrances, due to the fact that every new element which we use is a concrete historical object with innumerable dynamic connections; thus, we introduce our situation deeper and deeper into the concrete irrational reality. This difficulty is obviated by the *scheme*.

The scheme can be defined as a set of practical rules determining once and forever, in all its essential elements, a situation of a certain type. An exhaustive theory of the scheme requires a general theory of activity which cannot be given here. One important point must be noticed. The rules composing the scheme are evidently not external general formulae with which activity complies as a result of a self-conscious abstract reflection, but concrete, uniform, and permanent practical tendencies inherent and manifested in activity itself and spontaneously followed by the latter. Thus, the oldest, the primary schemes are *instincts*, with their permanent tendency and increasing ability of reconstructing fundamentally similar situations in varying circumstances, in this essentially differing from mere *habits*, whose uniformity is due to the recurrence of the same circumstances already schematically arranged. Of course, a rule or a scheme may be abstractly formulated; the principles which the technician learns in school, the laws as expressed by legislation and codified, are precisely such formulae of practical schemes, sometimes obtained by induction from practical situations, sometimes deduced from other already formulated principles. But the formula of the scheme is not the scheme, just as a term is not the object to which it applies. The entire reality of the scheme lies in the very fact of its actual application and is dependent on the number and variety of concrete activities which it succeeds in regulating. The formulated rules of technique or prescriptions of law are empty words unless applied in action. In fact, the mere act of "understanding" them, of applying them mentally, is already a beginning of their application; the mere thinking of a certain organization of objects is already organizing these objects. This explains how a new, abstractly formulated rule can become a real concrete rule applied in practice: its concrete technical or social use is only an extension of its mental use which has preceded its abstract formulation in words. But it needs many activities to pass from a mental application of the scheme to its full instrumental application, from situations constructed by the technician at his desk to the situations constructed in the factory with the help of human bodies and other technical instruments, from legal rules mentally applied by the legislator to these same rules applied by the judiciary and executive to concrete social situations. The auxiliary activities necessary to pass from the "planned" schematic organization to the "effected" schematic organization are a measure of the difference of realness between a mentally realized and an instrumentally realized scheme.

The way in which the scheme makes the exact reproduction of a situation possible independently of the concrete evolution of reality is by making this situation become the aim for which other instrumental activities have to co-operate. Instead of waiting to have auxiliary situations called for from case to case whenever the main situation fails to be constructed because of the lack of certain objects or connections within the given sphere of reality, which, as we have seen, leads to numerous complications and prevents the actual result from being ever identical with the expected one, we organize in advance all the auxiliary situations necessary to have our main situation appear. Each of these auxiliary situations separately does not have then to be exactly determined in advance, does not have to produce necessarily a certain unique result which would exactly fit into the ready framework of the main situation. For various auxiliary situations can co-operate in the course of their actual dynamic organization and their results, even if each of them should not be such as the main situation requires, can be step by step supplemented by others so as to realize finally together the main situation almost exactly as needed. Thus we avoid having the difficulty which we faced in reconstructing the main situation repeated for each auxiliary situation. And we can in a large measure base ourselves on whatever practical organization of reality is actually possible. If there is a possibility of obtaining by any combination of any auxiliary situations all the essential elements of our main situation, we actually do construct the latter; otherwise we do not, but may perhaps put such auxiliary situations as are actually possible to produce at the disposal of some other scheme. It is the scheme itself which, by determining once and forever the essential requirements for a given type of situations, permits us to judge in each case about the possibility or impossibility of its reconstruction and thus spares us failures.

We find again, on a wider scale, the same type of dynamic actual organization which is at the basis of each situation in particular; only here, instead of single objects, whole systems of objects, whole situations, are the elements which we organize. The main situation is the new status which we want to produce—new, of course, only within the limits of the present activity. The auxiliary situations are the pre-existing reality on the ground of which this status has to be made real. It would seem as if, the main situation being determined once and forever by the scheme, the status to be produced were in advance imposed as an aim on activity. And yet it is not so, since its actual acceptance as an aim depends on the actual preparation of the conditions necessary for its realization. The main situation as determined by the scheme is only a model, and it depends on present organizing activity which one of the many models existing in the practical world it will accept for the situation which it tends to realize with the help of other actually realizable situations. The model situation is not passively accepted. The whole first part of organizing activity consists in actively, though only mentally, reconstructing this situation in its content, as an aim, from the standpoint of and with reference to those auxiliary situations which are possible to realize in the given sphere of reality; and vice versa, in the measure in which the content of the future situation becomes determined and approaches to a certain schematic model, organizing activity selects and reconstructs mentally, from among the auxiliary situations which are possible to realize in the given sphere of reality, those which can be made to co-operate in realizing this model situation. When thus at a certain moment our activity has definitively accepted a certain schematically determined situation as an aim to be realized with the help of auxiliary situations, it is because at this moment the first, mental, part of this activity has been finished, all the auxiliary situations necessary to realize the model situation have been selected and mentally combined into a *system of situations* which, gradually realized with the help of various instrumental activities, will bring the aim, the given schematic situation, into reality.

The field of material technique is the one in which schemes have reached the widest extension and the greatest exactness. Every case of industrialization of a technical creation, that is, every case when a technical object has to be many times reproduced, requires schematizing activity, for such a multiple reproduction requires a model situation schematically defined once and forever as including very definite instruments and very definite materials, and in view of the continuous evolution of concrete reality this model situation can reappear time after time only if intentionally prepared in advance. Though a few of its elements, such as, for instance, artificial instruments, may last for some periods without very marked modifications, others, such as the physical materials, must be almost completely prepared again and again by specific, sometimes very complicated, activities, while others still, such as the organic conditions of the worker and the economic conditions imposed by his social environment, though more or less durable in their concrete historical realness, must be specially determined from case to case so as to be utilizable for this particular schematic situation.

The whole question appears with particular clearness in the early stage of industrial production when the higher form of practical organization of which we shall speak in the next section has not yet been developed; when there is neither a far-reaching individual specialization nor a wide social division of labor and co-operation, and the system of economic exchange has not yet embraced the whole field of technical instruments and materials and bears almost entirely on ready products. At this stage, each individual has numerous technical schemes, numerous models of situations at his disposal, and there is no principle which would compel him to work only for one of these models, to produce only one kind of technical values; at the same time, he could not specialize thus even if he wanted, for having to do most of the preparatory activities himself for each model situation, from case to case, he is very much dependent on the existing conditions for the realization of any of these model situations. Thus, we find the technical activities of an individual on a low level of civilization depending in an approximately equal measure, from case to case, on the present demand for certain definite technical products, and on the possibilities of producing which are offered by the existing conditions given within his present sphere of reality. The existing conditions make the actual realization of certain model situations easier than that of others; the actual demand for certain products is more insistent than for others; what the individual will then actually do, what kind of model situation will be selected by his present mental activity, and made the aim of his instrumental preparatory activity, depends on the actual dynamic combination of both conditions and demanded models, and will become settled only when the individual definitively adapts a certain model to certain actual possibilities and certain actual possibilities to a certain model.

Good examples of schemes are also found in the legal field. Any situation which civil or criminal law defines and which is expected to be solved by compensation or punishment would perhaps never be empirically realized without schematizing activity. To produce a definite juridical situation we need, first, a certain concrete set of social conditions to which a certain law will be applied; secondly, a set of social and legal proceedings constructing and solving their specific situations, collecting evidence, bringing the case to the notice of the court, organizing a sitting of the court, calling the parties and witnesses before the judge, etc. It has become the special task of the lawyer to construct the schematic legal situation on the ground and with the help of these other situations—some of them already given in social life and needing only to be redefined from the legal standpoint, some especially constructed by him for the actual purpose—by determining them with regard to one another and having them co-operate in creating all the essential elements of the situation as defined once and forever by the given law. The lawyer's activity results thus in the gradual dynamic organization of a set of actually realized or realizable auxiliary situations for the production of the required legal situation; all the other situations, that is, the pre-existing social conditions to which the given law appears as applicable and the auxiliary situations which bring these conditions within the reach of the court, constitute for the lawyer the material and instruments permitting him to realize the model situation defined by the law, and they become specially adapted to this aim in the measure the latter becomes determined. On the other hand, however, just as the primitive technician has many technical schemes at his disposal among which he selects during the first, mental, part of his activity the one which he is going to actualize *now* and *here*, taking into account the demand for certain results and the actual conditions permitting him to realize some schemes more easily than others, so the lawyer is acquainted with many different laws which he can actualize, but of which only a few prove on reflection applicable to the given conditions. And even this narrow field from which he can choose the model situation that will be his aim narrows still more as the progress of legal procedure, by introducing new auxiliary situations, imposes new conditions with which the lawyer's aim must comply; so that finally the legal situation aimed at becomes completely determined for him as the one which a certain particular law has regulated once and forever. Of course, the lawyer imagines that the situation is already given in fact and that he merely discovers it and brings it under the appropriate law, but this is the usual, realistic illusion of common sense which treats the results of activity as independent of activity simply because while acting it cannot reflect about the course of activity.

The first effect of the scheme upon concrete reality is thus to produce a more or less rational system which is wider than a situation. In each particular case in which the main schematic situation must be produced there is a system of auxiliary situations created, each connected with the others by the fact that its solution becomes one of the data of the practical problem which the demand for the realization of the main situation defines, and is combined with the solution of other auxiliary situations for this common result. Of course, the particular elementary objects included in different situations are only indirectly connected with each other; the rational organization which the scheme creates is not as close as that which unifies objects within a single situation. This is precisely one of the important points about the organization of reality: there is no other direct and immediate systematization of objects except the situation, and not the single object but a system of objects, taken as an indivisible whole, is the real unit of all wider and more complicated organizations which we find in practical life. The ultimate unit of the schematic organization is the situation, and the scheme itself with all the situations which it includes can become an ultimate unit in a still wider system. Each of the various situations which are organized into a system for the production of a model situation is in the course of this actual organization objectivated as one content and connected in this character with the other, equally objectivated, situations. This organization affects each auxiliary situation as a whole; in so far as the result of this situation must be combined with the results of others for the realization of the model situation, this auxiliary situation will have to be instrumentally solved at a certain moment and at a certain place, before, after, or together with certain other situations included in the same system: in short, there is an order introduced among the auxiliary situations. However, this order does not affect directly the objects included within these situations; each of the latter has its own special practical problem to solve and its solution follows its own particular way quite independently of the use which will be made of the result once attained.

But the scheme, while leaving untouched the internal constitution of the auxiliary situations, does influence the organization of the main situation which it regulates. By making this situation a permanent aim of schematizing activities, it gives it a still higher degree of definiteness than it could reach by itself, even if an exceptional permanence of circumstances permitted it to be reconstructed again and again without the help of a schematic organization of auxiliary situations. Since the schematized situation with all its elements is determined in advance once and for all, before being actually constructed, it is given from case to case as an object-matter of active thought, which the latter may realize or not in concrete reality, but which it should not modify in its systematic order, for such a modification would mean a substitution of another situation instead of the one required by the scheme. The composition and systematization of this situation appear thus as independent of any particular activity which reproduces it. This independence does not consist only, as in complexes stabilized by mere repetition, in a relatively strong suggestion of certain connections: the character which each element, thing or relation, possesses with reference to other elements appears as not merely given and real, but as necessary for this situation. There is from the standpoint of the scheme no other way possible of putting and solving the practical problem involved in the model situation than the one which the scheme has defined and which the auxiliary situations have to prepare from case to case. The activity which in a particular case actually will reconstruct and realize the model situation after having prepared it, is in advance deprived of all initiative; it must follow the lines traced by the scheme, precisely because all spontaneous efforts are concentrated in those preparatory activities whose common purpose is to make the exact realization of the demand of the scheme practically possible, and which would be deprived of their significance, would acquire the character of failure if the problem of the model situation for which they have worked were not put and solved in the required way.

In fact, under these circumstances there is no longer any problem left, since its solution is given in advance. When in a non-schematic situation the aim has to be realized with the help of given instruments and materials, its realization is a problem whose solution is not yet at hand, though all the data are ready. The result of the activity which is expected to realize this aim will have to comply with the conditions imposed by the situation, but how it will comply with them depends on the activity which will produce this result; in fact it depends on the nature of the modifications which it will bring into the given materials with the given instruments.

The result, at the moment when the situation is constructed, opposes itself to the materials and instruments; the latter already exist in their full content and meaning, the former is determined as to its content, but not yet as to its meaning; it is unreal as against the real situation and its realization is a task which activity will freely accept and fulfil. But when the situation is schematically objectivated in advance, the result is also objectivated in advance; the object which will be produced on the ground of the situation is as much defined, both in its content and in its meaning, as the instruments and materials with the help of which it will be realized; its level of realness is the same. Of course, while we are preparing the ground for a reproduction of the model situation, the solution of this situation does not possess full realness, is only mentally real; neither does the situation itself yet exist otherwise than mentally. The situation and its solution together constitute one aim of our preparatory activities. The materials and instruments necessary to produce a certain object and this object which will be produced with their help, with all their contents and meanings, are given at the moment when we prepare their realization as one content which our preparatory activity will make real. The result to which the future situation will lead is as definite, as completely characterized as this situation itself.

When preparing the realization of this situation, we do not separate the question, "How will this situation be solved?" from the question, "How will this situation be constructed?" The two questions are melted in one; we prepare the construction of the situation in view of the definite result to which we want this situation to lead; we prepare the result in preparing the situation. The determined situation appears as necessary to produce the determined result, and no other but the determined result can be produced when the determined situation is constructed; this occurs whenever and wherever this situation is prepared and actualized.

Thus, the actual dynamic finality of the *aim* is supplanted by a trans-actual static finality of *end* and *means*. The realization of a definite set of means is always and everywhere necessary for the realization of a certain end, and only a certain definite end is objectively realizable on the ground of a certain set of realized means. The situation and its solution being once and forever determined by the scheme and indefinitely reconstructible, the reciprocal determination of end and means is independent of any particular actualization of this whole system; it is based on the objective nature of end and means as determined by the scheme and becomes thus a *relation* of finality.

This is not all. Since the result of the instrumental activity which will solve the schematized situation is determined in advance, the modifications of pre-existing objects which by their combination will produce this result are also determined in advance. There is only one way of reaching the given end with the given means, and every step in this direction must be such as required; activity has no choice. The act ceases to count as act of creation bringing a new content and meaning into the world; it counts only because it starts, at a given moment and in a given place, an occurrence which is already fully determined in its objective nature, and has only to be realized once more in the given circumstances. The act would not count at all if the situations determined by the scheme were not parts of the concrete empirical world and, though meant to be identical in their composition and organization, did not differ from one another by their appearance at different *now*'s of the concrete duration and at different *here*'s of the concrete extension. As it is, acts are still necessary to realize empirically in actuality the modifications required by the schematized situation; but what is essential from the standpoint not of actual experience, but of the rational order of the situation itself, is only the determined nature of the modification, its real, not its ideal side. When a technical worker modifies a given material in a schematically prescribed way, it does not matter at all from the standpoint of the technical situation what he wants and thinks in doing it, what are the factors which have brought him to perform this action there and then, how much conscious effort and how much habit is involved in this action, etc.; what counts is a certain movement of his body which leads to certain movements of technical instruments, which lead in turn to a certain modification of the material.

As these modifications are completely determined with regard to the definite situation and to the result to which this situation is expected necessarily to lead, their character is no longer the same as in concrete activity; the situation being constituted by things with definite properties and relations, each modification is a disappearance from the situation of some property or relation and an appearance of some other property or relation. It does not matter that concretely those characters of objects which disappeared continue to exist as contents and meanings in memory, though with less realness, whereas those which appeared did not exist at all before being created, so that the act produces really more than it destroys: from the abstractly rational standpoint of the scheme which determines both the situation and its solution there is no difference of realness between destruction and production. Both ideally subsist forever in the scheme as equally necessary stages for the attainment of the end; both really appear whenever the scheme is applied in the concrete development of experience, and being fully determined in advance can bring nothing new except the mere fact of their appearance. They correspond to each other and presuppose each other, so that their appearance is one indivisible fact which, viewed from the standpoint of the means is a destruction, but viewed from the standpoint of the end is a production, and from the standpoint of the relation between end and means is a substitution of one property or relation for another, that is, a *change.* In so far, now, as this change is supposed to be only started in its actual appearance but not created in its objective nature by an act of thought, its progressive realization on the ground of the teleologically determined situation is a real *process.*

Each particular process is a necessary link of the development leading from the situation to the result, from the means to the end. The connection between processes is not dynamically created in the very course of activity, like the connection between creative modifications which are made step by step to combine in a common result, but is determined for all of them once and forever by the schematic definition of the means and the end; all that activity is supposed to do is to actualize this objectively existing connection. Each process has a definite position in a series of processes, the ground of which is that a definite process requires a definite status to start with, and except for the first process which starts with the given situation, each of the following ones is based on the status reached by the preceding one.

This does not mean at this stage of rationalization that the following process is the effect of the preceding process, since each process needs still an act of thought to be started; but it means that the following process cannot be started unless the preceding one has occurred. Since the whole series is objectively necessary for the realization of the given end with the given means, each process is objectively necessary for the following one. Supposing therefore the activities demanded by the scheme actually performed, supposing the schematic situation constructed and developed up to the end in accordance with the scheme, the whole series of processes is fully and exclusively determined in its actual development by the teleological system of means and ends, and each process within this series is fully and exclusively determined in its appearance by the following process for which it has to prepare the necessary status. In a word, the following process is the *final cause* of the preceding process, since if we presuppose a whole series of teleologically determined processes actually developing, every process in particular has no other direct ground for its appearance but the following process, though all of them together are grounded not in the end alone (which therefore is not a final cause) but in the total organization produced by the scheme. We see that the Aristotelian concept of final cause is, like many other ancient conceptions, quite unjustly neglected by modern thought, since it corresponds to a very real and very important empirical connection which is covered neither by the concept of aim, nor that of end, nor can it be reduced to that of mechanical cause.

When the realization of an end requires several distinct parallel series of processes, each of these series is teleologically necessary for each other and the connection of final causality is reciprocal between any two of these series.

It is evident that the practical possibility of applying the principle of objective teleological determination to schematized activity depends on the degree of perfection to which schematization has been pushed in actual life, on the efficiency with which preparatory activities have been performed and organized. If the same schematic situation has been repeatedly reconstructed during a certain period, the various auxiliary situations which have been used from case to case for this purpose appear as more or less closely connected with the main situation, so that the latter becomes gradually the center of a rather vague domain of reality whose limits widen with every new actualization.

This connection of auxiliary situations with the main situation which is left as a result of past activities must be, of course, clearly distinguished from the connection intentionally created between auxiliary situations in each particular case for the realization of the main situation. The latter brings forth, as we have seen, a rational system of auxiliary situations, whereas the former is not systematic at all, but appears as an unintentional consequence of the fact that all these auxiliary situations, though belonging to different rational systems, have served at different moments to actualize the same scheme. This connection between the schematic situation and auxiliary situations, like all empirical connections, grows in stability with each repetition; thus, the more frequently a certain auxiliary situation has been used for the realization of the main situation, the more closely it appears connected with it. Furthermore, this connection exercises a suggestive influence on future activities, so that we always tend to use in so far as possible from case to case the same auxiliary situations in preparing the same schematic situation, and introduce new auxiliary situations only when the old ones cannot be reconstructed *here* and *now*. Thus, the domain of reality which grows around a certain model situation is constituted first of all by the most frequently used auxiliary situations. Though it is forced, by the evolution of the concrete historical reality of which it is a part, to increase in complexity and variety by having new situations included in it, it tends by virtue of its own inertia to grow in stability by having its old situations fixed by indefinite reproductions. Both its growth in complexity and its growth in stability, while opposing and counterbalancing each other, help to give the model situation, the permanent center of this domain, a background of concrete experience and a field of concrete active influence which make this situation more and more real, more and more empirically important within the historical world.

A well-known example of such a domain of reality growing by the mere agglomeration of auxiliary situations is found in the indefinite but often very wide and strong social influence that an institution gradually obtains by the mere continuity of its functioning, quite independent of the objective importance of its social purpose and of the teleological perfection of its organization. The mere fact that all kinds of situations, some of them repeated innumerable times, have been used at various moments as subservient to the scheme which the institution realizes, leaves an always wider and deeper mark on social reality, a mark which, however irrational it may be, is very real, as everyone finds who attempts to substitute for the old institution a new, even a more rational one. Still deeper is that irrational but real influence which our instincts leave upon our "natural" environment, though here it is rather difficult to distinguish this unintentional unification of past experiences from the intentional unification and organization of future experiences which we shall study in the next section. An instinct, like that of food, in its continual manifestations, uses innumerable auxiliary situations which embrace a large part of the personal spheres of experience and reflection and constitute together a rather chaotic objective domain; and, in so far as this domain is composed of practical situations, the objects within its limits appear no longer as concrete historical objects but as things with definite properties and relations. Since similar partial effects are produced by all other instincts, the reality of our practical life, as we have inherited it from our ancestors and reproduced it in our own past, presents several different, more or less chaotic complexes of situations superimposed upon the chaotic complexity of the primary historical reality, and our objects, which are concrete, interconnected historical objects when viewed in their total duration and extension without regard to any particular practical interest, appear as interrelated things as soon as looked upon in the light of any past satisfaction of our instincts.

The scheme, while solving the difficulties to which the reconstruction of the situation is subjected in the present and unifying many past situations, raises the problem of the future, which it cannot solve alone. There is, indeed, no certainty whatever that a given scheme will in fact be permanently maintained in the face of the changing concrete reality. In each particular case its realization depends on a more or less spontaneous and original schematizing activity, and unless some higher organization is reached, the question whether the necessary activities will be performed at all in the future is entirely unsettled. In so far as the scheme bears not merely on the situation prepared and constructed at present, but on the situations which will be prepared and constructed at other periods of concrete duration, its continuation is not implied in the actual organization of reality over which this scheme presides, but can be only postulated by practical thought. The scheme raises the problem of the future in a way which precludes the easy solutions offered by those theories which try to explain our expectation of similar experiences by our habit of seeing similar experiences regularly return and are then forced to appeal to an immanent absolute rationality of nature in order to explain how the habit is formed and why the expectation is justified from case to case. There is no regularity whatever originally existing in concrete experience; all regularity must be actively produced and maintained, and this implies an active control of the future as well as an organization of the present and a unification of the past.

The greater our claims on the future in this respect, the larger the amount of regularity which we expect, the less we can rely upon the existing order of reality to fulfil these claims and our expectations must be based upon permanent tendencies of our activity rather than upon permanent characters of its object-matter. When all we demand is to have a certain object fit in the immediate future a situation whose other components are already at hand and systematized, we are concerned exclusively with the existing real characters of this object and rely upon them; only if it fails to satisfy our demand, we introduce a more or less organized activity to modify it according to our needs. When we want to reconstruct a whole schematically determined situation which does not exist yet within our present sphere of reality, we make the fulfilment of this demand dependent in varying proportions both upon pre-existing reality and upon our activity; we do not expect that reality will have everything ready and waiting for us; we rely on our activity to supplement whatever may be lacking in the given conditions. If now we want positively to maintain a certain schematic organization during an indefinite future in the field of actual interests, if we not only expect that it will be occasionally reconstructed when and where the concrete real conditions happen to be more favorable for its reconstruction than for the actualization of other schemes, but if we demand that it be continually reconstructed in a certain section of historical reality rather than other schemes, whatever the concrete conditions happen to be, then we evidently cannot rely upon reality at all. We can expect our demand to be realized only if our activity is not merely able to profit from case to case of favorable conditions in order to actualize the scheme, but capable of permanently realizing by its own spontaneous effort all the conditions sufficient and necessary for indefinitely repeated actualizations of this scheme. This evidently requires an organization of activities wider and more stable than the one which produces a system of situations.

THE PRACTICAL DOGMA AND THE SYSTEM OF SCHEMES

In all fields of practical life we find numerous examples of such a connection between schemes that the actualization of one scheme is accompanied or followed by the actualization of another, because the schematic situations are in some way permanently connected. Thus, in technique we see a factory producing materials or instruments which other factories use in their production; in the political field certain executive acts follow certain acts of legislation or jurisdiction; in the field of economics the performance of a certain professional work is followed by the payment of a fee, etc. The given actualization of one scheme constitutes an objective condition of the actualization of the other.

However, as long as this connection is merely the result of the fact that a certain schematic situation cannot be constructed in a given case without the help of another, the condition is neither sufficient nor necessary. It is not enough to do professional work in order to receive a fee; many other conditions are needed, which may be completely different from case to case, unless there is a stable customary or legal regulation of professional work in its relation to economic schemes. Nor is it necessary to do professional work in order to receive a certain sum of money in payment, for this result may be obtained in connection with many other schemes. In fact, we are still within the limits of the problem treated in the preceding section—the problem of constructing a schematic situation with the help of auxiliary situations which prepare the ground in advance. These auxiliary situations may be either new and especially created for the purpose, or may be themselves schematic situations reproduced for the purpose with the help of still other auxiliary situations; the system of situations becomes thereby more complicated, but does not change its essential rational form. When a hand-worker finds that a certain material which he needs is out of stock in his town, he may order it from elsewhere and thus put into action the complex schematic machinery of transportation; but there is no essentially new form of organization of his experience involved in this case, merely an introduction of a new situation into the old organization.

But the connection between schemes may also be such that an actualization or a series of actualizations of a certain scheme or group of schemes becomes a sufficient and necessary objective condition of an actualization or a series of actualizations of some other scheme or group of schemes, and reciprocally; not in the sense that this actualization should not require every time some spontaneous and original schematizing activity, some new arrangement of auxiliary situations preparing the ground, but in the sense that, in whatever way the main schematic situation may be reconstructed from case to case, it is meant to be reconstructed always whenever and wherever some other schematic situation has been or is being reconstructed, and vice versa. An agreement between employer and employee in which the latter is expected regularly to do certain work and the former regularly to pay him certain wages is one of the simplest and best-known connections of this kind. It does not preclude on either side schematizing activity; the employee must continually prepare for his work, make efforts to overcome external hindrances or his inability or his laziness, reconstruct from case to case the schematically determined situation by adapting to it his other personal experiences; the employer must periodically obtain, on the ground of other situations, the necessary money to pay the wages. But whatever may be the ways in which the respective situations are actualized, as long as the agreement lasts and excepting only very special circumstances, the regular performance of the work is considered sufficient and necessary condition of the regular payment of wages, and the regular payment of wages a sufficient and necessary condition of regular work.

A permanent connection of this kind evidently implies a practical principle superior to the schemes themselves, not merely postulating that either of the schemes be continued in general, but absolutely demanding that, whatever may be the concrete empirical circumstances, the continuation of a certain scheme (or group of schemes) A, be in the future accompanied by a continuation of a scheme (or group of schemes), B, and the continuation of B be accompanied by that of A. The significance of this demand may be in special cases qualified by various limitations and then the principle loses its indefinite bearing on all future experience, but even then the limits are self-imposed in advance and the claim remains absolute within those limits. In view of this absolute claim on certain future situations, we call such a principle a *practical dogma*.

In introducing this term, just as in using the terms "scheme" and "rule," we must avoid the intellectualistic suggestions which tradition seems to authorize. By dogma we do not mean a theoretically formulated principle, a concept, or a judgment, but a practical presupposition, often subconscious, a permanent attitude taken toward experiences and activities. It might seem at first glance wiser not to use such terms, which bring with them undesirable suggestions, but the disadvantage of introducing entirely new terms would be still greater; and we are justified in giving the old terms a slightly new significance by the fact that the significance which they were given in traditional definitions was not adequate with reference to the very object-matter on which they were made to bear. Thus, the rule has been taken to mean an abstract formula existing of itself and giving by its content certain indications to behavior by which the latter is influenced positively or negatively, that is, either consciously tries or consciously does not try to comply. But there is nothing which corresponds to this definition. That which exists of itself when the formula is produced is not a practical rule influencing, regulating behavior, but a set of ideas which can influence other ideas only when theoretically connected with them. The set of ideas becomes a rule of behavior only while and in so far as there actually is a behavior complying with it; it has no reality as regulating behavior except by and in this behavior itself. Similarly, by dogma, as traditionally understood, is meant the content of a religious or social belief, purely intellectual and devoid of any direct bearing on practice, from which only secondarily by a special ethical reasoning practical rules can be drawn. Now, there is no dogma in this sense; every belief is essentially practical, is the acceptance in conduct of a principle regulating a priori future practical experiences, mystical, social, aesthetic, etc., and its reality consists entirely in this active influence exercised on future activities. The abstract intellectual formulation of a dogma is something entirely different from the dogma as matter of belief; it is a set of theoretic ideas belonging not to religion or social life, but to philosophy or science. We are thus entirely justified in assuming the existence of a dogma whenever it manifests itself in its active influence, whether it has been theoretically formulated or not. This permits us to extend the use of this term to the total field of practical life and to call dogma every implicitly or explicitly accepted principle which unconditionally determines future activities in view of the maintenance of a certain complicated practical organization of reality, making it independent of any concrete empirical conditions by the very fact that it makes it rely entirely on itself in determining the actualization of its components exclusively with regard to each other.

The demand for a certain organization of reality put by the scheme alone is hypothetical: *if* and *whenever* the schematic situation is about to be actualized, it must be prepared in advance in all its essential elements. This implies a postulate that the schematic situation will be actualized, but an absolutely undetermined and practically inefficient postulate. On the contrary, the demand put on the future by the dogma is categorical; certain schemes, dependent exclusively on each other, must be continually actualized. There is no outside reason for their actualization; the only condition on which the continuation of one of them depends is the continuation of the other. The demand of the practical dogma is not justified by anything but the dogma itself.

Genetically, the dogma has, of course, originated in some preceding organization of activities; a whole dogmatically determined system of schemes may be still a part of some other wider system, conditioned by a more fundamental dogma, just as a new historical object may be only a variation of some pre-existing historical object. But just as the nature of the historical object as empirical object consists in its own content and meaning which it has in so far as distinct and self-existing reality, so the nature of the dogmatically determined system of schemes consists in its own specific organization in so far as it is independent, self-started system. Even if a system of schemes has originated as a part of some wider system, it is also a system in itself, and we must first know it as such before we study its origin. On the other hand, even if it is in some measure an independent and self-started system, it may be also in some measure a part of a wider system which will then, in so far as including several other systems, be much more complex than these. Thus, a dogmatically determined system of schemes may have many degrees of complexity, a feature which it evidently shares with the object, the situation, and the schematic system of situations. What makes in each case the unity of the dogmatic system is that there is always one dominant scheme, whose continued actualization is required to constitute a continually returning aim in view of which the other schemes are required to co-operate. This dominant scheme determines the *ideal* conditions under which the dogma demands that the other schemes be actualized, whereas the other schemes create the *real* conditions under which the dogma demands that the dominant scheme be actualized.

The primary, the oldest example of a practical dogma is the principle of hedonistic selection determining the organization of objects as personal experiences of a conscious living being. This organization is dogmatically imposed upon individual life; that is, even if the search for pleasure and the avoidance of pain should have a further and original justification in the conservation of the race, all consciousness of this justification is absent in personal experience unless secondarily developed by scientific theories, and hedonistic selection appears empirically as having its ultimate reason in itself. This does not mean that all organization of objects in individual experience is in any sense reducible to it, since all the innumerable existing schemes and systems of schemes, most of which are evidently quite independent of hedonistic selection, are equally actualized in individual experience. It means simply that the hedonistic organization is one of the dogmatic organizations of individual experience, the one in which the objects are treated exclusively as belonging to the individual's personality without regard to the impersonal systems to which they also empirically belong and which are also constructed by the individual. The hedonistic organization consists in an interdependence between the dominant hedonistic scheme tending to construct situations on the ground of which pleasure can be obtained or pain avoided, and all the "instincts," inborn or acquired, each of which tends to construct specific situations on the ground of which special ends are reached. In this interdependence, just as in that which exists between the aim and the situation, all instincts are made to co-operate for the continued realization of the hedonistic scheme, while on the other hand, the nature of the hedonistic situations which are realized depends on the nature of the instinctive situations which constitute the real conditions of pleasure. Life in its biological and yet conscious significance is for each individual precisely the continual actualization of the hedonistic scheme as aim and ideal condition of all the instinctive schemes, and the actualization of all the instinctive schemes, more or less reciprocally limited and interdependent, as a material and real condition of the hedonistic scheme. The organization is, of course, neither absolutely closed nor absolutely rational; but no empirical organization ever is.

Other examples are found in technically specialized industrial activities. When instead of one scheme for the production of a certain kind of values which are made at once ready for consumption, as in handiwork and in many non-specialized industries, several schemes are substituted each of which organizes only a special side of this production so that the value is made ready for consumption only by the co-operation of all these schemes, the whole system of schemes is determined in advance and unconditionally. Each of these special lines of industry can and should continue to produce as long as, and only as long as, the other special lines produce. All other special schemes of this system are ideally conditioned by one dominant special scheme—the one which makes the values definitively ready for consumption by *synthetizing* the partial results of other schemes—and this scheme in turn is really conditioned by all the others. Specialization requires thus continuous synthetic co-operation, which for each branch of industry is brought into effect by the fact that the managers of the more special and therefore interdependent branches explicitly or implicitly accept, in theory and in practice or only in practice, the principle of the necessary connection to be maintained between these lines in the future, independently of outside interferences. Because in this way every special line of production depends for its continuation only on the continuation of the other lines, the continuation of the total production is unconditional, the existence of the whole system in the future is, from the standpoint and within the limits of this system itself, dogmatically imposed, not made dependent on any conditions which may appear in concrete historical development of the empirical reality. Of course, the isolation of this system from the historical world is only a tendency which may fail in its realization and the system may be prevented from continuing by the lack of the necessary objects or by the non-performance of the necessary activities; but the same is true of the isolation of any rational organization from the concrete chaos of empirical reality.

The nature of the practical dogma appears with great clearness in the political field. A state is really a wide system of schemes in action, whose continual actualization is unconditionally demanded by the dogma constitution, whether abstractly formulated and codified or existing only as actively applied in custom. Within this wide system we find a large number of more limited and partly independent systems, some territorially, others functionally, specialized. None of the political dogmas determining these particular systems, nor even the constitution, are absolutely permanent, as we know; but as long as they last, their unconditional acceptance is not only demanded but practically enforced, that is, there are special schemes included in the state organization whose task consists in continually destroying such empirical hindrances to the permanence of the system as are most easily foreseen and schematized (disobedience to law, rebellion, treason, etc.). And we can follow here very well the way in which a dogmatic system imposes upon activity the realization of any particular scheme which it includes. For example, take a rule which orders every male citizen of a certain age to join the army when called by the government. This rule presupposes an indefinite repetition of a certain situation—the determined age reached, the call of the government received, the physical means of joining the recruiting station at the individual's disposal, etc. Those few social values, with the meaning given to them by social tradition, define the problem in an identical way for every individual and of every individual the same solution is expected. But the social values supposed to constitute this situation are concrete empirical objects entering into many other connections, which would prevent the situation demanded from ever being reconstructed if its reconstruction were not imposed as aim upon individual activities quite independently of the concrete conditions in which the individual finds himself when these values are given to him. The call to join the army at a given time comes into connection with a multitude of other values—home, family, career, present pleasures, etc., on the one hand, expected hardships, possible death in battle, etc., on the other. The actual situation spontaneously constructed by each individual under these circumstances would be entirely different from the one expected and the behavior solving these particular situations would be in most cases just the opposite from the one prescribed by the rule. But behind this particular rule, behind this one political scheme, there is a wide complexity of other schemes which act as social and legal sanctions of the rule, such as legal punishment, social contempt, on the one hand, and social approval, prospects of fame, moral duty, patriotism, etc., on the other. From among the many and various situations which these terms designate the individual himself, or, in the last extremity, the executive authority, is supposed in each case to select and realize a combination which will be sufficient to construct the real conditions necessary and sufficient for the realization of the model situation as demanded by the rule. The organizing activity preparing thus under the pressure of the whole political system everything necessary for any model situation prescribed by a political scheme constitutes the basis of all political obedience.

The system of schemes founded on a practical dogma is, as we see, first of all a system of activities rather than of objects, but of activities organized essentially in view of real, not of ideal, purposes, and therefore it results, just as the concrete action which organizes the situation or as a concrete schematizing activity which actualizes the scheme, in a systematization of objects. This systematization bears, first of all, upon the totality of the schematic situations which the dogma implies. The continual reconstruction of these situations in their reciprocal dependence is unconditionally demanded by the dogma, and even if for an individual who participates in the reconstruction only one of these situations can actually become an aim at once, from the standpoint of the dogma all these situations appear as one general, permanent, and complex aim imposed upon concrete activity. The unity of these situations appears thus as no longer dependent on their actual dynamic organization, as it is in the concrete system of auxiliary situations actually constructed for the realization of a model situation, but as given once and forever in its perfect rationality. Of course, in order to be empirically ascertainable, this unity must be actually reproducible by individual active thought in the same indirect way as a system of situations is. But it does not need to be reproduced by all the individuals who take part in its realization, nor to be reproduced by any individual in its totality. It is sufficient and necessary that some individuals, as, for instance, a group of industrial managers or political rulers, can each reproduce and actively maintain the rational organization of a *part* of the system, provided only such partial individual reproductions supplement one another so as to cover the total system. In the contrary case, if the system is not consciously and actively maintained in its rationality either by one individual or by several co-operating individuals, this rational organization soon loses its realness and the empirically given system degenerates first into a complex of schemes, then even into a mere complex of situations and single objects like those survivals of old institutions which exist in every society beside the vital and systematic actual organization. But in so far as the system is actively maintained and the schemes kept in their reciprocal dependence, the schematic situations appear as no longer actually interconnected, but objectively and permanently interrelated, for each of them is rationally necessary for all the others. The individual may exclude the dogmatic system from his actual sphere of reality or even impose a different system on his group, but he can neither change nor deny its rational organization in so far as the latter has been once produced. He can, indeed, make it more perfect if it is not perfect yet, but he cannot destroy its perfection when attained, though he may contribute to the destruction of the realness of the system as concrete complex of situations, or contribute to the substitution in historical reality of an irrational chaos for this rational order. For example, in industrial specialization and co-operation the technical situations constructed in different interdependent lines of production appear as objectively and permanently supplementing one another and constitute, with all the materials and instruments which they include, one common domain of technical reality, one definite isolated and rational section of the empirical world, which cannot be disturbed in any of its parts without being disturbed in its whole systematic unity. We may do the latter and destroy the realness of this whole branch of industry, but we cannot prevent its systematic organization from existing forever once it has been created, nor the situations, such as defined by the schemes, from being forever necessarily related with one another by the demand of industrial co-operation.

Such a rational stabilization of the system of schematic situations has a further effect upon the rationality of each situation in particular. We have seen that a scheme, by imposing the reconstruction of a definite situation as an aim, leads already to a determination in advance of the way by which this situation will be solved and thus introduces the teleological systematization of means and end, reduces the creative rôle of each act to the mere starting of a known and objectively determined process, and subjects the sequence of these processes to the principle of final causality. The situation contains already virtually its own solution, and activity is supposed merely to actualize this virtual solution from case to case. Now, when it is unconditionally demanded of a system of schematic situations that it be actualized indefinitely, even this limited rôle of spontaneous activity is ignored, and the development of the situation loses its teleological character. The schematic situation becomes determined not only in the nature of its construction and realization, but in the very fact of its construction and realization. Therefore its realization, which from the standpoint of the scheme was an *ideally* necessary outcome of its constitution, is from the standpoint of the dogma a *really* necessary result of its existence at a given time and place. From the first standpoint, the constructed situation *should* be realized in a way determined in advance; from the second, it *must* be realized in a way determined in advance. The constructed situation, in a word, is treated as including within itself everything necessary to have its virtual solution become actual, as necessarily bringing of itself a result determined in advance. Of course, activity must be always implicitly presupposed: the situation could not be constructed without the schematizing activity which selects and organizes auxiliary situations, and the schematizing activity would not continue to reconstruct the schematic situation time after time if it were not for the active influence of the practical dogma. But the situation once there, the fact of its solution is no longer a matter of choice; its existence having been unconditionally imposed upon activity and unconditionally accepted, its solution, being implied by its existence, follows also unconditionally. The whole series of modifications which will lead to the expected and demanded result are thus one complex process within which activity has nothing more to do, and which brings nothing new, since not only its nature, but its very occurrence was implied in the situation. In so far however as several objects are involved in this process and the change which occurs in one object is different from that which follows in another object, the process splits into a series, or several series, of different processes. Each of these processes, as we know, already is a necessary link of the series in the realization of a situation which is only schematically determined; but now, in the dogmatically demanded situation, its connection with the preceding and following process is no longer teleological, since the whole development of which it is a part is no longer treated as dependent upon activity, all activity having been performed in advance. The occurrence of a given process is thus no longer merely a teleologically indispensable condition of the occurrence of the following process, to which an act must be added in order to make it a sufficient condition: the whole development being presupposed as something that necessarily is going to happen and to happen in a determined way, the occurrence of a particular given process is both necessary and sufficient to have the following process occur. In a word, within the limits of the development implied by a dogmatically demanded situation each process is the *efficient cause* of the following process.

The principle of causality is thus the product of a highly developed practical organization, far from being the elementary and fundamental principle of all organized experience, as the eighteenth century assumed and modern idealism still continues to believe. History and sociology give us proofs enough that the original empirical attitude is to search for the explanation of each process in an act, not in another process; and an act can be neither a cause nor an effect, if we take these terms in their exact sense, as indicating a relation between real happenings. The most primitive application of the principle of causality is, as should be expected, found within schematic situations organized by the principle of hedonistic selection, the earliest practical dogma. We begin to expect definite effects from definite causes, to rely upon the natural sequence of processes, first of all within the situations formed under the control of our instincts, long before we succeed in organizing technical and particularly social situations which will then develop automatically. Any causality which we find in "nature," in the popular, non-scientific sense of the term, is always empirically a succession of processes in some instinctively organized situation which we expect—hope or fear— to be realized without the participation of our activity. For there is no practical causality except within the limits of one situation, which, of course, may indefinitely repeat itself.

Not only is there no causality possible in the concrete empirical development of the historical reality, but even in a practically organized reality an unexpected disturbance of the regular sequence of processes within a situation is not originally taken as the effect of a cause but as the result of an act, unless it can be interpreted as a process constituting a part of the development of some other dogmatically demanded situation. This is also the reason why in practical life we find neither the principle of an endless series of causality nor that of the essential homogeneity of causally connected processes. Since the development of a situation has a beginning and an end, there must be in it a process which is only a cause without being an effect and another which is an effect without being a cause. Practical reflection, unless influenced by scientific or philosophical theories, calmly accepts this circumstance, easily admitting a beginning and an end of the causal series. The first process which starts the development of the situation can, of course, be only the result of an act; but the act is excluded from the situation. The last process, the last modification of an object within the situation may become the starting-point of some other series of practical modifications, but this series, which must be started by a new activity, does not belong either in the situation. So the causal series is practically closed.

On the other hand, the most various processes can belong to it. In an industrial situation which includes men as elements, the only way in which the active, ideal factor can be ignored and the development treated as causal is to substitute, while determining the situation dogmatically, for each indefinitely repeatable act a bodily movement and a psychological process, and to introduce both of them into the causal series, the first as the effect of the second, which is in turn treated as the effect of some preceding material process. In the development of a political situation psychological processes, causally determined by material, economic, and other processes as motives, and themselves causally determining material, economic, and other processes, are the most important links of the causal series. On a higher level of organization, activity substitutes indeed more and more homogeneous causal series for heterogeneous ones; it tries to reduce, for instance, the entire development of a technical situation to mechanical processes. This evolution is brought by uniformizing the instruments used in the situations demanded by a certain practical dogma. Thus, machines are substituted for men in industrial schemes, physical coercion exercised through material instruments gives way to psychological influence exercised through social personalities in social schemes, etc. This facilitates the isolation of the given system of schemes from unexpected external disturbances which may interfere with the regular development of its situations, but it does not change the rational character of this development itself. The series of processes which go on in a factory appears as equally real and causal with regard to men as to machines, if we accept it as given and abstract it from the activity which has organized it and makes it run again and again in an identical order by keeping away all disturbances; it appears as equally ideal and concretely intentional if we remove this abstraction and take it as a part of the total evolution of our experience and reflection.

The second effect of the system of schemes upon reality is that this system becomes a center of unification of new situations. Every actualization of each scheme must be brought by an intentional organization of auxiliary situations, and since it is demanded of the schemes to be actualized again and again whatever may be the concrete empirical conditions, the dogmatic system imposes upon our activity an obligation to prepare such concrete empirical conditions for the future as will permit us to organize case by case the auxiliary situations of the demanded schemes. This preparation, of course, can be always only approximate and gradual. It consists in intentionally trying to maintain for the future such a composition and organization of the domain of reality within which the dogmatic system is developing as has proved up to the present sufficient and necessary for its continual actualization. This is done by avoiding within this sphere such activities as would modify it too much and by trying to counterbalance modifications which nevertheless occur. A conscious being who stays in a given natural and social environment as long as this environment remains in some measure uniform, who gradually reaches a routine of experience and activity so as to ignore in advance, not to notice and not to use, any new possibilities which the future may bring, who actively opposes unexpected modifications brought into his routinized experience and activity and who, when too much disturbed, may even, if possible, change his environment to a similar but more fixed one, offers a good example of such a stabilization of the future on the ground of the practical dogma of hedonistic selection. The permanent localization of an industry in a certain territory, the efforts made by its managers to maintain the means of communication, the prices, the labor conditions, even the social and political organization in a status which has proved propitious for their industry, the active opposition which every innovation provokes as long as the system runs satisfactorily—all this represents well the effect which an industrial dogma has upon the future. In the political field history gives us enough examples of an intentional perpetuation of given social, economic, intellectual conditions and careful prevention of all active modifications which may, directly or indirectly, make the continual actual preservation of the existing state system difficult. The practical dogma is in every field, just as it is known to be in the religious field, a foundation of conservatism, not merely because it demands unconditionally the maintenance of a given system of schemes, but because to assure and facilitate this maintenance it tends to control the future historical evolution of that part of concrete reality within which the system exists, by superimposing upon the concrete sphere of chaotically evolving historical objects a large body of unsystematized but interconnected and repeatable situations.

We understand now how it is that our common-sense reality, while being far from possessing that full systematic rationality which science tries to give it, while always only partially and fragmentarily rationalized and divided into numerous and never absolutely perfect systems, appears to us usually as a world of things, not a world of historical objects, why its relative stability strikes us more than its continuous evolution so that evolution seems superimposed upon stability instead of vice versa, and why at most moments of our conscious life we seem to find around us objectively and statically unified spheres of reality rather than actively and dynamically connected spheres of experience and reflection. The point is that most of our conscious life is spent in schematically constructing or in realizing practical situations imposed by some dogmas; that in our common-sense reflection we usually find ourselves in the midst of some practical activity and thus our present experience mostly converges toward some definite situation; that the section of our past experience which we now remember appears in memory as centralized around some scheme; that the section of our future experience which we now expect appears in this expectation as stabilized and unified by a certain dogma. Common-sense reflection, essentially practical in its character, never gets beyond the superficial standpoint of one practical system or another, and therefore cannot reach by itself, cannot even understand if shown, the concrete empirical reality upon which all the practical systems are built as a complex superstructure, objective and real indeed, but maintained above the rushing stream of the historical world only by a continuous positive effort of active thought. This maintenance is, indeed, not a mere preservation but a ceaseless extension of the maintained systems and creation of new ones, so that practical organization continuously penetrates deeper and deeper into the concrete historical becoming and more and more of the pre-existing chaotic reality becomes practically rationalized. But as the unorganized reality also continues to grow, practically constructive activity can never master the total concrete wealth of the historical chaos.

CHAPTER V

THE THEORETIC ORDERS OF REALITY

THE GENERAL FEATURES OF THEORETIC RATIONALIZATION

The imperfect and multiform organization of reality super-constructed by practical activity upon the world of concrete historical objects serves in turn as a foundation for a new superstructure, the rational order which knowledge imposes upon its object-matter.

We cannot, of course, give here a complete theory of knowledge which presupposes a general theory of activity and constitutes the most arduous task of philosophy. We shall limit ourselves to the minimum of indications necessary to understand the connection between knowledge and reality in so far as it affects the latter.

The fundamental points which must be kept in mind are that, on the one hand, knowledge constitutes itself a part of cultural reality, the domain of ideas, each of which has a content drawn from some other reality and a meaning due to its connection with other ideas; and that, on the other hand, each idea is objectified and stabilized thought, which at any moment can be actualized again as thought, as an activity of which reality is the object-matter. As a reality, the domain of ideas has a rational organization of its own, whose character is formally practical, that is, which manifests itself in situations, schemes, and dogmas, just as the rational organization of technical or political reality; and there is a special activity, which might be called theoretically practical, if such a term did not seem stranger still than that of ideal reality, which we have used to distinguish the domain of ideas from all other reality. The task of this activity is to create new ideas, both on the ground of real data and on the ground of pre-existing ideas. The instruments of this creation, with the help of which ideas become fixed and incorporated into the pre-existing ideal reality, are symbols, and the complexes of pre-existing ideas organized for the creation of new ideas are systems of knowledge. A system of knowledge, once ready, may be time after time actualized as a system of active thoughts bearing upon reality, and thus produce a more or less wide and complicated systematization of reality, which, since it does not tend to create any new objects within the reality upon which the actualized system of knowledge bears and includes no instruments, can be called a theoretic systematization in the original sense of the term, that is, a systematization by observation.

Now, this systematic theoretic order imposed by knowledge upon reality is *not* a copy, a reproduction of the systematic organization which knowledge finds ready and constructed by practical activity. A system of objects may be practically reproduced in the sense of being constructed again, as a schematic situation is, time after time; we know reproduction in this sense from the preceding sections and we hardly need to mention that the practically, even if only mentally, reproduced system is always still a practical system—technical, political, etc.—and not knowledge of a system. Or a system of objects may be reproduced in concrete experience without being practically followed in its organization, as a more or less complex datum; but such a "representation" of a system is not a knowledge of this system, but is this system itself becoming an object, an element of experience, with a given content and a meaning which it acquires in actuality. Reproduction in this sense, as a mere introduction of the system as a datum into the present sphere of experience and reflection, is not knowledge, any more than the reappearance of any object "in memory" is; we may call it *acquaintance* with the system, but acquaintance is only making objects accessible to individual theoretic activity, collecting materials out of which knowledge still has to be built. And when knowledge is built, both the way in which its elements or ideas are determined and the way in which they are systematized are completely different from the pre-existing determination and systematization of the objects upon which these ideas are based.

The content of the idea is, indeed, drawn from reality, since nothing but reality can be given; and yet the idea is not the reality which is its object-matter, but is objectified thought about this reality. This seeming contradiction, the necessity and the apparent impossibility of distinguishing the idea from its object-matter, has been one of the main stumbling-stones of the philosophy of knowledge, and there lies the source of that strange conception of ideas being subjectively psychological copies of objects, similar in content but different in being from their originals. This conception was the more readily accepted since it fell in with the practical distinction between real and unreal elements of practical activity of which we have spoken in the preceding chapter, and since moreover (a point which we shall discuss later) theoretic ideas when used for practical purposes are mostly actualized during the first period of activity when the aim is being constructed but waits to be realized, and when therefore activity is taken to be only mental from the standpoint of the second, instrumental, period. When, however, the study of concrete historical reality has forced us to reject the concept of representations as subjective copies of objects, we must search for a different and less arbitrary distinction between ideas and the reality from which they are drawn.

The whole difficulty comes from the prepossession that knowledge reproduces reality in its pre-existing determination and systematization, whereas the very difference between knowledge and its object-matter, and thus the very existence of knowledge as something distinct from its object-matter, are empirically manifested precisely in the specific and original determination and systematization which it gives to its object-matter. The act of thought which is the ideal ground of an idea cannot be given as object-matter, but its real results can be, and it is by its results as differing from the results of other acts that we recognize it and define it. In order to objectivate it as an idea, to oppose the idea as a specific object to the original object-matter of the act of thought, we must isolate the result of this act from the total concrete reality, stabilize it, raise it above the historical extension and duration of the sphere of experience to which it belongs. This is called theoretic *idealization* and requires the use of the symbol. The symbol is a real pre-existing object with which the given result of a theoretic act of thought becomes connected and, in so far as taken in this connection alone, can be treated as an object independent of its empirical context, and not as a mere modification of other objects. But that empirical result of the theoretic act, that real datum which the symbol helps to idealize, must be in some way different from the results of practical acts which construct practical systems of objects; otherwise there would be no difference between theory and practice. A symbolic connection is not limited to the field of knowledge; in fact, every concrete object might be called a symbol in that it has a meaning which suggests acts that lead to other empirical objects. A symbol in the special and definite sense of the term is characterized by the fact that it expresses an idea; but it can express an idea also only by suggesting acts which lead to some object-matter, and therefore the specific empirical difference which characterizes the symbol as a theoretic instrument must come directly from that object-matter which it symbolizes.

In fact, the formation of an idea implies as the first and indispensable condition the establishment of a connection between the given property, relation, thing, process, or even a whole system, if the latter in its entirety becomes the object-matter of knowledge, and other properties, relations, things, processes, systems, outside of the organization of reality of which the given object-matter is a part. This connection consists in the production, or reproduction, of a *uniformity*, that is, a community of determination between the objects which are being connected, quite independently of any differences which they may possess in the different real systems to which they respectively belong. Using traditional terms, we shall say that the first condition, the starting-point of the formation of an idea is *abstraction* and *generalization*. It is abstraction, in so far as the given object of theoretic thought, in order to be connected with other objects on the ground of uniformity, has to become isolated from the whole real systematic organization to which it belongs; it is generalization, in so far as it can be isolated from the real practical system of which it is objectively a part only by being connected with other objects outside of this system on the ground of some common determination, by being taken as one particular empirical manifestation of a super-systematic uniformity.

This uniformity of properties, relations, processes, things, systems, outside of their respective organizations, even in so far as it exists previous to theoretic thought, is clearly not a *real relation* or even a pre-existing practical connection between them, but the result of the fact that they have been determined in a similar way each in its particular organization; that a certain similar kind of connection has been at various times and in various places established between each of these objects which we generalize and some other objects which may be quite different from case to case. The source of this uniformity of objects can therefore be only an ideal uniformity of the acts which have determined them, and the theoretic thought which connects objects on the ground of their uniformity follows in fact the traces that certain ideal characteristics of active thought have left upon the reality which this active thought has created in the past. But the full demonstration of this proposition belongs with the theory of active thought.

What is evident here is that the isolation and subordination of the particular to the general by which, using particular real data as material, we construct the content of an idea does not correspond to any pre-existing *real order*. In practical reality, as we have seen, all direct rational determination of objects is within a situation, and if objects present similar characteristics, it is as inseparable elements of situations, not as variations of common real essences. An actually given object appearing in individual experience may be indeed a particular variation of the total concrete historical object; but a particular property, relation, process, thing, is not really a variation of more general property, relation, process, or thing; and if a system may be considered as a variation of some other system, it is only if taken with regard to its form, to the nature of its organization as determined by the same kind of active thought and not with regard to the real matter it contains.

The content of an idea is thus constructed as a unity of all these particular determinations of reality which become connected by theoretic thought on the ground of their uniformity, as variations of one more general determination. We know, of course, that theoretic thought seldom, if ever, actually embraces all the particular determinations which may be subordinated to the same general determination, all the "particulars" of a "universal"; but in so far as the idea can be actualized again and again, the system of determinations which it creates may be said to contain *virtually* all the particular determinations of this common form which will ever be found in experience. Between the content of several ideas again some more general uniformity may be found and these ideas subordinated to one common idea whose content is directly constituted as a unity of their contents and indirectly as a unity of all these determinations of reality which they have unified.

The content of the idea roots thus in reality by the nature of its materials, but rises above and outside of reality by the nature of the unification of these materials, to which no real systematic unity of objects corresponds, only an ideal uniformity of the acts that have determined them in the past, which is the genetic source of the common form of these objects, though the latter belong to different real systems. And the more general an idea, the more evident is the lack of any pre-existing real connection between the determinations which are unified in it, the more indubitable the ideal ground of this unification; if anyone should doubt whether empirical "rednesses" or empirical "tables" are not interconnected really, there can be hardly any doubt, except on the ground of mediaeval realism, that only a common form, no real bond, unifies all the empirical "colors" or empirical "pieces of furniture," when theoretic thought begins to connect them as members of a class.

But it is not enough to give to the idea a content; it must acquire a meaning for science, become a full element of the ideal reality by being connected with other pre-existing ideas. Only by this connection, as part of a system of ideas, its content becomes definitively stabilized and determined as independent—on its ideal, if not on its real side—of the concrete evolution of reality in extension and duration, so that the real data on which it is based may evolve and even completely disappear from actual experience, while the idea will persist together with the system of knowledge into which it has been incorporated. In so far as ideas must be expressed in symbols, since without a symbol a thought cannot be objectivated as an idea, symbols are also indispensable instruments of the systematization of ideas, because actual connections of ideas can become stable relations only if expressed in relations of symbols; at the same time the meaning of the symbol itself, as of an instrument, can be stabilized completely only by this use in relation with other instruments-symbols to express a system of ideas.

The systematic connection by which ideas acquire their scientific meaning is, of course, not subordination of the relatively particular to the relatively general, since this already determines their content, but analytic or synthetic subsumption of the relatively concrete to the relatively abstract. A system of ideas is either the product of an analysis of an idea into several different ideas, which are precisely therefore assumed to be simple within the limits of this system, or the product of a synthesis from several different ideas of an idea, which is precisely therefore assumed to be compound within the limits of this system.

We use the term *concept* exclusively to indicate an idea which is, and in so far as it is, analyzed into or synthetized from other ideas. The concept is clearly not exhausted by the ideas into which it is analyzed, nor is it fully created by a synthesis of other ideas. It must always have a content of its own independent of these ideas, which cannot be obtained otherwise than by the observation of reality and is always a unity of uniform empirical determinations common to many real data; if it has no real foundation, it has no content and therefore is not a distinct idea but a mere complex of different ideas. The analysis or synthesis is not supposed to determine its content, but to give this content a meaning, to establish a connection between it and other ideas; in analysis its content has been already created beforehand, whereas in synthesis it remains empirically unknown and will have to be created by empirical observation after its meaning has been determined, and thus after certain rational conditions have been imposed on this creation. On the other hand, the ideas into which the concept is analyzed or from which it is synthetized are not exhausted by their connection with the concept; each of them has an empirical content which would remain even if the concept were not there and which may serve for the analysis or synthesis of many other concepts; the connection with the concept and with the other ideas into which the concept is analyzed gives only a definite scientific meaning to the given content of the idea. If it has no content drawn from reality independently of the concept, then it is not a separate idea but a mere part of the concept.[1]

A concept which has been or will be analyzed into or synthetized from other ideas can, as we know, play the part of a simple idea, an element of analysis or synthesis, with regard to some other concept; and vice versa, an idea which was treated as simple element in one system may become an analyzed concept in another. In this way, indefinitely complicated scientific systems may be constructed by a hierarchical subsumptive organization.

What is the connection between this systematic order of ideas and the pre-existing organization of reality? We see, indeed, that just as the content of particular ideas has a foundation in reality, so the relation between ideas as manifested in synthesis and analysis is based upon reality as upon its original material. The relation between the concept of a thing and the ideas of properties into which it is analyzed has its real ground in the coexistence of the properties corresponding to these ideas in the empirical things; the relations between ideas in the theoretic definition of the concept of a certain type of situations is founded upon the internal unity of each situation of this type as including certain really interrelated things and developing in certain teleologically or causally ordered processes; the relation of ideas in the

[1] Evidently there can be no theoretic idea of a unique practical element, that is, of a thing, property, relation, process, etc., which exists only within one system of reality, though there can be ideas of unique historical objects, for example, historical personalities, which belong to several different rational systems of reality and have some common determination in all of them.

theoretic definition of the concept of a certain type of scheme is drawn from the systematic organization of the situations as conditioned by each scheme of this type, etc. But the rational ground of the coexistence of properties in a particular thing, of the coexistence of things, relations, and processes in a particular situation, of the coexistence of situations in a particular scheme, is completely different from the rational ground of the systematic organization of the ideas of the properties as analytically or synthetically connected with the concept of a thing, of the organization of the ideas of things, relations, and processes as analytically or synthetically connected with the concept of a situation, of the organization of the ideas of situations as analytically connected with the concept of the scheme.

The empirically given thing has the properties which it has because it is determined with regard to other things contained in the situation; the concept of a thing is analyzed into certain ideas of properties because empirical things belonging under this concept, which on the ground of a certain common form that they possess have been made the material of this idea, possess properties of certain classes, none of which, however, is necessarily limited to things belonging under this concept but may be also found, with the same general form, in things belonging under other concepts. The empirically given particular situation contains the things, relations, processes, which it does contain because it is so determined with regard to other situations in the realization of a scheme; the concept of the situation is analyzed into certain ideas of things, relations, processes, because the empirical situations of a certain class, which, on the ground of a common form or a similarity of organization which they possess, are the material of one idea, include things, relations, processes, whose common forms can be found empirically manifested not only in situations of this class, but also in situations of other classes. And so on. In short, science can indeed reconstruct theoretically any empirical, practically rational organization of reality, but only by isolating it from the wider organization by which it is determined, by ignoring the real factors which made it what it is, by taking it as granted, as self-existing material of a concept.

Then, having thus severed the real links which unified it with a wider system of reality, it determines its entire constitution from the standpoint of an entirely different rational systematization. Just as in the formation of an idea each particular empirical datum which constitutes its real material becomes connected with many other empirical data which present the same general form, to whatever systems they may belong, so in the formation of a system of ideas each particular empirical organization which is its material becomes variously and more or less closely connected with many other empirical organizations, with which it may have had no real connection whatever but whose elements present forms similar to those of the elements of the given organization. When an empirical situation becomes not only the object-matter of theoretic generalization but also that of theoretic analysis or synthesis, when it serves not only as the material of an idea but also as the material of a system of ideas in which its intrinsic practical organization will be theoretically reconstructed, then it not only becomes theoretically connected with those situations which have an organization similar to its own, and thus are taken as belonging to the same class, but also with all those situations which, however, they may differ from it in their general form, possess some particular things, relations, processes, formally similar to those things, relations, or processes which the given situation includes.

The same will happen on a higher level when theoretic thought undertakes to reconstruct the connections which it had at first ignored between the situation and other situations in a schematic system of situations. It will then have to reconstruct theoretically this schematic system of situations in its internal organization, and in doing this it will ignore the connections which may exist between this particular scheme and others, if this scheme is a part of some dogmatic system of schemes. Instead, it will first of all create an idea of a schematic system of situations of which the given one will be a particular case and thereby connect the latter, not with the schemes with which it is really connected, but with all those which present some characteristic uniformity. Then it will analyze this idea, taken as a concept, into ideas corresponding to the particular situations included in the schematic system and their reciprocal determinations, thus connecting the given schematic organization with all those which, even if perhaps completely different from it in their general form, include similar situations. It may push this analysis still farther, analyze the idea of each situation, taken as a concept, into ideas corresponding to the particular things, relations, processes, included in these situations, and thus connect indirectly the schematic organization with all those that, even if their situations should be different, have at least similar things, relations, or processes within their situations.

Finally, if theoretic reconstruction reaches the dogmatic system of schemes, beyond which the real practical systematization never goes, or if in the given field practical organization has not yet reached a level of systematization higher than the situation or the scheme, then, of course, knowledge has no pre-existing practical connections to ignore; it only creates a new order, but always of a different type from the organization found in practical experience, always based on ideal uniformity instead of real determination.

Of course, this creation of an order of reality different from the pre-existing practical systematization of this reality is not the aim of knowledge in the course of the construction of systems of ideas. The latter are constructed for the creation of new ideas, and while having a foundation in pre-existing reality, present a rational organization of their own which, being the product of organized creative activity and resulting from the combination of various materials and instruments for the attainment of definite common results, has within itself the same fundamental forms as the organization of technical, hedonistic, political systems. But knowledge has the privilege of being not only a closed and specific organization of objects, but of being also able to become at any moment an organization of active thoughts which bear upon other fields of reality; and in this bearing, that is, not as static ideas but as dynamic thoughts, imposes upon these other fields of reality an order which these fields did not possess. A system of knowledge when applied to reality as object-matter of actual theoretic reflection, when regulating our observation, establishes between the many real empirical data which are its object-matter a set of systematic connections, which like all connections have a certain objective realness. This theoretically imposed rationality cannot attain by itself the same degree of realness as a practically established organization, since theoretic thought when directly applied to reality uses no instruments. However, such as it is, it is evidently sufficiently real to influence in a very marked way our common empirical real world, and with the growth and systematization of knowledge, all the domains of historical reality which knowledge has influenced appear to us empirically more and more permeated with a type of rationality which can be only the product of theoretic reflection.

Now, the important feature of knowledge as system of thoughts bearing upon reality is that it makes the rational organization of reality ever wider and more perfect by continually tending, self-consciously or not, to the ideal of a *complete theoretic rationalization* of the real world. This ideal has found its most radical expression in those philo-

THEORETIC ORDERS OF REALITY

sophical theories which look upon the real world exclusively in the light of theoretic activity; however, it plays a more or less important part in every philosophy in so far as the latter attempts to give a consistent rational conception of reality as a whole, and in every particular science in so far as it tends to realize it within the particular domain of reality which constitutes its material.

The way in which this ideal is approached differs in various branches of knowledge in so far as some of them neglect entirely the rôle which practical activity has played in organizing the world and take only the last real results of this activity, treating them as self-existing and self-determined in their rationality, whereas others take into account and try to reconstruct theoretically some existing practical systems, either stopping at the situation, or rising to the scheme, or, finally, taking even the dogmatic system of schemes into consideration. Of course, each branch of knowledge, by the very nature of theoretic idealization, has to ignore whatever practical organizations there may be superior to the one which is its special object-matter: if its object-matter is things, relations, or processes, it ignores the situation, and *a fortiori* the scheme and the dogma; if it idealizes situations, it ignores schemes and dogmas; if its method is specially developed to study schemes, it ignores dogmas.

But whatever kind of organization is its object-matter, knowledge takes this organization as it is in those systems which have pushed it to the highest degree of perfection, and assumes that the rational form of this organization represents a type of rationality which is universally present, if not in all reality, at least in those sections whose order appears as more or less similar to the one accepted as a model.

More than this. Science often appeals to practical activity to construct especial *artificial models* of rational organizations in the form of classified collections or experiments, and takes these models as representative of the real order universally latent in empirical reality, or in certain parts of reality at least. Since, as a matter of fact, reality does not grow up to these expectations and lacks the necessary uniformity and perfection of order, science uses two assumptions to justify its claims: the assumption of *approximation* and that of *interference*. The first, found whenever we want to reconstruct theoretically a concrete fragment of reality with the help of abstract ideas, consists in accepting the general principle that, although reality does not present a perfect order, still it more or less approximates it, and the problem in each case is simply to determine the rational limits within which the imperfect rationality of experience can be placed. Thus, the variety of empirical organic bodies cannot be perfectly defined as constituting an ideally rational system of species, but an approximate systematization, based upon the assumption of a majority of average individuals approximately realizing the essential characters of the species, is rationally possible.

The other assumption, used when we analyze a concrete fragment of reality[1] into ideal abstract elements, consists in treating the imperfectly rational empirical object-matter as the product of an "accidental," purely matter-of-fact (explicable only by the total concrete reality) combination of perfectly rational real components which in this combination, interfering with each other, cannot manifest fully their several rational essences. No causal law needs ever to be exactly realized in experience because it is always possible to assume that its working has been interfered with in the given case by some other causal law, which

[1] When we speak of theoretic analysis or synthesis of reality, it is evidently only an abbreviation. What is analyzed or synthetized is the concept based upon the total object-matter which is being theoretically reconstructed; since the concept implies a real ground, the abbreviation can be used without inconvenience.

in turn never needs to be perfectly applicable to unprepared experience because of other possible interferences, and so on indefinitely; whereas at the same time it is usually possible at least approximately to reconstruct practically the model situation, the isolated closed system within which it has proved to work, and thus to test it by experiment.

THE PHYSICAL ORDER

The theoretic ideal of the perfect rationality of the world, like every other ideal, continually evolves, and in every historical epoch as we well know finds expression in many partial, imperfectly interconnected and within themselves not always perfectly systematized, scientific and philosophical theories. But all these theories, whatever may be their object-matter and their own systematic organization, can be classified into a very limited number of types with regard to the general, *categorical forms* which they tend to impose upon reality. The origin of these categorical forms of theoretic reflection lies in the forms which reality acquires in those fundamental types of practical systems which we have studied above. These practical forms which in empirical reality are never perfect and develop only under very definite conditions, as we have seen in the preceding chapter, when generalized and idealized by science as categories become in their actual application to reality *methodological presuppositions*, helping to create perfectly rational systems of knowledge on the ground of an imperfectly rational reality, and thus to raise the latter also step by step to a higher level of rationality. If formulated as general affirmations about reality as a whole, justifying the belief in the attainment of the theoretic ideal by the assumption that reality is rational itself, they claim to be ontological truths a priori—a claim which, as we shall see, must be rejected.

The oldest and the most firmly established set of such methodological presuppositions, which precisely therefore has been most frequently ascribed an ontological validity—whether with regard to absolute "noumenal" or to "phenomenal" reality only, is immaterial—is the one that constitutes the formal foundation of that branch of knowledge which ignores entirely practical systems and takes as its object-matter the ultimate elements of reality. These it treats as if they were all perfectly determined in perfect rational situations but without regard to the situations themselves to which they owe whatever determinations they really possess. This branch, to which all natural sciences of the material reality belong, without exactly splitting into two distinct parts, tends nevertheless to a division of problems into two groups, each of which presupposed an elementary order of reality of a somewhat different type. On the one hand we have a *static* order of things, properties, and relations; on the other hand, a *dynamic* order of causally determined processes. Let us examine the most frequent forms of each of these orders separately.

In the static order, processes which of course cannot be ignored also have to be logically stabilized; this is done by analyzing them into *states of things*, so that each process is taken as a succession of states. Now, a state is a property of the thing, and in this way the category of property is divided in two: permanent properties, qualities, including quantitative determinations when taken as belonging to the thing itself and not as expressing merely relations; and changing properties, states. This type of rationalism, as we have said, most frequently passes from a methodological to an ontological application of these categories, and it does this by an implicit or explicit reasoning which can be briefly resumed in this manner. Because any empirical complex of objects can be theoretically reconstructed as a rational system of things, qualities, states, and relations, all reality objectively is constituted by things, qualities, states, and relations. In the most radical philosophical expression of this ontologism the thing becomes a substance, the property an attribute, the state a modus.

The fundamental characteristics of the thing as object-matter of theoretic reflection are: isolation from and limitation against other things, self-identity, independence of the actual connections within which it is taken. Now, these formal characteristics, which are ascribed to the thing for the purpose of present scientific reconstruction, can be assumed as belonging really and objectively to any particular thing in the measure in which this thing has been already fully determined within a static situation, so that no new determinations are supposed to be added to it by the total situation and thus, in defining theoretically the thing as now given and ready, we do not need to take the situation of which it is a part into account. But suppose now we ignore, not only for particular theoretic purposes, but absolutely, the fact that things are determined by special practical situations and are what they are only within the limits of these situations; suppose we claim that all the objects of which concrete empirical reality is composed are by themselves ontologically things or substances, isolated and limited, self-identical, independent of actual connections. What will be the consequences?

Isolation and limitation, if neither taken as dependent on practical activity which maintains the object as limited or distinct from others, because it makes it determined by others, nor as dependent on theoretic activity which reconstructs the object as isolated or separated from others, because others are ignored for the time of this reconstruction, but as absolute, real characteristics of the thing itself, as static features of reality, are possible only in space. We find in many empirical situations spatial order, more or less pure, substituted for concrete extension; but it is theoretic thought which, by ignoring the particular, variable, and practically limited character of each such empirical spatial organization, constructs the unique, absolute, homogeneous space as the common receptacle of objectively isolated and limited things, superimposing this abstract rational extension upon the concrete irrational extension of the historical world.

The thing becomes thus a material or quasi-material object, occupying one and only one position in pure extension at a given static moment and spatially separated from other objects; it is determined as *this* thing by its position in the one common space and the space which it occupies is determined by it. Extension becomes thus something external to the thing itself; the latter has only so much of it left as it possesses within one particular situation where it is supposed given only in one abstract objective *here*, and it is not entirely inextensive only because it is simultaneously determined from the standpoint of all the other objects included in the situation, each of which has its own distinct *here*. The theoretic thing is, like the concrete historical object, taken as element of an extensive reality, but since its own extension is limited in advance, its participation in the total extension of the world cannot be internal, based upon the intrinsic extensiveness of its own content and meaning, as it is in the case of the historical object, but external, consisting exclusively in its occupying a definite portion of the one rational space. Therefore, if something exactly similar in content can be localized simultaneously in two different positions of the one rational space, it is two different things. But since it is evidently impossible to substitute space for concrete extension as a milieu of all experiences, since the total empirical content and meaning of a concrete historical object, continually growing, can never be exhausted by any number of similar or dissimilar, specially localized, and rationally determined things, for all those variations of a concrete object which are not determined as isolated elements of perfect material situations and cannot be interpreted as things with definite spatial positions, theoretic reflection adopts a qualification which we have already found in practical organizations applied to particular fragments of empirical reality, but which in knowledge leads to a distinction cutting the whole world in two. The object which, having one position in rational space, is simultaneously present at various *here*'s of the concrete extension, is taken as a complex of one thing and several subjective representations.

Similarly, the self-identity of the thing as logical subject-matter is theoretically justified by the fact that the thing in theoretic reflection, for the special purpose of the actually constructed system of ideas, is raised above change; and it is practically possible within the limits of one situation, if practical activity maintains this situation identical against the evolution of empirical reality. But the only way in which the thing could by its own virtue, independently of theoretic or practical activity, remain really, materially self-identical, would be if it were changeless in duration. Since, however, concrete duration is the product of activity and implies necessarily continual growth of historical reality, science has to substitute for this irrational duration a pure rational time, an empty form of existence which exists quite independently, whether objects in it change or remain changeless. In this objective time the thing has a definite period of duration; it is at all only as long as it is self-identical, remains unchanged—unchanged, of course, in that which constitutes its objective nature as *this* thing; once changed, it is no more, and a different thing begins to exist instead. Thus, duration, like extension, is put *outside* of the thing whereas it is *within* the concrete historical object. Philosophy, by substituting the substance for the thing, goes still farther and denies even that the empty time, the pure external duration, is a receptacle of substances; it is only supposed to include the *modi* of the substance. A real substance therefore can have no beginning and no end. Remnants of this conception are found up to the present in the principles of conservation of matter and of energy. And in so far as the scientific order of self-identical things lasting for definite periods of time cannot cover empirical duration, in so far as an object continues or begins to exist in concrete duration after it ceased or before it began to exist as thing in rational time, the same distinction is applied as in the contrast between concrete and spatial extension. An object that is given before or after it had existed as a thing is a distinct phenomenon, a subjective representation of the thing.

Finally, the independence of the thing from the connections in which it is given is again logically justified in so far as, in idealizing the thing theoretically, in incorporating it into a system of ideas, we ignore all modifications which active thought, even our present theoretic reflection itself, may bring into its content and meaning by connecting it with other objects; it is possible really and practically in so far as practical activity makes the thing independent of all other determinations except those which it has received within the closed situation with reference to other things included therein. But as absolutely real characteristic of the thing, independence of all connections would be possible only if the thing as long as self-identical possessed a complete self-sufficiency, if its relations to other things did not affect it in itself. This implies a complete externality of the relation to the thing. The thing as such cannot be affected by any relation; relation can influence only either its spatial position or the period of pure time in which it is localized, but not its own objective nature. The philosophical substance, for example, the monad of Leibniz, is not subjected to any relations whatever. Any dependence of the object on the empirical connections into which it is brought that does not destroy its self-identity and yet is not reducible to a mere change of localization in time or space is classed as subjective; if the thing is differently given in different connections, it is not that the thing has become a historical concrete object, which varies in varying complexes, but that there are various psychological copies of it, various mental images taken by different persons or by the same person at different moments.

It is clear that a world of ontologically pure things-substances could be only the object-matter of aesthetic contemplation or intuition, not of scientific logical thought, which has to analyze and synthetize idealized things. But when we introduce into reality any ontological category supplementing that of the thing, this means that we are making a concession in favor of experience at the expense of rational consistency, that we have to deprive the thing-substance of its rational inviolability for the sake of the creation of an empirical science. Though there is no logical reason why anything that may disturb the rational perfection of the real thing-substance should not be put out of the way and transferred into the all-suffering and always ready psychological subject, yet as there could be then no science of empirical reality, some of these disturbances, in a proportion which varies from period to period and from science to science, are left with the objective theoretic order of reality to be accounted for.

And thus, although things similar in some respects in strict logic cannot be taken as being in any sense objectively unified if they are spatially distinct and isolated from each other, still since things absolutely isolated and therefore absolutely unique would give no ground whatever for analysis, we must assume that their partial similarity is an objective link between them in spite of their spatial isolation. The common quality is objectively one in many things, overcomes their plurality, makes it less absolute. Since it exists simultaneously in spatially separated and distinct things, it is extensive, and yet not spatial, for it is not localized and isolated in space. Through it, a minimum of empirical extension is indirectly re-introduced *into* the things, which represents an intermediary stage between abstract spatiality and the full concrete extension.

While the quality of a thing within a particular situation possesses a reality of its own, but only as this particular quality determined from the standpoint of other things within this situation; while the idea of a quality possesses a generality of its own, is one in many objects, but only in so far as idealized, whereas its real basis is always a plurality of particular qualities in particular situations, the quality as ontological category must possess both the reality of the particular quality in a situation and the generality of the idea. It is real because it belongs to real things; it is one in all the things in which it is found because it is not in each case taken as the product of a situation, but as existing by itself. Thus, within the plurality of spatially isolated and limited things there must exist a plurality of general qualities cutting across the static order of things, having each a non-spatial unity and differentiated from others in that special way which we call precisely qualitative distinction. In philosophical rationalization these objective qualities are either mere empirical attributes of substances, if emphasis is laid on the absoluteness of the metaphysical substance, or self-existing metaphysical essences, if substances are treated as no more than empirical things. They are as self-identical in time and as independent of all connections as things. They can be rationally systematized, and their systematic order serves to define things rationally; as we know, ancient and mediaeval science was mainly science of qualities. A thing, to remain self-identical, must possess all the qualities by which it is defined; and therefore any empirical variation of an essential quality which is not a change of the thing is a subjective illusion. And unless the category of the state is also ontologically objectified, a strict rationalism of things and qualities which assumes a purely static order will classify as subjective all those properties which cannot serve to define things permanently, all non-essential qualities which a thing may alternatively possess or not possess while in all other respects remaining the same.

Of course, the introduction of the category of state, though ontologically it represents a new break in the rational perfection of the thing and even of the quality, is again indispensable if we wish to rationalize at least a part of the empirical processes on the ground of the static order of things. Now, the ontological state, like the ontological quality, possesses both the reality of the particular changing property within the situation and the generality of the idea of this property; it is objectively the same real state in all the things in which it may be found. But it does not simultaneously, or rather timelessly, coexist in various things; it may pass from thing to thing, and thus possesses a kind of concrete duration which is not merely the occupation of a certain period of pure time, but implies a becoming in the form of this very passage from thing to thing. In so far as a thing is subjected to certain states before or after other things, duration ceases to be completely external to it; the thing begins internally to participate in the duration of its states; it is becoming itself. Since, however, as a principle, a change of state is not supposed to affect the self-identity of the thing, its participation in concrete becoming is only superficial, is accidental, not essential to it. The passage of states from thing to thing appears as only a half-real becoming, a μὴ ὄν, to use in this connection again the wonderfully expressive Platonic term, something that seems to be and yet rationally should not be. To make it completely real, it must be conceived as a manifestation of objectively real relations between things. A thing cannot acquire a new state by its own essence, but if the appearance of this new state is provoked from the outside by something that tends to disturb this essence, if it is a *reaction* to the *action* of another thing, it is in so far real even though, or rather because, the essence of the thing is not disturbed by it (Herbart). The action in this sense is, of course, itself a state of that other thing, appearing at a given moment of its existence. An empirically given state is ontologically real only if it is a link of a relation, either an action provoking a reaction or a reaction to an action. A modification of the content of an object which can be interpreted neither as determined by nor as determining another modification of the content of some other object is classed as merely subjective.

The ontological relation, real and affecting the thing, is thus a necessary supplement of the ontological state, and it is also indispensable if we want to take in some measure at least into account the modifications to which the content of the object is subjected in various connections. Thus, to the external and formal relations of space and time are added internal and material relations by which a thing is modified in its state under the influence of other things. These active, internal relations do not possess the real unity in plurality which is given by theoretic rationalization to qualities and states. In so far as real, a material relation between two things, manifested in a given action and reaction, is unique and particular, localized in space where the things are, localized in time as the respective states when they come to these particular things. A material relation between things in theoretic rationalization shares thus the uniqueness of the concrete active connection, without, of course, being treated any longer as the product of an act of thought. The very terms of action and reaction preserve the trace of the origin of this category in the actual determination of objects by human acts. But the physical relation is treated as real only in so far as it constitutes a determination of a state of one object by a state of another, just as vice versa a state is treated as real only if it is the link of a physical relation. Therefore the connection which lacks the reciprocity of determination implied in the principle of action and reaction, the actual connection by which only the content of one object is modified, is from the physical standpoint only subjective.

If now all these categories of the static rational order are only used as methodological presuppositions for the solution of specific scientific problems, and their ontological formulation is only a figure of speech meant to express nothing but the permanent form which a certain type of the rationalistic ideal preserves through all the variations of its content, then things, qualities, states, and relations simply supplement one another in the theoretic reconstruction of any particular fragment of reality. If, however, they are meant to express the universal objective order of reality as a whole, each one of them excludes the others and an ontology based on these categories is a set of contradictions.

Thus, we can isolate any single quality or any combination of qualities from the content of an object and treat it as one in many objects for the purposes and within the limits of a certain scientific problem without impairing the reality of these objects, because the concrete object has content enough for many qualitatively determined things and we cannot exhaust it in any theoretic system, however wide and complex the latter may be. But if we think of all the objects as being in themselves once and forever qualitatively determined things and of all the qualities that ever were and will be the ground of scientific analysis as objectively real, then the entire content of each thing will resolve itself into qualities and either isolated things or common qualities will be unreal, as is historically shown by the insoluble opposition of objective idealism and empiricism on this point.

Similarly, as long as we treat within a certain scientific investigation certain determinations of the object as changeless qualities, others as changing states, the changelessness of the former and the changeability of the latter are correlative and limited, qualities are bound to remain changeless and states are bound to change only with regard to each other and within the limits traced by the special problem of this investigation. But if we want all the determinations which ever have or will be treated as qualities to be qualities ontologically, there can be no states left; and if all those which have been or will be treated as states were states ontologically there would be no qualities. Either of these contradictory assumptions contradicts in turn the assumption of the reality of the things. The opposition between things and qualities has been formulated above; that between things and ontological states is equally clear. Suppose we have excluded qualities: then the thing will be analyzed into states, common to many things. The analysis is methodologically unobjectionable if reality is defined as the concrete historical reality, for no theoretic system can exhaust the total duration of a concrete object, and the latter will have always enough permanent existence left outside of the modifications which we have isolated as states. But if objects are rationally determinable things and if all their determinations which can ever be treated as states are states, the thing is completely decomposed into states, just as it was before decomposed into qualities.[1]

Both the ontological quality and the ontological state each separately excludes the other and excludes the thing. But they cannot exist without the thing; they have any significance at all only in so far as limiting the ontological absoluteness of the thing. A world of qualities is as impossible as a world of states. The knot of contradictions is already inextricable; and it becomes still more intricate when we introduce the ontological relation into reality in general. In the opposition between pluralism denying all

---

[1] The objection that even after the abstraction of all qualities or states from the thing something still remains—the manner in which these qualities or states are combined in the thing—is irrelevant, for the manner of their combination is itself, from the standpoint of consistent ontology, a quality (compare the modern German concept of Gestaltqualität) if permanent, a state if changing.

objective realness of relations and monism rejecting all independent realness of things, qualities, and states, and melting them into one great whole of indefinitely complicated relations, the mutual exclusion of the relation and of the other ontological categories is historically manifest. If, indeed, a relation or group of relations is methodologically used to explain certain particular determinations of the concrete object, the object still preserves enough independence to be itself. But if, forgetting the limitation of all such explanations to a particular theoretic problem, we want to claim that all relations which have been or will be found objectively real and used to explain the empirical determinations of rational things, are ontologically real, then no state, no quality, and no thing can preserve its ontological reality. And since relations cannot exist by themselves, we reach an absolutely irrational mystical One, a Being which is identical with Non-Being.

The second type of the naturalistic ideal, that of a dynamic order of causally determined processes, is much simpler in its logical constitution. It implies, of course, a dynamization of things, properties, and relations, the first being conceived as empirical complexes of continuous processes, the second as general continuous processes more or less lasting, found in many complexes at once, the third as relations of functional dependence between elementary processes entering into different empirical complexes. By isolating causally related processes from empirical situations, theoretic rationalism makes causal relations independent of the specific organization imposed upon the situation by a system of schemes, and therefore absolute. Every process, elementary or complex, is thus taken to be a link of a causal series, necessarily determined by some other process, also elementary or complex, and itself in turn determining necessarily another elementary or complex process. There can be neither a beginning nor an end of the series, since the existence of the determination is not conditioned by anything. Space and time are only in so far necessary for the rational system of processes as this system tends to substitute itself for the system of things, and thus takes over such spatial and temporal problems as the latter involves. But by itself, the system of processes does not imply any definite conditions of extension and duration and therefore may be adequately expressed in terms of mathematical functions, substituting, of course, quantitative for qualitative determinations of particular processes and general types of processes. Anything in experience that is not a rationally determinable process, that appears either as a static thing, quality, state, relation, or as a concrete content or meaning, is in advance classed as subjective.

Here again the same distinction must be made as with regard to the application of the categorical order of things to reality. If the dynamic order of processes is used methodologically as a presupposition permitting the theoretic rationalization of any given natural becoming, it is perfectly justifiable, particularly since the static order of things does not permit us to attain the highest level of rationality in treating processes, even when it takes the latter into account as changes of states. It is thus a theoretically indispensable supplement of, often a substitute for, the methodological static order of things in treating special scientific problems. But when conceived ontologically as the ultimate and universal order of reality, it not only contradicts and excludes, by reducing it to subjectivity, the order of things, but also contradicts itself if we apply it to the total becoming of empirical reality in general. For causal explanation presupposes that the special form of the process which we want to explain already exists in experience. In the practical organization of reality it is determined in advance, and what we want to explain is only its appearance at a certain moment of the development of the concrete situation. In scientifically determined reality, in a perfect system of processes, it exists independently of duration and extension, and what we want to understand is only the causal relation between a process of this special form and other processes.

By implying the possibility of an indefinite repetition of a causal relation between processes of a certain type in space and time, the principle of causality implies an absolute existence, independent of space and time, of the *types* of these processes. And, clearly, the appearance of a new type of a process cannot be explained causally, for a new type of a process, like a new content, is an absolute addition to empirical reality, whereas the process as effect is equivalent in its reality to the process-cause, so much so that a branch of empiriocriticism has proposed to substitute the principle of equivalence for the principle of causality. The appearance of a new type in the effect would mean that the cause was not merely a process determining another process, but in some, however slight, measure a creative act. An agglomeration of processes, however long, could produce a new type, a new "essence," however insignificant, a new kind of qualitative change, for example, only if during every process a little reality appeared out of nothing, if in the effect there were a little more than in the cause—an assumption which contradicts the principle of causality.

The historical evolution of reality shows continually the appearance of new types of processes. Materialistic evolutionism itself must admit that the immense majority of the very processes found in the material world and now causally explained have appeared during evolution; most physical and chemical and all biological processes, according to its own doctrine, could not have existed in the original state of the material reality. But even putting materialistic metaphysics concerning the genesis of the pre-cultural world aside, at every moment we find new absolute beginnings of new forms of processes—in industry, in our own organic activities, in social life. Of course, materialistic evolutionism will not stop in its causal explanation when it finds a new form of a process started by conscious beings. It will search in the organism and back again in the inorganic material environment for the causes of the process. But this is ignoring the problem.

The whole point is not that a process of a definite formally ready kind appeared at a certain time and place, but that a type of processes which did not exist before appeared in practical experience. Once we have accepted creative activity as the source of practical situations within which processes are found, the problem is perfectly clear. A new modification is created by a new act, stabilized and objectivated in a repeatable situation, and once objectivated, becomes a content with a definite practical meaning—a new concrete object which, like all objects, grows in reality as part of concrete experience and may even be given and enter into practical systems *as an object*, without being reconstructed again by activity. This development can often be followed almost to its end in the automatization of bodily activities. It may be shortened by creating a process as a real object with the help of instruments, as when a movement, first consciously performed by man, becomes a part of the dynamic organization of a machine.

Now, all this evolution of new processes is incomprehensible on the ground of the ontological principle of causality. For the purpose of a particular scientific investigation, nomothetic science can help itself out by the assumption that a certain specific process which it is investigating is not really new in its essence, but is a combination of simpler processes, each of them old and known in its form. But this assumption has no validity when applied to the world in general. For as long as we deal with one or a few processes and are interested only in reducing these to old and known elementary causal series, we can ignore the fact that, when the process is thus analyzed into a combination of old processes, the novelty of its type is not explained but only changes its logical character, so that instead of a new type of process we have a new form of the combination of processes. But this fact cannot be ignored when we claim to treat in the same way the total becoming of reality.

Suppose that we have succeeded in analyzing all the processes of the world into combinations of a limited number of eternal, or rather untemporal, types of processes. First of all, we shall be forced then to put into the subjective, psychological field all the empirical side of these supposed combinations of processes, all the "appearance" of novelty and simplicity which these assumedly complex combinations of old processes present in experience. For instance, if we want to reduce all processes to combinations of movements, the empirical content of chemical changes, of changes of lights and colors, of sound, smell, and taste, etc., become "subjective." And even then, the ontological problem still remains unsolved and causal evolutionism still contradicts itself; for there remains always to explain the new real foundations which correspond to these new subjective data, the appearance of new forms of combinations of the eternal elementary processes. The formula of the problem is changed, but the problem remains as insoluble as ever.

THE PSYCHOLOGICAL ORDER

The order assumed by the naturalistic variation of the theoretic ideal is not only the oldest and the most firmly established in knowledge, but also its various aspects have been most thoroughly and consistently developed, and the specific tendency of theoretic systematization of reality, the tendency to neglect in so far as can be done the pre-existing practical organization, has here found its most radical expression. In other branches of knowledge, the theoretic ideal is as yet less definite. There are still many problems to solve as to the form of this ideal in each group of sciences, and we hope that the attention of logic and methodology will be turned in the future rather to the elaboration of these other indispensable and practically most important but badly neglected forms of theoretic rationalization of reality than to the continual perfectioning of the naturalistic ideal. But as such a special elaboration is not within the scope of the present sketch, we shall limit ourselves to pointing out a few general questions concerning the presuppositions of each of these non-naturalistic orders and their relations to the naturalistic order and to one another.

The naturalistic order itself implies, as we have seen, the existence of "subjective" representations, images, data of consciousness, or whatever else we may call them; indeed, it can be maintained at all in application to empirical reality only under the condition that everything which does not comply with it is excluded from "material" reality and put among these immaterial psychological phenomena. In this way, a psychological domain is erected outside of the physical domain and grows in wealth with the growing rigorousness and simplicity of the material order, which forces us to treat more and more empirical data as subjective.

It is impossible to put clearly the problem of the theoretic rational order of the psychological domain without having first excluded two most important and in a measure contradictory errors which have been made, and are only too often still made in interpreting psychological reality. First of all, it cannot be sufficiently emphasized that the psychological domain is originally only a theoretically separated part of the empirical reality, a part which is indeed only negatively determined, since it includes everything which is left over from materialistic systematization, but which even in this purely negative original determination does not include all the *empirical world* outside of material nature, but only all reality outside of material nature. It does not therefore include *active thought*, which manifestly cannot belong to any order of reality whatever but possesses an entirely different order of its own, and has neither more nor less connection with physical reality than with psychological reality. Meanwhile, because psychological reality by opposition to physical nature is classed as "subjective," that is, as limited to the sphere of experience of an individual, and because the same individual to whom these "subjective," "psychological" determinations of reality are ascribed is also a source of activity, we find a relatively early identification of the "subject" as sphere and receptacle of psychological, physically unreal experiences, and the "subject" as source of activity. There were, of course, also other factors active in the history of this identification which we cannot follow here; but the identification once achieved, we have the peculiar problem of the subject-object dualism, which in the history of human thought belongs to the same class as the squaring of the circle or *perpetuum mobile*. On the one side there is the physical nature, self-existing and purely real; on the other side the subject, a receptacle of all experiences which are not nature, and a source of all activities.

But here the problem does not stop. On the objective side, together with nature, all other kinds of rational objective reality are put—the state, the system of theoretic ideas, religious trans-material realities, etc.—for each of them, just as material nature, leaves irrational remnants for which realism finds no other place than the subject. And on the side of the subject, since the latter is taken to be a source of activities and activities deal not only with experiences that do not conform with the objective order, but also and in the same line with such as do conform with it, such empirical data as are already included in the objective order become also put into the subjective sphere, together with experiences excluded from the objective order; and the subject becomes thus a receptacle for all experiences. And then an interesting antinomy begins. For, on the one hand, the totality of the objective orders includes the individual subjects themselves whose consciousnesses, connected with their bodies, appear as determined in all their parts by objective reality, and on the other hand the individual subjects include and determine by their consciousnesses the objective reality. Either of these two opposite standpoints can be developed philosophically with equal consistency, but neither can be reduced to the other, and their reconciliation is impossible.

If, indeed, philosophy accepts the affirmation that all objects are dependent on consciousness as included in it, then necessarily consciousness, as condition of everything else, becomes absolute. The world is then dissolved into mere data of consciousness, and the objects and objective orders must be reconstructed from these data and their subjective connections. All depends then, evidently, on the question how we conceive the data of consciousness and their connections. We may completely neglect the specific character of individual consciousness as it appears when opposed in theoretic reflection to the objective world, and simply treat as datum of consciousness everything just as it is given, with all its relatively subjective or relatively objective characteristics. We reach then the philosophy of "immanence." But the whole significance of the subjectivistic view is drawn from the specific character of the subjectively given objects and connections as against the objective world; if the subjective experiences and the objective world together, with all their specific characters, are equally immanent in consciousness, the concept of immanence loses all significance, becomes an empty qualification of all and everything. The theory of universal immanence cannot be overcome by any arguments, not because it is rationally perfect, but because it is rationally meaningless.

Suppose now we want to preserve all the specific characters of subjectivity as individual subjectivity, we evidently cannot deduce the objective world as it is given to the individual along with and opposed to his consciousness, from this very consciousness. We can only deny this objective world and treat it as a mere appearance, as an illusion of the individual subject. This is pure solipsism, which is as invincible rationally as the philosophy of universal immanence, though for different reasons: it simply refuses to accept any premises which would make a discussion possible, since any discussion whatever demands the recognition of some ground transcending individual consciousness.

Much more productive philosophically was the middle way of objective idealism, in which the effort was made to deduce the objective world from consciousness by conceiving consciousness as bearing in itself sufficient foundations of objectivity without ceasing to be the subject, though no longer the individual subject. In this class we find the Fichtean absolute Ego and the Kantian transcendental unity of apperception, the concept of a social consciousness as sum or as resultant of individual consciousnesses, and finally the phenomenalistic doctrine of a world of data from which the principle of consciousness is excluded but which has the same formal character as the succession of data in individual experience viewed in the act of self-reflection, only without the limitation in extension of individual experience.

But in spite of the undoubted importance which this method had in provoking philosophical productivity, it shares the weakness of all half-solutions. Whereas at first glance it seems to unify the opposite viewpoints, on closer investigation it proves to have simply divided the difficulties which separate them and thus made the opposition less conspicuous. As far, indeed, as the super-individual consciousness transcends the individual either by its absolute rationality, as in the Kantian and Fichtean idealism, or by its extension, as in the sociological and phenomenalistic conceptions, the individual must take toward it the same attitude as toward the objective world, and we have the same antinomy as before, only with a more limited application. And on the other hand, in so far as the super-individual consciousness preserves some subjectivity, our reflection about it must conceive it in the same way as it conceives the individual subject, as dependent on the same objective world which we try to deduce from it, but transcending it either by the incalculable richness of its content—in transcendental or absolute idealism —or by the perfection of its form—in theories which try to reduce rational objectivity to social objectivity or logical order to associative order. And the antinomy repeats itself once more.

If, on the contrary, philosophy in developing its systems tries to remain on purely objective ground, then consistently it is the objective world which becomes an Absolute. And the development of problematization becomes almost exactly parallel to that which we see in subjectivism. The pantheistic inclusion of the individual subject with all its characteristics in an absolute objective unity is a perfect counterpart of the doctrine of immanence and leaves, like the latter, the real problem completely untouched. More important historically than (on the subjective side) solipsism, though not less one-sided, is the essential tendency of post-Socratic philosophy to exclude in some way the fact that the character and order of all elements constituting the objective world vary when these elements are given in the individual process of experience, and vary even from individual to individual and from moment to moment. This tendency leads to a division of the entire world into a positive side, representing the objective absolute order, and a negative side, representing a mere disturbance of this order by the individual subject; this negative side is treated then as unworthy or incapable of being investigated, precisely because it is supposed to involve no positive order, all positive order belonging by definition to the objective world. A modern expression of the same tendency is found in radical materialism and its treatment of consciousness as "epiphenomenon," only this doctrine is incomparably narrower than the ancient doctrines were, because in the materialistic conception the objective world itself has been deprived of most of its content.

The deduction of the subject from the object brings with it again the original antinomy, though in a somewhat different form. The subject, being entirely the product of the objective world, is by the very essence a "subject for the object," that is, can and must be only a perfectly adequate subjective counterpart of the objective reality; otherwise we should necessarily come to the conclusion that the objective reality, being experienced by an inadequate subject, is in fact a subjective world. Meanwhile, the subject supposed produced by the objective world is precisely the individual, limited, and imperfect subject, distorting the objective reality in the process of his experience. This was, for example, the paradox of the doctrine of divine creation: God created men to understand and glorify him and to be happy, and men were essentially incapable of understanding him, with the rare exception of a few saints unwilling to glorify him, and mostly condemned to wretchedness. Quite analogous is the paradox of modern evolutionism: individual consciousness has developed exclusively as instrument of adaptation to objective reality, and it is quite unadapted to objective reality, leading all the time human beings, with the rare exception of a few modern scientists, to various absurd notions about reality and to a very irrational behavior. And if we try to avoid the paradox by putting some intermediary link between the individual and the objective world, a rôle which in the doctrine of creation was played by the religious system connecting man with God and in the doctrine of natural evolution by the scientific systems through which the individual can understand the world and adapt himself to it, then our paradox repeats itself twice on a smaller scale, since the individual is not perfectly adapted to the system of religion or science and the system of religion or science is not perfectly adapted to its supernatural or natural object.

Finally, it is evident that, once we have opposed subject and object to each other as ultimate principles of the empirical world, any common principle to which we want to reduce them must both transcend experience, since we treat the process of experience as essentially subjective, and be irrational, since rationality belongs according to our premises essentially to the objective side of the world. We reach thus such conceptions as the "One" of Plotinus, the "Will" of Schopenhauer, the "Life" of Bergson, essences whose cognition demands some mysterious act of ecstasy, direct apprehension, or intuition, in which subject and object become unified, while the real problem is left as it was. For not only can we not understand how subject and object evolve out of this mystical essence, but when they are already there, the old antinomy reappears, since their common trans-empirical and irrational ground does not change anything at all in their reciprocal relations within the given world. The most consistent is the solution of Hegel, who simply accepted both the traditional opposition of subject and object and the necessity of having them reunited, and postulated this reunion as a continuous alternative passage from one to another; but such a solution of the problem is evidently only a formulation of its insolubility.

The conception of the subject as opposed to the objective world can have thus no ontological significance, though it is perfectly justified methodologically. In other words, there are no phenomena essentially belonging to the subjective domain as against others essentially belonging to the objective domain, but when studying any fragment whatever of the concrete world as possessing a certain order we can always make a separation between certain sides of objects or thoughts, which from the standpoint of this order are treated as objective, existing or subsisting in accordance with the given order, whereas other sides of the same concrete objects of thoughts may be qualified as subjective relatively to the first and from the same standpoint.

There may be therefore as many different ways of separating empirical phenomena into subjective and objective as there are possible theoretic orders of the objective world; the psychological subject which we obtain by excluding from real objects and connections everything which does not fit into the physical order, is only one of these methodological conceptions and has nothing in common with any conception that might be formed on the ground of a theory of thought by excluding from the domain of objective thought all acts which do not fit into a certain logical order. And if instead of starting with the physical order of reality we assumed, for instance, the social order of reality as fundamental, our conception of the subject would be also that of a subject of experience, not of a subject of thoughts, but it would be entirely different from the one which has historically developed. This historical development was almost entirely due to the fact that human knowledge started with material nature and reached the highest degree of perfection in studying material nature, so that the psychological domain, originally defined by opposition to the physical order, has remained fundamentally the domain of personal experiences as opposed to natural reality; the one special conception of the methodological subject which has been formed from the naturalistic standpoint has absorbed, so to speak, all other possible conceptions of a subject of experiences, though not perhaps those of a subject of thoughts.

Of course, the psychological domain as long as only negatively determined by opposition to the natural world has neither definite limits, since it is simply all reality that is not physical, nor a definite form, since it is simply defined as not possessing the physical form. But the theoretic ideal of perfect rationality of the world compels us to give an internal limitation and a rational form to this remnant of the physical reality, which is in fact much wider and richer than the physical reality itself, and that is what we do in psychological theory.

It is precisely in psychological theory, in the attempts to introduce scientifically a rational order into the psychological domain as a special domain of reality, that we meet the second fundamental error concerning the character of this domain. This error consists in applying to psychological phenomena principles created in constructing the order of material nature, and in trying to incorporate the totality of these phenomena into that very nature from which they have been excluded, so as to attain a monistic view of reality. As we have seen, the only justification of the assumption that there is a duality of psychological "representations," "perceptions," "remembrances," "associations," etc., on the one hand and material nature on the other hand is precisely the impossibility of including the whole concrete empirical reality in the physical order, the necessity of cutting off a part of it; the psychological phenomena are not excluded because they are distinct by their essence from the rest, but they are treated as distinct by their essence because they are excluded from the physical order. Being a receptacle of all that seems irrational from the standpoint of the naturalistic principles, the psychological field evidently cannot be rationalized with the help of these very principles. This is so clear that even the most radical naturalism never tried to apply its rationalistic presuppositions to psychological phenomena taken directly as individual experiences. But it failed and still fails to notice the contradiction when it goes at this problem indirectly, by substituting for each psychological phenomenon something to which formally one of the categories used with reference to the material world could be applied; and it does not see that in this case either the irrationality seemingly removed from each psychological phenomenon in particular will continue to exist in the connection between these phenomena, or if these connections become rationalized, the system of reality thus obtained does not correspond any longer to the psychological domain, but to something entirely different. This is precisely what happens when psychology, instead of taking as object-matter the psychological phenomenon itself, the "subjective datum," that is, that which is given to the individual, that object or connection which the individual experiences but which cannot be incorporated into the natural order, begins to study the *fact of the appearance* of this datum in individual consciousness. It substitutes then for a certain experience as the individual himself perceives it, the occurrence of a certain experiencing as the theorist who observes this individual reconstructs it.

This occurrence, this "psychological fact," is then categorized either as a state or as a process. The difference between these two categories, which at first seems to be, as in the material world, only a difference between a static and a dynamic view of the psychological reality, has here still other logical consequences. For a state is essentially the state of something and therefore the use of this category implies the assumption of a psychological consciousness which, even if it is not defined as a "soul," as a substance of which those states are the modi, even if it is supposed entirely exhausted in its reality by its states and existing only in them, is nevertheless a basis of unity of all its states, is at least a common field, an empty receptacle for all of them. On the ground of this concept, all the facts of experiencing which the observer finds "in" the given individual belong together as states of this individual's consciousness, and only this consciousness as a whole belongs to the objective world. But the consciousness as a whole is evidently an absolutely irrational chaos, since it is merely a projection of the total individual sphere of experience and reflection upon the screen of naturalistic categories, without even that order which the individual at least partially constructs within his sphere; for this order as realized by the individual within the empirical chaos of his experience appears indeed as existing and objectively real to the experiencing and acting individual himself, who knows nature only from his experience and reflection and for whom there is no other objectivity than the one he produces or reproduces, but it does not exist from the standpoint of the psychologist who observes this individual's experiencing and for whom this individual's reflection is not an objectively valid activity constructing or reconstructing an objective rational order, but merely a plurality of psychological states. The irrationality remains, of course, exactly the same if instead of states of consciousness we interpret facts of experiencing as states of the individual organism.

The concept of the psychological process can, indeed, escape this difficulty, for the process is a self-sufficient ontological category and does not have to be made dependent on the existence of a common entity—a soul or consciousness. But here another and in a sense an opposite difficulty presents itself. For if conscious processes as processes of experience do not belong together as mere modifications of one consciousness or one body, they must belong together on some other ground. Otherwise there would be no reason and no possibility for a science of the psychological reality as distinct from the rest of reality. A process of experiencing would have a significance only in connection with the experienced object; the introduction of this concept would correspond not to a distinction between "objective" and "subjective" phenomena, but merely to the fact that, besides the individual's having certain phenomena given to him, somebody else (or this individual himself when retrospectively reflecting about it) is aware, as social observer, of these phenomena being given to this individual, and is aware of it as of an occurrence happening in connection with some other occurrences within that part of empirical reality which is given to him, the observer. In order to give these processes the significance of elements of a specific psychological reality, it is indispensable that one conceive them both as interconnected and as at the same time distinct from other processes.

But this is clearly impossible. For the only way in which they can be interconnected is by being referred to, dynamically centralized around, the same individual. Such a centralization of real processes implies that the individual must be a real object to which processes converge from other objects and from which they emanate to other objects. He cannot be a consciousness, for then these processes would become states of consciousness; he can be only a body. But what processes can there be centralized as psychological around the body? Evidently not the processes going on in the material environment of the body, since these are already classed as natural processes. Can they be the organic processes? The naturalistic schools which first tried to reduce psychological phenomena to processes of organic adaptation accepted this idea. But the organic processes are not what we mean when we think of the processes of experiencing. On the contrary, when the facts of experiencing are conceived as states of consciousness, the psychologist takes into account the organic processes of biological adaptation as going on alongside states of consciousness and always accompanying them; this is the well-known psycho-physiological parallelism. Unless then the processes of experiencing are kept as "epiphenomena," which means simply a recognition of their irrationality and a denial of any real or ideal connection between them and the material natural order, they have simply disappeared as a consequence of the attempt to rationalize them, without leaving anything instead as object-matter. And besides, if we should interpret experiencing as a biological adaptation between the individual organism and his environment, it is quite illogical to conceive it as a process. There are no processes going on between the organism and the environment; there are only *relations* between organic processes and processes going on in the environment. The organism from the standpoint of the dynamic natural order is a set of continuous processes; a phenomenon of biological adaptation is the causal determination of an organic process by an extra-organic process or vice versa. A certain science is, of course, free to study such relations between organic and extra-organic processes instead of studying psychological phenomena, that is, experiences as given to the experiencing individual. But such a science is not psychology; it is a part of biology. The behavioristic school does good work in studying organic behavior instead of conscious data; but this does not mean that it reduces psychology to a study of behavior, but that it has left the field of psychology to other schools and gone over into the biological field.[1]

The exclusion of certain phenomena as psychological from the domain of material nature was, as we have seen, due to the implicit assumption of the naturalistic method that reality is constituted by objects and connections uniformly determined in accordance with the same perfect rational order and that therefore we can study them while ignoring the variety of actively constructed situations in which they become determined. It is consequently evident that, if we meet phenomena which do not fit into the natural order, it is either because these phenomena are not rationally determined at all, or because their rational determination differs from that

[1] The concept of psychological process may be applied, as we have seen in the preceding chapter, to non-material links of a *practical* causal series, because in practice there is no definite separation between the physical and the psychological order; but this separation once made necessary by the development of physical science, all processes from the theoretic standpoint must be classed as physical. Therefore the elementary causal fact in nomothetic psychology is never reducible to a functional dependence between processes, but must be stated in terms of dependence of the appearance of an attitude *in toto* upon another attitude and a social value (see p. 280).

which is assumed as common to all objects or connections of the naturalistic type and requires therefore the reconstruction of the situation for its adequate understanding. The conception that any phenomena are not rationally determined at all is opposed to the rationalistic ideal of every science; therefore a science which wants to study those phenomena which naturalism rejects must decide for the second part of the alternative and consider these phenomena as fully apt to be theoretically rationalized under the condition of having the situations to which they belong theoretically reconstructed. Such a science will then put upon situations the same claim of perfect rationality which naturalistic science puts upon objects, ignoring again that most of the situations are rationally imperfect and that those which approach perfection owe this to the organizing schematic activity.

In fact, every particular psychological problem which we state, not in terms of states or processes but in terms of individual experiences, is a problem of situations instead of being a problem of objects. What we ask ourselves when we investigate individual experience, not as integral part of the natural world but as divergent from the natural world, specifically personal, belonging to the actual sphere of this particular individual, is not "What is this reality?" but "How does this individual at this moment experience this reality and why does he experience it as he does?" This implies the well-known empirical statement that a certain reality can be experienced differently at different moments and by different individuals. But we cannot accept for scientific purposes the whole enormous complexity of the concrete, non-rationalized empirical world, which would force us to admit first that there is not a single individual experience identical to another and that the explanation of the individual's actually experiencing a certain reality in a certain way must be sought in the total sphere of this individual's experience, past and present. If we want to rationalize personal experiences theoretically, we must search first for some objective similarities between some of these experiences at least, which would permit us to generalize them in some measure, to ignore their variations within certain objectively determinable limits, and yet to take enough of these variations into account to justify the distinction between the uniformly determined natural reality and its personal aspects. We must have, secondly, more or less rational and objectively determinable, limited sections of personal experience to which we could refer particular experiences of an individual and thus explain the particular aspects which a certain reality assumes for this individual at this particular moment without being forced to take his entire concrete personality into consideration.

The situation—which may not be perfectly in harmony with the demands of the natural order, but which nevertheless is in some degree rational—gives us both a ground for the generalization and a ground for the explanation of personal experiences. A reality is supposed to assume similar aspects in similar situations, and if it has a certain aspect for the given individual at the given moment, it is because it is determined for his actual experience by some actual situation of which it is a part. Therefore whenever similar situations are found, we expect similar experiences of given reality, and, on the contrary, in different situations we expect different aspects of this reality to appear. Vice versa, whenever we find similar experiences of a reality, we assume the existence of similar situations, whereas different experiences of the same reality point to the existence of different situations. The objective natural reality—thing, property, relation, process—viewed from the psychological standpoint, does not bear in its self-identity a sufficient or even a necessary condition of being always and by everybody experienced in the same way; nor is an objective difference of natural realities sufficient to guarantee a general and permanent difference of their representations. To make the first experienced in a similar way and the second in a different way, we must have them included in similar situations; in the contrary case the self-identity of the first may result in a non-identity of representations, and the very difference of the second may lead to an identity of their aspects.

To heighten the rationality of its order, psychology implicitly or explicitly assumes that in a certain measure similar situations and similar experiences are perfectly identical, and in repeated laboratory experiments tries to approach this identity as far as empirically possible by artificially and systematically isolating a certain situation from concrete experience, and at the same time varies situations in definite ways so as to obtain a more exact definition of the corresponding variations of experiences. Wherever it cannot create identical and stable situations experimentally, it constructs them by abstraction, implicitly ignoring or explicitly excluding such personal variations as can have no scientific significance at the given stage of psychological systematization. It constructs thus analytically, as a theory of psychological elements, classes of experiences corresponding to definite realities and reconstructs out of these elements synthetically, as a theory of psychological complexes, classes of situations which by their specific forms are supposed to determine the ways in which certain groups of realities are experienced. Of course all this work is no longer a reconstruction of the original practical situations, but of situations qualified as psychological by the assumption of an existing natural reality to which all experiences are supposed to refer.

But besides this static order of psychology there is a dynamic psychological order possible, leading, just as does the dynamic order of nature, to a determination of causal laws. In the dynamic order of nature the original elements are modifications of objects as against the static natural order of which the original elements are the objects themselves.

A parallel difference can be found between the static and the dynamic orders in psychology. The former bears upon the data of individual experience as distinct from natural things; its original materials, the concrete object-matter upon which it draws, are contents of objects. The static order ignores the meaning as such; if it has to take into account the difference between the natural relation of a thing to other things and the connection which the individual establishes between this thing as object of his experience and other objects, it either treats this connection as a relation which the thing acquires in the personal situation in which it is given, or if this cannot be done, it turns the meaning into a content and treats it as an aspect of the thing in personal experience. The first happens, for instance, when we distinguish the order of "apperception" of objects in personal experience from their natural order; the second, when we treat the emotional meaning which objects acquire by their connection with a whole personal organization of life as an emotional content attached to these objects by the individual.

The psychological experience as such when statically rationalized can have no meaning, for it is inclosed and already determined within a situation. But without meaning there can be no dynamic order of personal experience, for only in so far as an object has a meaning for the individual can it have an active influence upon other objects of his experience. A psychological datum does not lead to any modifications of other data. And it is impossible that natural reality should influence psychological becoming; physical objects cannot be the causes of psychological effects, since they are objective standards with which psychological experiences do or do not comply, depending on personal situations. A physical object could influence dynamically psychological objects only if, by becoming itself a psychological object, it brought a meaning with it into the psychological domain; but physical objects have no meanings. In order therefore to have a rational order of psychological becoming, we must have somewhere objects which are at the same time determined rationally by situations—for only then they can be psychologically rational data—and are nevertheless dynamic concrete historical objects with meanings.

Now, such objects can be only *social*. The social object is determined as element of situations, but of many situations constructed and reconstructed again and again in the experience of many individuals; in so far as determined within each situation, it is a thing; in so far as varying in fact from individual to individual and still the same, it is a historical object and the fact of its actually being connected all the time with various other objects gives it a meaning; it opens possibilities and suggestions of acts which neither the psychological datum nor the natural things can do. We shall return to this question. The fact is that objects can have meanings for *psychologically* conceived individuals, can suggest changes of psychological phenomena as such only if they are social; only the social reality which, though objectively determined, is still dynamic, can exercise an influence upon psychological reality. A dynamic psychology, searching for laws of psychological becoming, must be a social psychology.

The psychological problem is here no longer started by the divergence of content between individual experience and the objectively fixed material nature, but by the divergence between the meaning which an object has in the experience of one individual and that which it possesses for other individuals. Of course, the implicit or explicit assumption is that the object has for the individual the meaning it has, because the individual connects it with certain other objects and determines it with reference to them as an element of a definite situation. Therefore the difference or similarity of the influence which it has upon the personal experience of various members of the group depends upon the difference or similarity of the situations into which they introduce it, which they accept as the ground of its determination. Individual acceptance or non-acceptance of a certain situation with its consequences as to the determination of objects is psychologically not to be explained, for it would demand a complete reconstruction of individual past; we simply find the situation accepted, and this is a fundamental psychological fact. From the standpoint of this acceptance, the fact of having a certain meaning given to an object, a meaning conditioned by the situation into which the object is being introduced, becomes itself a psychological occurrence, a personal *attitude* taken toward this object.

The attitude toward the object, being dependent upon the constructed and accepted situation, a modification of the situation by the introduction of some new object or group of objects will change the attitude and produce a new attitude instead. Assuming now classes of identically defined situations common to a given social group and socially common objects, social values determined by these situations, we can always say what objects have to be brought to (or excluded from) a given situation as accepted by the individual in order to produce another definite situation; we can say what social values have to be used to influence the individual at the time in order to change a given attitude into another definite attitude. On the ground of the general tendency of the rationalistic ideal which consists in searching in the given field of reality for the order which we find in the most perfect instances of systematic organization, we shall presuppose, as a methodological principle, that all attitudes are conditioned by perfect situations and every situation belongs to a socially uniform and once and forever determinable class, so that the appearance of every attitude can be explained on the ground of some pre-existing attitude by the influence of some social value (or group of social values) which have changed the old into the new situation. Thus, we have the formal basis for laws of psychological becoming whose general formula is not, as in natural causality, constituted by two elements, a process determined in its appearance by another process, but of three members, an attitude determined in its appearance by a pre-existing attitude and a social value.[1]

On the ground of these laws, the psychological evolution of an individual or of a race may be reconstructed as a dynamic synthesis of situations taken in the course of their construction, though, of course, psychological laws, just as physical laws, can account only for the appearance in a certain sphere of psychological reality of attitudes and social values which have already existed in experience, not for the creation of new ones, which have to be treated as mere accidental results of combinations of the old or as approximate repetitions of the old. Psychology cannot reconstruct the concrete development of psychological experience in general any more than natural science can explain the concrete development of natural reality in general.

And psychology, which must presuppose for the purposes of its theoretic systematization a perfect uniformity of analogous situations from moment to moment and from individual to individual, must also ignore, as we have seen, cases in which the order which it presupposes does not exist. It must be therefore supplemented by some other science, just as it has itself supplemented the sciences of material nature. Its own partial success in rationalizing phenomena which natural science could not rationalize has proved due to the fact that it took objects within the situations in which they are determined and which the physical order ignores. Since all order of objects is due to situations, psychology can go

[1] Cf. William I. Thomas and Florian Znaniecki, *The Polish Peasant in Europe and America*, Vol. I. Methodological Note. I am resuming here and trying to put on the general ground of a philosophical theory of reality a methodological conception of social psychology and sociology which Professor Thomas and I have developed together, in the work quoted above, for positive scientific purposes.

back to the practical origin of the natural order in individual experience and explain thus why in certain cases individual experience harmonizes with the scientifically postulated order of natural things or processes, whereas in other cases it does not. Though from the naturalistic standpoint explanation seems needed only in cases of disagreement between individual experience and the natural order, yet this explanation would be impossible except on a ground which permits us to explain also cases of agreement. In the same way, if we want to supplement psychology in cases which it cannot handle because they lack the required order, we must have a standpoint which would permit us also to understand the origin of cases which it does handle because they do present the expected order. But no science of reality can understand the absolute origin of any rational order from a complete or partial empirical chaos, since every science of reality must presuppose the order which it postulates ready and existing in its most perfect form. Only a theory of activity can explain the gradual genesis of any type of order from concrete historical reality. On the ground of the sciences of reality, to explain the origin of an order can only mean to explain the rational organization of the systems in which this order is manifested as a result of their determination by some wider and more comprehensive system of which they are a part.

This shows that it would be a fundamental error to try to supplement rational psychology with its implicit or explicit postulates of a certain perfect order by some more vague and more subtle kind of psychological investigation which would reject all presuppositions of perfect uniformity of psychological data, attitudes, and situations, and try to describe as exactly as possible individual phenomena in their original variety. Such a descriptive psychology, provided it did not, as frequently happens in such circumstances, introduce unconsciously postulates as far-reaching as those on which psychological generalizations are now based, could be only either literature or a mere preparation of materials, which scientific psychology would then use according to its own methodological presuppositions.

THE SOCIOLOGICAL ORDER

The only way in which problems left aside by psychology can be made the object-matter of another science is by taking into account the dependence of situations on schemes. All uniformity of situations being the product of their schematic determination, the empirical existence or non-existence of that regularity of individual experiences and attitudes which psychology must postulate can be rationally explained instead of being simply accepted as given only if we interpret each particular case as a result of the empirical realization of schemes. Of course, in order to make our explanation rational for cases in which the required order is not present, we must make use of the supposition that different schemes when simultaneously realized in a certain section of experience interfere with each other. This supposition is parallel to that of physical science which assumes that, when certain causal series are simultaneously developing in a certain section of experience, they interfere with each other and none of the respective causal laws are directly manifested in experience. The difference between the applications of the principle of interference to reality when treated as natural and self-determined, and to reality when taken as consciously human and determined actively by practical schemes, consists in the fact that a natural law when interfered with by another law is supposed to be fully realized nevertheless, but in combination with the interfering law, whereas if two schemes interfere with each other, this means that neither of them is actually realized except in so far as the interfering one permits. However, in spite of this difference, the principle of interference permits us to assume that all individual situations are perfectly determined by schemes, though in particular cases a situation may be subjected to the common determination of several schemes and thus present an accidental mixture of incomplete organizations, each of which would conform perfectly with the schematic type if it could be completed and were not stopped on the way by the interference of the others.

Since psychology has already put situations on the ground of particularized personal experience as opposed to the general natural world instead of taking them as they originally are, that is, within the concrete empirical world of historical reality, this new rational order of schemes by which the psychological order of situations must be supplemented becomes defined theoretically with reference and in opposition to particularized personal experience, and it is not a direct reconstruction of practical schemes as superimposed upon the historical becoming of the total of concrete experience. In other terms, this new extra-psychological reality is as relative to the psychological reality as the latter is to physical reality. It is the specific reality which is common to psychologically differentiated and isolated individuals—common not because composed of self-existing trans-psychological things or processes, but because determined by super-individual schemes. In a word, it is the *social* reality.[1]

It seems hardly necessary to develop here at great length the arguments showing the necessary independence of the

[1] Since the present volume deals only with the problem of reality, it is evident that in discussing the methodological presuppositions of psychological and social sciences we have in mind only those among the studies now included in the bibliography of these sciences which treat their object-matter from the realistic standpoint, as psychical or social reality. In fact, however, many investigations classed as psychological and sociological are based on idealistic, not on realistic, presuppositions, and their actual object-matter is activity. These, as we shall try to show in detail in another volume, belong into the domain of philosophy of culture, which thus covers the field of traditional philosophy, a large part of what is now called sociology, and much of the object-matter now dealt with in psychological monographs.

social order from both the psychological and the physical orders. The very fact that there are schemes in empirical life guarantees a specific object-matter to social theory in so far as the latter is the only science of reality which does deal with practical schemes determining practical situations uniformly for various individuals and at various moments. And it is clear that a science which reconstructs reality as a rational order of schemes cannot be identified with or subordinated to a science which reconstructs it as a rational order of situations or of things.

Furthermore, since a social order, super-individual and yet working within individually diversified and psychologically isolated spheres of personal experience, must be admitted, precisely so as to allow us to understand phenomena for which personal experience in its psychological limitation offers no sufficient ground of explanation, it is self-contradictory to reduce the social to the psychological and vice versa. We can indeed abstractly conceive society as a synthesis of psychological individuals just as we can conceive the psychological individual as synthesis of social schemes—laws, customs, mores, religious, intellectual and aesthetic beliefs, economic institutions, technical traditions, etc. But in either case we lose from sight the very condition without which neither particular psychological nor particular social phenomena can be the object-matter of science: the existence of both a specifically social and a specifically psychological order. By conceiving society as a synthesis of psychological individuals we preclude the possibility of a rational solution of all particular problems which can be solved only with the help of common social schemes acting in and through individuals and yet existing independently of each of them. By conceiving the individual as synthesis of social schemes, we preclude the possibility of the solution of all those problems in which the continuity of personal life or the uniformity of experiences in all conscious individuals independent of the social groups to which they belong are the necessary pre-suppositions.

Finally, it is perfectly clear that we cannot divide or classify empirical phenomena into such as are by their onto-logical essence psychological and such as are essentially ontologically social, since every phenomenon can be treated from either of the two standpoints. In general the problem of the relation between the psychological and the social, if put on the ground of an absolute ontological distinction between these two domains, is as insoluble as the problem of the ontological relation between the natural reality as the "object" and the psychological "subject," and leads to similar contradictions. But as a methodological distinction of two different rational orders, with no limits of application traced a priori, but each used whenever in a particular case it helps better than the other to attain the rationalistic ideal of science, the separation of the psychological and the social is as indispensable as that of the physical and of the psychological.

In this field, however, the battle has been fought and won by the very progress of positive sociological investigations. More dangerous seems to be the position of the sociological method when it meets the traditional self-assertion of naturalism. Indeed, when viewed from the standpoint of the psychologically isolated personality, the social seems to share with the natural its super-individual, trans-psychological character. Thence the easy temptation to reduce it to the natural by assuming that whatever in the individual's psychology transcends the limits of personal experience or individually developed behavior has its source either in the biological continuity of the race or in the natural environment, and that the super-individual social order is thus reducible to the co-operation of common racial features and geographical influences.

If we omit here the metaphysical problem of inherited active tendencies, which belongs in the philosophy of activity, and limit ourselves to the empirical aspect of the question as concerning the order of social reality, the error of these naturalistic claims is perfectly evident. The objectivity of biological or geographical phenomena is an objectivity of things and processes; the objectivity of social phenomena is an objectivity of rules. The former, that is, the individual's own organism and its natural environment, are supra-personal as given materials and instruments of personal activity which he can use efficiently for his aims only by taking into account their pre-existing real characters. The latter, social institutions of all kinds, are supra-personal because they impose a definite form upon personal activity and compel the individual to choose definite aims and to select definite materials and instruments for their realization.

Therefore there is and can be no correspondence whatever between the biological or geographical order or their combination on the one hand and the social order on the other. The same race in the same geographic conditions develops the most heterogeneous forms of social organization at different periods of its historical existence; different races in different or in similar geographic environments show both similar and different institutions without any regularity whatever. Of course, the question of the nature of the materials and instruments given to activity may and usually does condition the selection of those schemes from among the given ones which permit the group to organize activity most efficiently for the accepted purposes and under the given conditions, and such relatively most efficient schemes are apt to be perpetuated and developed; but the character of the social schemes from among which the selection is made is no more determined by natural conditions than is the artistic style of a painting determined by its object-matter. And even independently of those self-evident philosophical considerations, from the standpoint of a purely empirical scientific method a sociology which, on the ground of a few approximate parallelisms between certain natural conditions and certain social forms, speaks of the natural, that is causal, determination of social organization by biological or geographical factors, leaving aside all the "exceptions," which are incomparably more numerous than these facts which seem to corroborate the supposition and are entirely inexplicable on the naturalistic basis—such a sociology has certainly not gone beyond the stage of the "philosophy of history" of the eighteenth century.

But on the other hand, the more recent attempts to deduce the natural from the social order as one of the "oldest social traditions" (expression of Le Roy) are also unjustified. For, although the foundation of the natural order is laid by situations which reach their rationally perfect form only when determined by schemes, yet these situations themselves could not constitute a natural order without the generalizing abstracting activity of theoretic thought. Furthermore, even in the practical organization of reality, perfect situations and permanent empirical systems of perfect situations, such as the natural order of reality presupposes as its empirical basis, can be attained only if the schemes themselves are systematized by practical dogmas, whereas the social order as such does not imply any more comprehensive organization than the scheme. Finally, the most important argument against this sociological standpoint is that the social order itself is not a primary order of reality, but is a theoretic superstructure raised upon an imperfect and fragmentary type of practical organization, and a superstructure which could have no separate existence in its typical form except in so far as supplementary and opposed to the psychological order which, as we know, is not primary either. The practical schemes by which situations are determined assume a specifically *social* character only by contrast with the specifically *personal* psychological situations. Originally situations are not personal and schemes are not social; concrete objects and connections of the historical reality and practical systems

of reality may be either limited to the spheres of experience
and reflection of one individual, or extending to all the individuals of a group, or even covering the common domain of
experience and reflection of many different social groups between which there is no social bond whatever. The distinctions between social and psychological, psychological and
physical, are distinctions between correlative orders within
the same empirical real world, each independent of the
other though all together dependent, first on the concrete
historical reality, secondly on practical activity which organizes and rationalizes it in part, and thirdly on theoretic
thought which pushes this rationalization as far toward
unity as it can go.

Of course, in numerous particular cases it may be possible
to show how a certain systematic organization of physical
reality has grown up within the experience of a social group
under the influence of a socially recognized scheme which has
been determining for many centuries individual practice and
individual theory. Such special sociological investigations,
up to the present pursued only occasionally and almost
limited to the French sociological school, should certainly
become more frequent, not only for theoretic, but also for
practical social purposes, for they contribute much toward
strengthening the faith in the power of social culture and
toward undermining naturalistic fetishism. But the possibility of such sociological studies does not prove the social
origin of the natural order as such, any more than the demonstration of the fact that the presence or absence of certain
natural materials has contributed to the growth or decay
of certain social institutions proves that the social order has
its source in the natural order.

The rational character of the social order has been as
yet only imperfectly determined by sociological investigations
and methodological studies, precisely because of the continual
extension to their field of either psychological or naturalistic

views. We can therefore only outline those presuppositions which are logically indispensable for the constitution of a social science as supplementary and distinct from other branches of knowledge. The fundamental presupposition 'is, as we have seen, that social reality is formally constituted by schemes, by social rules, formulated or not, giving uniform and permanent definitions of personal situations. But these social rules as opposed to psychological experiences and attitudes are no longer conceived as concrete dynamic tendencies, as they originally are from the practical standpoint, but as static practical principles imposed upon the individual. Their active, dynamic character, by which they actually determine in each particular case the reconstruction of the schematic situation with the help of auxiliary situations, has been separated here from their formal, static, generally standardizing character, because the actual reconstruction of the schematic situation is now a psychological, personal matter, whereas the general standard which this reconstruction must follow is social, supra-personal. When the social rule is reflectively objectivated and formulated in words, or when a set of rules connected in any institution becomes attached to a common social symbol, the rule or the institution acquires for the individual who takes an attitude toward it the character of a specific social value superadded to its original character of a scheme.

Social values constitute the matter of social reality of which the schemes are the form. They are a specific product of the social order, intermediary between the concrete empirical objects composing historical reality and the things of natural reality. The scheme, by determining socially personal situations, determines also, of course, the objects included in these situations in a way which is formally general and stable and in so far similar to the determination of things; the social object is thus clearly distinguished from the concrete historical object which lacks one general and stable determination, but has many particular and changing determinations. But at the same time this determination, as social and opposed to the psychological variety of personal experiences, appears as a standard imposed upon individual experiencing of this object rather than as an absolutely real form inherent in the object itself; and a standard may be complied with or not. We cannot therefore exclude from the object as socially determined, as part of the general theoretically rationalized social reality, the variations of individual experiences which disagree with its social determination in the way we do with some particular variations in constructing particular practical situations and with all disagreeing variations in constructing the theoretic order of physical reality. These variations belong in some measure to the social object, not indeed as integral components of its content and meaning, as they do in concrete historical experience, but as psychological influences which affect the efficiency of its social determination, make the latter appear more or less valid individually; the social requirement that the object be commonly and permanently defined in a certain manner may be more or less realized in fact. And thus, if such divergent variations increase, the social determination of the object may be judged as no longer in conformity with the way in which the object commonly and actually appears to individual members of the group, and the object may receive a new determination. By this possibility of having its general and stable determination changed to another, equally general and stable but different, the social object is most clearly distinguished from the physical thing whose determination is supposed purely objective and unaffected by a change of personal experiences. Therefore, if we are forced to change the determination of a physical thing, we characterize this change as a discovery of the real nature of the thing and by opposition to this real nature qualify the preceding, rejected determination as a merely social product.

The second fundamental theoretic presupposition about social reality is that, since the influence of social rules upon psychologically isolated individuals is logically possible only under the assumption of social communication between them, a social rule extends only as far as the necessary social communication reaches, that is, mostly over social groups limited in extension and duration. Here again the rule, theoretically qualified as social, distinguished itself from the original practical scheme as realizing itself in concrete historical reality. Since in the latter individual spheres of experience and reflection are not isolated from each other and since social communication, as we have seen in a former chapter, is not the condition of the community of experiences but, on the contrary, is conditioned by it, a practical organization of reality can pass from individual to individual without any need of conscious social influence and a scheme has originally no limits of application. Furthermore, since the social values are such in so far as determined by schemes, their extension and duration, unlike the extension and duration of concrete historical objects, become equally limited to a certain social group.

Social reality is thus divided into sections, each section formed by the social rules and values common to a certain intercommunicated social group. While these sections are, of course, not entirely isolated, certain rules and values can be communicated from one group to another, still their isolation is sufficiently marked to have social theory accept, for each such section, the principle of spatial localization elaborated by the naturalistic view of the world. The principle is not applied to the relations of rules and values existing within the domain of experience of one social group; these rules and values are socially extensive because coexisting in the experience of many members of the group, but in so far as they are social, not physical objects, they are not spatially isolated nor limited with reference to one another. But spatiality is presupposed for the relations between groups; each group with its total civilization becomes geographically localized. This idea of a geographic separation of civilization shows more clearly than anything else the relativity of the social order to the physical as well as the psychological order; while in historical reality geographic spatiality is conditioned by the concrete extension of the empirical world and the "geographical environment" exists *within* historical experience as a part of the world of cultural objects, from the special sociological standpoint concrete extension becomes included in the pure rational space and divided into sections with reference to the external, formal extension of the world of natural things.

The totality of social schemes and social values coexisting in a section of social reality limited to one group, embraces a great variety of cultural phenomena—political, economic, religious, moral, intellectual, aesthetic, hedonistic—and does not constitute in any sense one rational system, and the evolution of all these schemes and values does not manifest any one fundamental law. The rational theoretic order of social reality relies therefore as much on idealizing abstraction and generalization as that of psychological or physical reality. Out of the concrete complexity of the social life of a group single elements have to be theoretically isolated and a new systematic organization constructed from them.

Here again we find the possibility of two different orders, a static and a dynamic one. The distinction has become popular since Spencer expressed it, but the rather inadequate formulation which this philosopher gave to it prevented its importance from being sufficiently realized, so that in many sociological works we find it entirely obliterated. And yet there are two entirely different sets of problems implied in it—as different as the problems of the nature of things and those of the functional dependence of processes in the physical domain. On the one hand, we may study the objective

nature of social schemes in the effect which each of them separately tends to have upon individual experience and behavior;
that is, we investigate the perfect type of situation as it is
defined socially by the scheme and as, in accordance with
our presupposition of a perfect social rationality, it would
always be realized in individual life if it were never interfered
with by the influence of other schemes.　In doing this, we
should not, of course, limit ourselves to a given formulation of
a scheme as it may be offered by the legal code, by religious
or aesthetic canons, by current moral sayings, by theoretic
judgments expressed in spoken, written, or printed words,
by economic contracts, etc.; but we should try to reconstruct
comparatively, by a study of cases which can be considered
approximately typical, what would be the actual working of
the scheme if it did work perfectly.　Thus isolated from its
social context, the scheme may present such far-reaching
analogies with certain schemes found in other social groups
that the formation of a class becomes possible.　Furthermore,
schemes which differ in detail as to the particular nature of
those objects and connections which they demand for the
construction of their situations may still be similar with regard
to the more general character of their material and to the
broader outlines of the organization which they impose;
thus, we can subordinate particular classes of schemes to
general classes and reach a static classificatory systematization
of social phenomena, of which every section of social science
and every general system of sociology offer examples.　If we
want then synthetically to reconstruct, with the help of this
static analytic system, any particular concrete fragment of
social organization, we have only to find what schemes are
actually working there and how their coexistence affects
each of them, how they supplement or interfere with each
other.　By studying comparatively the influence of various
schemes upon each other, we reach a definition of various social complexes which can with more or less approximation be

reduced to a relatively limited number of fundamental types. Every concrete social personality, every concrete institution, every artificially or half-artificially isolated fragment of a wider social group (a territorial unit like a village, a town, a city ward; a family group; a professional organization; a social class, etc.) is such a social complex of various working schemes, approximately reconstructible and reducible to types.

As against the problem of this static reconstruction, the problem of a dynamic order, of a rationally determinable evolution of social schemes, must appeal to completely different principles. Social reality by itself, in so far as it is perfectly social, its schemes general and stable, and its values determined by schemes, does not include any factors of evolution. To say that the cause of a social fact must be sought in another social fact, if by fact we mean, as the school of Durkheim does, the social rule in its active determination of individual experience and behavior, is as self-contradictory as would be a principle according to which the cause of a substance should be sought in another substance. A change of social schemes in a group can occur only if the old scheme has ceased to correspond actually to the prevalent experience and behavior of individual members and the new scheme has begun to correspond to them instead. This passage from the old to the new implies a period when neither the old nor the new is perfectly social, when individual experience and behavior with regard to the given values are very imperfectly determined socially, because they are determined by two different rules at once. This period of individualization is a necessary stage of every social becoming. The factor which works during this period, which makes the old scheme lose its determining power and the new scheme acquire determining power, cannot be defined in terms of social, but in terms of psychological reality. It is the *attitude* of the individuals who accept the situations imposed by the new scheme and reject the definition of the old scheme that brings the change. From the sociological standpoint the attitude alone cannot produce a new social rule directly from personal situations; the question of the absolute origin of the social order from non-socialized experience and reflection cannot be solved by sociology as a science of reality which presupposes an already existing social order. What individual attitudes as such can do is only to substitute within the limits of the given group one social rule for another, to modify a pre-existing social definition of personal situations so as to make it conform better with the actually experienced and constructed personal situations. The appearance of a new social scheme in a group can be explained therefore only on the ground of the combination of two antecedents: a pre-existing social scheme and an individual attitude. We have here a condition which is parallel with that found in psychological explanation; there also the appearance of a new individual attitude required two antecedents, a pre-existing attitude and a social value. Thus, while the static psychological and the static social orders are entirely distinct from each other and can be treated separately, the corresponding dynamic orders encroach upon each other; causal explanations of the psychological demand the use of social elements and vice versa.

The laws of social becoming following the general formula scheme-attitude-scheme (or, if we objectivate the scheme as a specifically sociological value, value-attitude-value) will certainly present various degrees of generality, just as do causal natural laws. These varying degrees will permit us to organize them into an abstract system. With their help, any concrete social becoming may be conceived as the result of a combination of several laws, and types of such combinations may be approximately distinguished. But this is still a question of the future, and the same point must be emphasized here which we have already raised when speaking of the natural and the psychological dynamic orders. A theoretic reconstruction of social becoming based upon the concept of laws evidently cannot pretend to explain the appearance of absolutely new forms of social schemes, since the law as such is always a law of repetition. It can only explain how a scheme, already pre-existing in concrete experience, became socialized, realized, and applied in a certain group at a certain epoch, but not how it appeared in the empirical world in general as a result of a new and spontaneous schematic determination of situations which were not schematized before.

THE IDEAL ORDER OF REALITY

The social order, static or dynamic, cannot cover entirely its field of reality any more than the natural and the psychological orders can exhaust their fields. There is always some irrationality left over, manifested in the impossibility of reconstructing theoretically any given static section of social reality, any given social becoming, otherwise than approximately. No concrete fragment of the social world can be synthetically reconstructed in its completeness out of schemes or laws of change—neither the total civilization of a nation, nor the cultural life of a class or of a locally isolated community within the nation, nor the concrete reality of an empirical institution with all the manifold interests of its agents and its public crossing one another in the most various and unaccountable ways, nor even the relatively limited sphere of cultural existence of a social personality. And even in so far as our synthetic reconstruction goes, we are unable to account fully either for the coexistence within the given concrete section of social reality of such schemes as we find working together or for the co-operation within this given concrete part of social becoming of such laws as we find developing together. We can construct abstractly perfect classificatory systems of hierarchically ordered schemes; we can hope to reach some day perfect abstract systems of hierarchically ordered laws; but when we have to extend our abstract, rational order to the concrete, social world, we find that it applies perfectly only to artificially isolated, and therefore also more or less abstract, combinations of schemes or causal series, whereas, as soon as we want to reconcile concreteness and rationality, the best and only methodical device which we can apply is the concept of the *type*, which has neither a perfect rationality, for there is no reason fully accounting for the fact that a particular type contains certain particular rational elements in a certain specific empirical combination, nor a perfect concreteness, for every concrete fragment of social reality only approximately realizes the type.

Sociology by itself is unable to overcome these difficulties, for its scientific task is to supplement psychology in rationalizing personal experience and behavior as personal and its very existence is bound to the concept of inter-personal or super-personal reality superimposed upon and therefore relative to the division between concrete psychological individuals. Therefore, in separating for sociological synthesis fragments of social reality from the whole to which they belong, we must keep on the ground of psychological personalities and follow the lines traced by their psychological isolation and social interaction; we can, in other words, separate sociologically, for theoretic reconstruction, a section of social culture from the rest, only together with the men who participate in it, who are controlled by it psychologically or are modifying it, and it is the fact of this fragment's being the social reality of certain men which permits us to treat it as a distinct fragment. Therefore back of every sociological concrete object-matter, however limited it may be, there is always the whole complexity of human personalities; however much this complexity may be reduced on account of the exclusion of the natural world from it and because of psychological rationalization, it is still irrational enough to prevent any part of reality into which it is introduced from ever being exhausted by any theoretical order.

A full and rational scientific synthesis of a concrete fragment of social culture would be possible only if this fragment
itself were already empirically, practically rationalized; if
it included only objects perfectly determined by situations,
situations perfectly determined by schemes, those schemes
themselves in a limited, rationally exhaustible number and
variety, and all belonging together not by the mere fact of
their empirical coexistence but by a common rational determination with regard to one another. Now, these conditions
are approximately found in a dogmatically organized system
of schemes. The political organization of a state, a system
of religion, a style of art as developed in particular works,
the system of ideas constituting the ready body of a science
as taught in schools, the economic organization of a trust,
the technical division of labor and co-operation in a branch
of industry, are examples of fragments of culture whose complexity can be assumed theoretically exhaustible and whose
systematization is approximately rational. And the social
order, even within the limits which it is rational, presupposes
implicitly a dogmatic stabilization and imposition of schemes
upon social life; otherwise there would be no ground for the
assumption that any scheme will continue to work within
a given section of social reality until causally supplanted by
a different one.

In so far as we succeed in subdividing a sphere of social
civilization into such rational fragments, the difficulties
connected with the synthetic reconstruction of sections of
social reality are evidently removed. But we are no longer
in the domain of sociology. The reality with which we deal
is no longer social in the exact sense of the term, for in the very
measure in which we want such systems of schemes to be
rationally perfect, we must abstractly exclude the concrete
complexities of psychological individuals as their empirical
foundation and limit the manifoldness of social schemes by
which these psychologically separated complexities are united

and determined socially. Our object-matter is no longer the group or the personality as typical combination of various social schemes. Men count exclusively as bearers of the given system, as underlying foundation upon which the system becomes realized in extension and duration. From the standpoint of a perfect state organization, a human group is not a concrete historical nation with multiform half-chaotically combined spheres of cultural interests, but exclusively a body of political beings, subjects, or citizens, determined only with regard to their rôle as governed or governing, as participating in the realization and maintenance of the state system. From the standpoint of a religious system, men are not a concrete gathering of individuals whose lives are determined not only by religious, but also by hedonistic, aesthetic, intellectual, economic, political, and similar schemes; they are an organized church, a body of purely religious beings whose only significance is to make the religious system a historical reality. From the standpoint of a ready system of art or science, they are not a scattered plurality of complicated and various personal types, but united and relatively homogeneous spheres of artists plus the public, of masters plus students, defined exclusively in view of their task of realizing and perpetuating the historical existence of the given art of science. From the standpoint of an economic system of schemes, they are *homines oeconomici*, the abstract human entities whose experiences and attitudes are exclusively determined by this system of schemes so that the latter can be realized; from that of a technical system, they are exclusively technical workers, planning minds, or executing hands, etc.

Of course, when we ask ourselves how a given system of schemes can be realized psychologically or sociologically, or what is its psychological or its sociological significance, we have to reintroduce the psychological individual or social type; but then the system itself is no longer a perfect rational order of definite schemes, but a disconnected set of psychological experiences or social values, to be rationally recon-structed by psychological or sociological methods. It is hardly necessary to mention that a psychological reconstruc-tion cannot by any means follow the rational organization of such a system of schemes, but breaks the latter up into an indefinite plurality of personal subjective data or attitudes. These data are classified alongside other experiences of each psychological individual who in his own way perceives or conceives the system—experiences which have nothing to do with this system as objectively closed and rationally organized —and these attitudes are dynamically connected with other attitudes which belong to entirely different domains. But it is worth emphasizing, in view of the growing tendency to ignore this super-sociological or extra-sociological order for the benefit of sociology, that a sociological reconstruction of a political, religious, economic, aesthetic, system is as impossible as a psychological one.

The conditions of scientific development in the field of social culture have been different from those in other fields. Whereas the scientific recognition of the psychological order followed that of the physical order and the realization of a sociological order came later still—an evolution which, as we see, corresponds to the logical connection between these three types of the rationalistic ideal—the recognition and scientific treatment of dogmatically determined systems of schemes of the kind illustrated by our examples preceded often by many centuries any methodical attempts of a sociological treatment of the respective domains. Thus, the theory of the state was already highly developed in Greece, whereas consciously socio-logical studies of political schemes hardly go back farther than Spencer's *Political Institutions;* a historical theory of scientific systems begins with Aristotle, if not with Plato, whereas a sys-tematic sociological treatment of intellectual schemes has been started just recently; economic systems are methodically studied by English economic science of the eighteenth century, whereas a sociological study of economic schemes is scarcely more than thirty years old; and so on. The reason of this will become clear when we realize—a point which will be treated presently—that the rational organization of these systems from the theoretic standpoint appears as an order of reality which, while supplementing and continuing other orders, differs from them, in that reality by its own pre-existing nature does not contribute anything to its formation; this order is an immediate and full manifestation, in the field of reality, of the logical organization of active thought. The systematic order which logical thought, by virtue of its own organization alone, tends to produce in reality and which it always would produce if not forced to comply in some measure for its own purposes with the re-existing real conditions, began to be abstractly studied long before the study of those real orders in which the pre-existing concrete reality cannot be neglected had reached the problem of the sociological order. For it is always the first impluse of theoretic reflection, in its efforts to reach the ideal of perfect rationality, to ignore the limitations which reality by its concreteness imposes upon rationalizing thought. It is not strange therefore that idealistic theories of the state, of science, of religion, of economics, etc., have been evolved before sociology started to treat these domains as subjected to its own order. Under the influence of the empirical current predominating in intellectual life during the past half of a century, the consciousness that the sociological order could be extended to fields in which up to then an ideal order was assumed and that this extension yielded unexpected and interesting discoveries, resulted in the widespread belief that there was a new and better method to be substituted for the old within political science, economic science, theory of knowledge, theory of art, etc.; whereas this extension meant that concrete empirical phenomena which were already the object-matter of these older sciences could be made also, when differently defined and taken in a different connection, the object-matter of a new science, sociology, without ceasing to be treated as realizing an ideal, non-sociological order.

The difference between the two orders becomes immediately clear when we begin to analyze sociologically the composition or the becoming of any one of these cultural systems of objects. For, if we isolate the various schemes which constitute a given political, religious, economic, or other system and study each of them separately with regard to the definition which it gives to personal situations, we shall find a great variety between the schemes in one system, which makes it evident that it is not any particular similarity which brought them together. Thus, a political system may include not only many dissimilar schemes of legislation, jurisdiction, and execution, often incorporated from completely different political groups, but also schemes of economic organization (governmental business enterprises), of intellectual and moral education (school control and press censorship), of religious institutions (state religion), etc., which cannot be classed as political by themselves but assume a political form only in so far as and because incorporated into the state system. Similarly, a religious system may not only contain religious beliefs and rites of the most heterogeneous character, but also include schemes by which it tends to control morality, art, science, politics, economics, etc., and which have a religious sanction only because subordinated to a religious dogma, as schemes whose permanent realization is claimed as necessary for the maintenance of the whole religious system in historical reality. In short, when we construct a classificatory order of schemes as we do in social statics, this order will cut across all the existing dogmatic systems of schemes, will put into one class schemes belonging to different systems and into different classes schemes belonging to the same system. From this standpoint the coexistence of certain schemes rather than others in a given political, religious, economic, dogmatic system will seem as equally "accidental," equally matter-of-fact, as the coexistence of certain schemes in the sphere of social culture of an individual or a group. The static sociological order cannot account for the rational connection of schemes in a dogmatic system; and the dynamic sociological order, on the other hand, cannot account for the exclusion of schemes which make at each moment of its existence the dogmatic system rationally exhaustible. For, from the standpoint of social causality, each of the schemes included in a political, religious, economic system appears as dynamically connected with schemes which are completely outside of political, religious, economic life, as influencing them and influenced by them, so that a causal explanation of the social origin or disappearance of any of these systems or an adequate account of all the social consequences of its existence, its development, or its decay would require practically a dynamic synthesis of the entire social life of the group within which it is realized.

The rational theoretic order based on the existence of dogmatic systems of schemes must be therefore entirely different from that which sociology postulates. Its nature will be best understood if we remember, first, that the dogmatic system manifests a tendency of active thought to subordinate reality completely to ideal demands, to control it independently of pre-existing real conditions. Secondly, we know that the dogmatic system is the highest type of practical organization of reality and, unless it is a part of another dogmatic system, is never practically conditioned by any other real organization. Therefore, while the physical object draws its determination from the situation, while the psychological situation is stable and uniform as a result of the scheme, while the continuity and generality of self-identical schemes in social life presupposes that these schemes are determined by dogmas, the determination of the dogma is purely ideal; whatever rational perfection it possesses is directly derived from the logical systematization of the activity which constructs it and not from any superior systematization of reality. For these two reasons we call the theoretic order based upon dogmatic systems the *ideal* order of reality.

The ideal ground of this order manifests itself in the methodological presuppositions made by the sciences which construct it. A scientific study of dogmatic systems must, of course, postulate a perfect rationality of its object-matter, like every branch of knowledge which tends to realize the rationalistic theoretic ideal. And since it is evident that no dogmatic systems found in empirical reality are ever absolutely perfect, any more than other types of practical organization, a science which studies these systems must first of all idealize them, reconstruct them analytically as if they were perfect. Now, in view of the fact that their organization tends to be entirely independent of pre-existing reality, and approaches perfection in the very measure in which it succeeds in controlling reality completely, in subordinating it unconditionally to the demands of thought, a perfect dogmatic system would be one constructed by thought absolutely freely on the ground of an accepted dogma, without any regard to the given real conditions. Therefore a science which postulates an absolute rationality of the order based on dogmatic systems must assume that the rational organization of every system which it meets in experience possesses and manifests a perfect *rational essence*, follows with an ideal necessity from the dogma which it is based upon quite independent of the empirical conditions in which it is realized. Given, therefore, a certain practical dogma and a certain field of reality to control, the theorist can construct a priori a perfect system of schemes for the control of this reality and assume that, if these schemes were fully realized, the given field of reality would be fully controlled in accordance with the demands of the dogma. Of course, these schemes may as a matter of fact never be realized practically, because active thought may be unable so to organize as to overcome the obstacles which the reality to be controlled puts in the way of their realization; but this empirical lack of realization does not impair the intrinsic perfection of the rational essence of the system as constructed by the theorist.

Given a certain constitution and a reality—a social group—to be politically controlled, the political scientist can construct theoretically a perfect state system in which every scheme is rationally founded upon the constitution and which thus represents the rational essence of a state possessing such a constitution. The problem of the actual realization of each scheme in particular and of the system as a whole is completely different and has nothing to do with this problem of rational essence; on the ground of the latter the political scientist can say only that if, by whatever concrete empirical organization of human activities, all the schemes rationally demanded by the constitution are ever realized, the social group will be completely controlled in its political life in accordance with the constitution. Similarly, given a certain scientific or philosophical principle and a domain of empirically founded knowledge to be controlled by theoretic systematization, the theorist of knowledge can construct a rationally perfect scientific or philosophical system of concepts which will represent the rational essence of a theory based upon this principle. It will then be a completely different problem whether such a system of concepts is realizable in fact, whether in view of the already realized and fixed body of knowledge it is practically possible to give old ideas such interpretations or to produce by observation such new ideas as will give to the system the empirical foundation which it requires. But suppose this is done, the given domain of knowledge will be completely controlled from the standpoint of the given principle. In another field again, on the ground of the dogmas accepted by the classical or by the materialistic schools of economy and of an economic reality to be controlled by these dogmas, economists build rationally perfect systems of schemes which, if neither of them expresses the rational essence of economic life in general, correspond at least essentially to some empirical dogmatic systems among all those which can be found in the concrete complexity of economic organization. Again from the purely rational standpoint it does not matter whether the classical or the materialistic or any other economic system will ever be completely and adequately realized in the empirical world; this depends on the question whether our activity will be able to realize all the conditions necessary for the continuous actualization of the schemes demanded by the dogma.

The political scientist, the economist, the theorist of art, of religion, even the theorist of knowledge usually claims that in constructing a perfectly rational system he follows empirical data and does not act a priori. This claim is, of course, in some measure justified. First, the scientist usually does not attempt to construct rational essences or political, economic, aesthetic, theoretic, moral, religious systems which are not at least partially realized in the empirical world, and thus he limits the field of his theory to the historically given practical organizations; though this limitation is not general and the theorist, under the influence of practical considerations, often intentionally transgresses past and present empirical reality and builds non-existing systems in the expectation that these will be realized in the future, still this is not considered a properly scientific activity. Furthermore, in order to construct the rational essence of any system, the scientist must be acquainted with the practical activities to which the organization of empirical systems of this type is due and with the reality upon which these activities bear. He cannot construct a political system, a moral system, a religious system, an aesthetic system, by theoretic reflection alone, for the rational organization which theoretic reflection creates in reality is not the same as the rational organizations which political, moral, religious, aesthetic activities create. He must practically realize what political, moral, religious, aesthetic activities are; that is, he must be able to reproduce these activities mentally, though not instrumentally. It is precisely because, and only because, these activities can be reproduced, or produced, mentally that he can substitute for his scientific purposes a rationally perfect dogmatic practical system for those rationally imperfect ones which are instrumentally realized in the historical world. The actual subject-matter of his science is not the empirically given and fully real system which has been or is being constructed by others with the help of instrumental activities, but a model system of the same type which he practically constructs himself with the help of activities of the same class, only mental. Mentally performed political, economic, moral, aesthetic activities do not meet such obstacles in the pre-existing reality as instrumental activities do, and therefore a mentally constructed dogmatic system of schemes can be at once rationally perfect and can serve as material for the theoretic determination of the rational essence of systems of this type. Such a mentally constructed practical system corresponds, in sciences of ideally ordered reality, to the experiment in physical science; it is an artificially created model of perfect rationality.

When a political scientist determines the rational essence of an absolute monarchy or of a democratic republic, he performs a double activity: first, he performs practically, though only mentally, all the activities which a political sovereign would have to reproduce instrumentally in organizing a state in accordance with a certain constitution; secondly, as a theorist, he reconstructs this mental organization scientifically, using this time all the materials and instruments necessary to produce a fully objective and rational system of ideas. The problem of the empirical bearing of a science of the ideal order is not how a dogmatic organization existing in the empirical world can be theoretically reconstructed in general; we know that it can be in so far as its schemes are practically limited in their number and complexity; but the question is, "How can all the existing practical organizations of a certain class be theoretically systematized?" And this depends on the question of how far such political, economic, aesthetic, or religious systems, serving as basis for the theoretic reconstruction of rational essences, actually correspond to the instrumentally realized political, economic, aesthetic, or religious systems. Since every science tries to reconcile rationality with concreteness, to reach a theoretic systematization as perfect as the reality upon which it bears permits, and to keep as closely in touch with empirical reality as its rationalistic ideal allows, the normal tendency of political science, of economics, of theory of art, of theory of religion, will be on the one hand to construct such model systems as would correspond each to as many as possible empirical organizations; and on the other hand to take as far as possible into consideration and to explain rationally the deviations which each of these empirical organizations present as compared with the model system which is assumed to express their rational essence.

The first tendency leads to a hierarchical classification of rational essences with regard to the generality of their empirical application: for example, the rational essence formulated in the concept "state" has a wider field of application than those expressed by the terms "absolute monarchy," "constitutional monarchy," "republic." The general scientific concepts reached in this domain are those which serve as ground for separating the sciences of cultural systems from one another. Thus, at the basis of the separation between the political and economic sciences lies the assumption that there is a common rational essence of all political systems and a different common rational essence of all economic systems. Neither of these rational essences can be reduced to the other, and thus all efforts to reduce the political to the economic, like the one which historical materialism has tried, are rooted in a misunderstanding. Of course, in the concrete social life of a group we can find innumerable relations of partial dependence between particular political and particular economic schemes, and vice versa; but the study of these relations is the task of sociology, not of political or economic science, and involves, as we have already seen, an isolation of the schemes thus connected by social causality from the several different systems in which they are connected with other schemes by a rational determination for the fulfilment of the demands of the respective dogmas. Since the fundamental difference between the sciences of the ideal order of reality and sociology is that the object-matter of the former is the dogmatic organization of schemes which the latter ignores, by treating schemes of rationally different systems as causally dependent on one another and thus dissolving the systems we simply substitute sociology for political or economic science.

With regard to the deviations of empirical systems from their rational essence, sciences of the ideal order began first by assuming generally that, since all rationality of these systems comes from the logical order of thought, all break of rational order comes from the irrational empirical reality and therefore cannot be rationally explained. This is the stand taken by ancient science. But modern science in its effort to reconcile concreteness with rationality can no longer be satisfied with such a summary solution. The latter is, moreover, in disaccordance with the very principle of the ideal order which is not supposed to be dependent on real conditions. In the very measure in which we assume that active thought is able completely to control reality, we cannot admit that the latter puts in the way of dogmatically determined systems obstacles which active thought is *entirely* unable to overcome. From the standpoint of the ideal order, the imperfect realization of a rational essence in an empirical system of schemes must be taken to be the result of an incomplete formal organization of the activities whose task it is to realize this essence within the given sphere of reality, not as the result of insuperable material hindrances. However, the sciences of the ideal order cannot study the absolute origin of this order in creative activity; just like all other sciences, they must assume the order on which their investigation bears as existing and ready before it becomes the object-matter of theoretic reflection, even if it should be only mentally realized by the scientist himself, for the existence of this order is the very foundation of theoretic rationalization. An attempt to explain by the nature of active thought why the latter succeeded or did not succeed in organizing a system perfectly would lead to the whole problem of the logical order of activities, which is beyond the reach of any science of reality. And since there is no higher organization of reality by which its dogmatic organization is determined and explicable, the sciences dealing with dogmatic systems cannot be supplemented by any other sciences of reality and have thus to rely exclusively on the ideal order itself to explain the imperfections of this very order.

This means that of the two principles with the help of which theoretic reflection tries to reconcile concreteness with rationality, the principle of approximation and that of interference, the sciences of the ideal order have to reject entirely the first and give to the second a form and development which it does not possess in any other branch of knowledge. These sciences cannot admit that the rational essence of a dogmatic system may be realized only approximately or that for any reasons such a system may fail in attaining perfect rationality; but they must assume that any number of dogmatic systems of a similar or different type may coexist, each perfectly developed, in a given section of the cultural world. And thus, if in the political organization of a group we do not find

some of the schemes realized which the constitution demands,
if a system of science or philosophy which we are studying
seems to lack some of the concepts required for the full
theoretic application of its fundamental principles, if an
empirical economic system does not show in practice all the
schemes necessary for the realization of the dogma, we must
assume nevertheless that these schemes do exist and that if we
do not find them in observation, it is because they have not
reached the same degree of realness as those which we do
observe. We must implicitly suppose that the political
schemes which, though required by the constitution, are not
manifestly realized in the group, nevertheless already exist
within the total sphere of civilization of this group. We
must implicitly assume that the concepts which, though
demanded by the principles of a philosophic or scientific
system, are not formulated in words, nevertheless already
exist in the domain of knowledge; that the economic
schemes rationally necessary for the perfection of an economic
organization are already there in economic life, though we
cannot find them. Such assumptions are implied in the very
fact of treating an empirical system as identical with the
ideal system theoretically reconstructed by the scientist,
though they do not involve, of course, any positive supposition as to where and when the schemes whose existence
we postulate have been realized. Sometimes, indeed, such
an implicit assumption becomes the starting-point of a research, and we often find in fact that the political schemes
which at first glance seem to be lacking really exist in the
political practice of the group or of some of its members,
though they are not formulated; that the concepts which
are not expressed in the works of the scientist or the philosopher have been in fact constructed by him, though not made
public; that an apparently incomplete business organization
already includes a plan for more complete development.
In other cases, the theoretic reconstruction of a system as

rationally perfect becomes the starting-point of a practical activity which will realize in the empirical system the schemes that seem to be lacking and will thus make it express fully its rational essence; the study of the political organization of a country gives the initiative for new laws, and the critical analysis of a scientific system starts new observations. But from the purely formal rational standpoint such questions have a secondary importance: for the rational perfection of the system it does not matter by whom and under what conditions its schemes have been brought into existence nor how much reality they possess, provided they exist already— and they certainly do exist at least mentally at the moment when the theorist begins to investigate them.

On the other hand, if in a given domain of cultural reality we find together with schemes necessary for a dogmatic system other schemes which do not belong to it rationally, we must assume that there is another system existing in this domain with more or less realness, and that these superfluous schemes are a part of it. This is a very frequent case. In every social group we find several different political, economic, religious systems existing together, and our task is then to separate them and to reconstruct each in its rational perfection. We have consciously attempted to do it elsewhere;[1] more or less clear illustrations of this method can be found in many historical monographs.

Following these two postulates in which the principle of interference expresses itself in the sciences of the ideal order—the postulate that in each empirical system its total rational essence exists, though not always with the same degree of realness, and the postulate that each scheme which does not belong to a given system must belong to another—every science of the ideal order can approach a complete theoretic exhaustion and systematization of its field. These sciences

[1] W. I. Thomas and Florian Znaniecki, *The Polish Peasant*, Vol. I, Introduction, particularly studies on religion and on economic life.

are the only ones which find in their way no empirical real concreteness necessary and yet essentially impossible to overcome, since their object-matter is originally as much rationalized as practical reality can be, and their method, by ignoring the degree of realness which their order possesses, leaves to them only such irrationality to deal with as comes not from the pre-existing real chaos, but from the imperfect organization of activity.

But it is evident that there can be only a static, not a dynamic, ideal order of reality, since the ultimate factor of all evolution here is active thought, and therefore no order of reality, however highly idealized, can explain it. There is no possible *scientific* theory of the evolution of political organization, of morality, of economics, of knowledge, of religion, of art, of technique. Science can follow the succession of different systems in history; it can dissolve these systems and explain sociologically the origin of each scheme composing them; but a dogmatic system in the intrinsic essence of its organization is for science a rationally analyzable but genetically inexplicable datum, whose source lies beyond the reach of science, in creative activity.

THE PROBLEM OF THE UNITY OF KNOWLEDGE

The rationalistic ideal of knowledge, when applied to reality in so far as already in some measure practically organized, finds, as we see, a double limitation. First, none of the general presuppositions by which philosophy tries to determine once and forever the essential character of objects and their connections, by qualifying them as physical, or psychological, or sociological, or elements of ideal systems, are anything more than methodological assumptions, objectively justified by being approximately realized within certain practical systems and apt to be theoretically postulated beyond these systems, but unable to become ontological truths about reality in general. This means that there can be no systematic philosophical theory of reality as of a rational whole—beyond, of course, a mere study of the forms which reality acquires as object-matter of practice and of knowledge, like the study we have attempted here. Even the possibility of our present study, as we shall see in another work, is ultimately due to the fact that all forms of reality, even though entirely different from the forms of active thought, are directly or indirectly derived from them. All that can be done by theoretic reflection about reality is to reconstruct rationally, on the ground of certain methodological presuppositions, fragment after fragment of the empirical world, thus approaching indefinitely to the ideal limit of its complete theoretic exhaustion. And even if this limit were ever attained, still there would be no place for a philosophical ontology based on the general nature of reality besides the sciences based on the particular empirical phenomena. For, when gradually reconstructing reality scientifically on the assumption of a certain formal order, we unify indeed disconnected fragments into one rational system and thus generalize this order; but the unity of the system is directly and in itself a unity of knowledge, not of reality, and becomes a unity of reality only as a dynamic connection superimposed upon the disconnected practical world when the ideas constituting the theoretic system are actualized as thoughts in application to reality.

A rational order, by being generalized by science, does not become one inherent order of reality absolutely imposing itself upon our thought; it exists only as a set of innumerable particular suggestions offered by objects, beside other suggestions, as a plurality of specific meaning which in each particular case thought is free to follow or not, and which it regularly follows only when logically determined by the system of knowledge which has created those meanings, when applying again in actuality this system to its original object-matter. Therefore the methodological presuppositions with the help of which we construct our theoretic system never can become ontological truths bearing upon the entire reality covered by this system; they remain methodological forever, they serve to "rediscover" rational determinations of empirical reality every time the ready system is actualized by being applied to experience, just as they served to "discover" them when the system was first constructed. The specifically "theoretic" suggestions which the objects offer —their suggestions to be taken in accordance with their scientific determination—may grow more and more powerful with every application of the system; but the theoretic order is always actually being extended only to particular objects or groups of objects and for particular purposes, never actually applied to all objects at once, in general and absolutely, independently of specific theoretic or practical problems.

This first limitation of the theoretic ideal should not be taken in the Kantian sense. It is not merely the Kantian world of things-in-themselves, but also the very world which Kant qualified as phenomenal and which philosophy was supposed to master in the very essence of its order, which is in fact inaccessible to philosophical reconstruction—for the "forms a priori" which theoretic reason imposes upon it are not in fact necessary forms of our "phenomenal" reality, are not transcendental conditions with which experience must conform. What makes precisely all attempts of philosophy to construct an absolute theory of empirical reality hopeless is that any forms of reality which it may find assumed in scientific research are *partly* objectively realized before science and *partly* not, and that science by postulating their perfect realization imposes nothing upon reality absolutely and unconditionally, but only gives to itself the task of trying step by step to superimpose upon the imperfect real order a more perfect one. These forms are not in any sense the necessary conditions of experience, or even of organized experience, for concrete experience lacks them and practically organized experience never perfectly realizes them. If they are *now* the universally used methodical assumptions of *our* science, it is because our science in its historical development has not only accepted the general ideal of rationality, but also the specific tendency to advance toward this ideal by the way of extending and perfecting in its own systems the pre-existing practical organization of reality, instead of taking some other, logically equally possible way. Perhaps an adequate history of science would even show that it has often tried in the past to branch off into different lines. Now it is so stabilized in its fundamental tendencies that for a long time there is scarcely any possibility of its changing its methodological ground; and if it changed this, it would no longer be science in the historically accepted sense of the term.

But the very fact that the forms which science uses as its methodological presuppositions are neither the necessary forms of experience nor those of knowledge, and are only imperfectly realized in practice, gives a significance to the future progress of science which it could not possess under the Kantian conception. For, if historically developing science were only getting from reality the order which non-historical absolute reason had for all time put into reality, what would be the objective importance of such work? Whereas by actually superadding to the imperfect rationality of reality a growingly perfect one, science performs a creative function which has an objective significance even apart from its practical applications, by introducing something new into the world.

But even the ideal limits toward which scientific progress tends lack, as we have seen in the preceding sections, that absolute perfection of rationality which philosophy used to require by believing in *one* theoretic system of reality. Not only is it true that reality cannot be exhausted in one theoretic system *now*, but it never will be, even if all its fragments and aspects ever should become completely rationalized theoretically in particular scientific researches. For the results of scientific activity, by the very nature of the methodological assumptions which determine the ways of stating and solving scientific problems, can under no condition be unified into one system of knowledge. We have followed the division of scientific fields as it has actually developed in history and we have found that, when science takes as fundamental the physical order of reality, that is, an order based exclusively on the perfect practical form of objects and connections but ignoring the practical organizations within which they receive this form, it must add to this order three other entirely incommensurable, though supplementary, orders, built with entirely different methodological presuppositions, so that reality presents four different rational aspects based upon the fundamental forms of different stages of practical organization: the thing, the situation, the scheme, the dogma.

Suppose now that, by some radical modification of the entire body of our scientific knowledge, science should ever accept as fundamental not the physical order of things, but the ideal order of dogmatic systems corresponding to the highest stage of practical organization; suppose that the sciences of cultural instead of those of natural reality should constitute the rational basis of our theoretic reflection. Since the dogmatic system contains all the subordinate stages of practical organization—schemes, situations, and things— there would then be no reason for supplementing this order by the social, psychological, and physical orders; for all the social schemes, personal situations, physical things, and processes would find place and rationalization within the scope of an order of dogmatic systems, if the latter were not reduced, as they must be now, to an ideal order ignoring pre-existing concrete reality, but were studied in all the details of their practical development in the historical world. A full knowledge of cultural reality would be a rational knowledge of entire reality as practically determined, and yet, even then, scientific unity would not be attainable. For on the ground of cultural reality we have several entirely different types of rational practical systems, such as theoretic, aesthetic, moral, religious, political, economic, technical; and supposing even that each of these types should be theoretically reduced to a perfect rational unity, the scientific systems constructed on the basis of these different types would still remain entirely separated and different from one another. And since each of these systems, if fully developed, would extend over the entire reality—for it is clear that the entire reality could be viewed from the theoretic, the aesthetic, the moral, the religious, the technical standpoint—we would have still as many different incommensurable and disconnected theoretic aspects of reality as there are theoretically irreducible types of cultural systems of schemes.

Thus, the concept of a theoretic rationality of the entire real world, even if taken as an ideal of knowledge, must reconcile itself with a pluralistic interpretation of science; it can mean only that if the ultimate limit of scientific development were ever attained, every fragment or aspect of reality would be scientifically determined by *some* rational system of ideas built from the standpoint of *some* rational order. The concept of a *realistic rational monism*, of *one* theoretic system embracing all empirical reality, is not even an ideal: it is a chimera.

There is, however, one imaginable objection against this pluralistic conclusion, on a ground which has already been used to maintain the possibility of reconstructing concrete reality, at least in its most important features, by one science. Does not the limitation of each of the scientific orders outlined above come from the very fact that none of them deals directly with the original concrete world of historical objects, but with one-sidedly and narrowly determined, isolated fragments of this world—practically organized systems? And is there not one prominent branch of knowledge whose object-matter is the total historical reality in its primary empirical concreteness? Is not therefore *historical* knowledge, in the widest sense of the term, the one and the only knowledge which can reconstruct theoretically the whole reality without any distinction of abstract and incommensurable orders? The problem is very interesting indeed, and we regret not to be able to give it here the whole attention it deserves, but to be obliged to limit ourselves to a few general remarks.

First of all, there can be a question here only of a history of reality; the problem of a history of activity does not bear directly upon the theoretic reconstruction of reality as a whole. Most of what is called history is history of reality, cultural and natural. Now, it is clear that the history of reality does not work upon the presupposition of any general historical rational order, distinct from the special physical, psychological, sociological, and ideal orders. The only presupposition which distinguishes it from each and all of these special sciences is that in concrete historical extension and duration some or all of these orders are interconnected and melted in a general creative becoming, in a continuous development of the new which cannot be explained on the ground of any definite rational order and can be only approximately reached from case to case, as an imperfectly accountable synthesis of several orders. Even natural history, already limited by the naturalistic viewpoint to one abstract side of historical becoming, cannot work within its limits on the assumption of one historical order as such, but on that of an imperfectly rationalizable synthesis of the static order of things and the dynamic order of processes. And we know that cultural history needs all of the scientific orders together to reconstruct any past historical object or set of historical objects. We find physical, psychological, sociological, ideal presuppositions at work in every historical investigation, whether its task is the biography of an individual, or the history of a group, or the reconstruction of any past concrete domain of art, religion, literature, science, etc., in their historical connections with other domains of th cultural world.

All these methodological presuppositions can be used in two entirely different manners, depending on the purpose of historical investigation. Historical reconstruction of the past may be nothing but an auxiliary activity preparing materials for other, systematic, sciences; or it may be an aim in itself, for which other scientific researches with their specific methods are merely auxiliary activities preparing instruments. In the first case history of the past plays the same rôle as observation of the present: it brings within the range of the scientist select data which he will use for physical, psychological, sociological, cultural, generalizations. Its object is not reconstruction of historical reality in its empirical concreteness, but selection and collection of such abstractly isolated fragments of reality as can be treated from the standpoint of a certain theoretic order. In this sense, historical investigation is in some measure a part of almost every scientific research, since we seldom find everything we need to construct our theoretic systems within the immediate reach of our present practical experience and must rely more or less on realities which are no longer practically actual, or not practically actual within our part of concrete extension, so that we must reproduce them indirectly, "mentally," with the help of other experiences or testimonies of other people. There is nothing in history when thus used which would justify its conception as of one separate and independent branch of intellectual activity. A psychological, sociological, political, aesthetic, theory based partly or even entirely upon the reconstructed culture of past peoples does not belong in the sphere of "historical science" any more than does a physical or astronomical theory using the experiments or observations made a few years ago by a scientist who since died.

History as separate and self-determined pursuit appears only when the most exact possible *reproduction* of historical objects as such becomes its *fundamental interest*, and all the methodological presuppositions and theoretic generalizations of other sciences are used for the sole purpose of obtaining with their help the most adequate possible *acquaintance* with the past, either by excluding on their ground suppositions about the past which would not fit into our world in so far as already determined by its practical organization and in some measure by its theoretic orders, or, more fruitfully, by supplementing with their help such insufficient and incomplete data as can be directly obtained by oral or written tradition. But history in this sense is not theoretic reconstruction: it is *creative continuation* of the past in the most emphatic sense of the term. A historical work is, of course, by its rational form, its symbolic expression, its material existence as a book, a new cultural object. But the ultimate significance of its content, of the subject-matter of historical thought, is not to be an aesthetic picture of historical reality as opposed to the reality pictured, but that reality itself, brought to life again with the help of its present remnants as materials and theoretic ideas as instruments. Without this creative revival, without this conscious reproduction, past culture would after a time disappear completely from the sphere of our experience; it would lose almost entirely its realness without being exactly annihilated. Reproduced by history, historical objects reappear in our experience with a new real influence, become actualized again, usually indeed—as we have seen in a previous chapter—with different connections, in different complexes and systems, often much less important practically than they used to be. Sometimes, however, they become even more important; who does not know, for example, how much more social influence the social personality of a national hero or of a religious founder often has when historically reproduced than when still materially and psychologically existing?

Because of this actual, present reality of historically re-created values, we can in some measure justify the principle brought forward first by German methodologists and recognized more or less generally since—the principle of axiological selection of historical object-matter. Since the ultimate problem of history is not theoretic study, but real preservation and revival of historical objects in their empirical concreteness, it is only natural if each historian, each nation, each epoch, tends to reproduce first of all historical objects which seem to them most worth preserving because of the influence which they still may have upon future cultural life when historically revived. The danger of such a selection, if too uniformly and consistently pursued, lies only in an undue limitation of the field for a time, which may result in a general narrowing of the cultural interests and views of the individual or the group; this danger is particularly imminent if the standards of selection, instead of being sincerely accepted as purely personal or national, are claimed to be absolute. German historiography of the nineteenth century and the consequences of its influence on the social and cultural life of the German nation constitute perhaps the best known and most radical proof of the importance of this danger.

In so far as the problem of the actual historical reproduction of any selected historical object or set of objects is concerned, several methodological questions are raised which cannot be discussed here in detail. The first, chief point is that, since the ideal of history is the revival of past reality *as it was* and a total reproduction of concrete historical objects in their whole content and meaning is practically impossible, history must try to reproduce at least all those characteristics of each concrete individual historical object which were most important at the time of its full realness; that is, those in which its own determination by other objects and its influence on other objects were most widely and most durably manifested. This has nothing to do with the application of the concept of type to historical reality (Rickert), which results not in general historical reproduction of the concrete but in special sociological theoretic reconstruction. The second point is the necessity, imposed by the same ideal, of avoiding as far as possible all additions to the reproduced historical object and of determining its content and its meaning in a way which as closely as possible reproduces its past determinations. This possibility is also limited by the very fact that, in order to have a cultural object which no longer belongs to our sphere of reality actually given, we must often in some measure re-create its content with the help of now given contents; but the arbitrariness of our reproduction can be indefinitely diminished by taking the historical object in connection with other objects of the same period and the same domain of concrete extension, by reproducing it as an element of a whole past civilization and thus supplementing the deficiencies in the reproduction of its contents by a more exact determination of its meaning as it really was. It is always difficult to trace the exact dividing line between re-creation and new creation; history will always border on art, and often may pass the border. But their methodological tendencies as conditioned by their ideals are different; precisely because history does not want to be art but intends to reproduce *pre-existing* reality, it makes use of scientific concepts which art in its desire for creation of *new* reality must ignore.

In every empirical historical investigation we find both intentions characterized above—that of preparing materials for some science and that of reviving historical objects— more or less intimately coexisting. Historical preparation of scientific materials demands reproduction of the past with more or less concreteness, and reproduction of the past with the help of scientific concepts is possible only by a synthesis of various abstract aspects of past historical objects. Not the result of historical investigation at a given stage, but the direction in which it progresses, characterizes it either as a preparatory, scientific activity or as a specifically practical, re-creative activity. It is the former, if we see it progress from the concrete historical chaos toward a rational system-atization of phenomena determined from the standpoint of some theoretic order; it is the latter if it advances from a provisional systematic organization of phenomena in accord-ance with various theoretic orders toward a reproduction of the concrete historical chaos. Only in the first case it is essentially scientific; but then the order which it introduces is always a specific, limited, abstract order, one of those which we have outlined above. In the second case, though it uses science, it consists in empirically practical, not in ideally theoretic, creation and the realization of this aim is the more perfect, the more exactly the chaotic historical reality is reproduced. Thus history cannot furnish us with a universal theoretic order of concrete reality independent of its prac-tical organization and superior to all special scientific orders, since in so far as it is theoretic, it must treat concrete reality from the standpoint of some abstract and special scientific order; whereas in so far as it tends to embrace reality in its historical concreteness, it is not theoretic and does not order it at all.

THE INSTRUMENTAL RÔLE OF SCIENCE

We have considered knowledge in its reference to the practical organization of reality as to its object-matter. But in speaking of historical reproduction we have already approached a different connection between theory and prac-tice, which is the opposite of the former; the results of science can become the object-matter of all kinds of practical activity. This question has become actual particularly because of the emphasis put by pragmatism upon the practical application of knowledge, and we regret the necessity of dividing it and limiting ourselves exclusively to that side of it which concerns the rôle played by ready scientific ideas in the construction of practical systems, postponing to a later time the connection between practical and theoretic activities as such, and in particular the question whether and how theoretic activity originates and develops in the course of practical activity and vice versa. In whatever way a scientific idea has been produced, whether for the satisfaction of a practical need or for the realization of theoretic ideal, it certainly can be taken out of the theoretic system of which it is a part and used for practical purposes. The problem is what this use consists in and how it influences the theoretic and the practical organization of reality.

It is evident, first of all, that theoretic ideas are used exclusively in the non-instrumental period of activity during which the system of reality—the future situation, and similarly also the future schematic system of situations, and the future dogmatic system of schemes—is constructed; but as yet it is constructed only "mentally"; it has not passed into the state when instruments begin to be used for the realization of the determined aim on the ground of the selected pre-existing reality. This period, during which the aim is being determined and the materials and instruments chosen, is, as we have seen, practically qualified as subjective as against the period of instrumental realization. Of course, when we speak of it as of a definite period, preceding the period of instrumental realization, it does not mean that all the "subjective" activities must be performed necessarily before any "objective," instrumental activities can start, since in fact they usually overlap each other more or less; non-instrumental activities are scattered among instrumental activities and vice versa; but the more rationally organized activity becomes, the more clearly are the mental and instrumental acts segregated, and the more distinct is their separation in time. When the first, non-instrumental part of practical activity makes use of theoretic ideas, this use is called *planning*, and the second, instrumental part assumes, with reference to the plan superimposed upon the practical organization of reality, the character of *fulfilment*.

In planning, the theoretic idea is used as a specific instrument by which the connections mentally established between the objects, or systems of objects, from which a system is constructed acquire at once an objectivity intermediary between a simple actual "imagined" connection and one already realized with the help of other instruments in the practical world. The connection established with the help of ideas does not cease to be dependent on thought, does not resolve itself into static properties and relations, or a causally conditioned process; but, although dependent on active thought for its actual realization, it is founded on the rational order of reality as to the meaning and content which it gives to the connected objects. Planning, while still qualified practically subjective in so far as actually performed by an individual, has at the same time an objective aspect in so far as the individual, while performing it, acts on the ground of his knowledge of the objectively organized and rationally determined reality.

The idea can play the rôle of an instrument for planning because of its double character, both ideal and real. As objectivated thought, it can be actualized in its essential content at any moment, while on the other hand its content, being based on a more or less wide area of rationally determined reality, transcends the actual spheres of experience and reflection of the individual who actualizes it, and being objectively stabilized in its generality is very little dependent on the particular modification which the individual may give to it in the course of his present experience and reflection. Therefore, by treating the particular object actually given to him as an element of a theoretically defined class embraced by an idea and by determining its content and meaning on the ground of this idea, as supplementing and controlling his present experience and reflection, the individual raises this determination above the limitation of the *here* and *now* and makes it independent of any "nonessential" connections which the unique and irrational development of his personality may bring with it.

Of course, the individual's determination of practical objects is always made with regard to his actual practical intention and in connection with other present objects. It is always only a certain aspect of the given object, or system of objects, that he is interested in—the aspect by which this object can be incorporated into the situation which he wants to construct or by which this system can become a part of some wider system that he is planning. The constructive side of planning always is and remains practical; the aim is spontaneously qualified, the practical materials and instruments spontaneously selected, by practical, not by theoretic reflection. But every practical determination given to an object with reference to other objects, every practical qualification of the aim with reference to the already selected and defined instruments and materials, every choice and practical definition of a material or an instrument relative to other materials and in view of the aim as already determined, are subjected in perfectly purposeful activity to the theoretically reflective control of ideas, to theoretic criticism. Any practical determination which cannot be justified theoretically, which cannot be treated as a particular application of a general idea or of a synthesis of general ideas, but seems merely the result of the concrete actual set of personal tendencies and experiences, is excluded as subjective, as unwarranted by the rational order of reality, and only those determinations are admitted into the plan which have stood the theoretic test. The plan is the common result of practical production and theoretic criticism; on its ideal side it represents an expurgated theoretic reconstruction, a model copy of the actual practical system of objects on the ground of which the aim is to be realized; on its real side, it is an objective, perfectly rational order introduced into the partly subjective, imperfectly rational organization of reality which the individual, or a number of co-operating individuals, has actually reached at the moment when his aim is ready, his instruments and materials selected, and fulfilment begins. The real empirical organization as we find it in practical life, is, of course, never completely identical with the plan, in that it always contains practical features which would not stand the test of theoretic criticism; but such features are not supposed to influence instrumental activity; the practical problem which the latter will solve is supposed to be entirely expressed in the plan.

When activity passes to the fulfilment of the plan, this fulfilment becomes in turn a practical test of the applicability of the ideas which have been used in building the plan, to the particular practical conditions to which they have been applied. The plan is evidently realizable only if it takes fully and adequately into account the pre-existing real nature of the instruments and materials in their reciprocal relation with regard to the realization of the given aim. An idea may be based on such characters of the empirical object or system of objects as either do not possess a sufficient degree of reality to serve for the realization of the given aim, or else, even if sufficiently real, are irrelevant for the given practical situation, or group of situations, because they do not correspond to the requirements of other objects, or systems, on which the realization of the aim will be based. The first case is found, for instance, if the savage, in his plan of a technical situation, makes use of his knowledge of the magical properties of things. The magical properties are not entirely unreal since they have at least a recognized existence within the spheres of experience and reflection of the given social group for many generations; the degree of their realness is quite sufficient to reach with their help an economic, a political, a religious aim, but it is not on the same level with that of physical properties and therefore, since a technical aim requires instruments with a high degree of realness, their introduction into a technical situation is a mistake. The second type of mistake is committed, for instance, when an inexperienced technical worker selects for the given technical situation a certain kind of material on the ground of his general knowledge of such physical properties of this class of material as may have served to realize the given aim in other situations in connection with different other materials and with the help of different instruments, but are of no use in the present situation because they are not the properties which this material is required to possess in view of the nature of the instruments and of other materials which are in this particular situation at the disposal of the worker.

But those mistakes are practical failures, not theoretic errors. The mistake does not consist in judging that the given objects as members of a class possess properties which they do not possess, for they do possess them in some degree at least, since these properties have entered into the definition of the class to which these objects belong; but it does consist in trying to use them on the ground of these properties for the realization of a certain practical aim in connection with certain other pre-existing objects with which they cannot be used for this purpose. Theoretic reflection can show only whether, by assuming the possession of certain properties by certain objects, I am "illusioning myself"; that is, whether these objects possess these properties only within the limits of my present personal experience and reflection, or whether these objects are "really" such as they seem to be *here* and *now;* whether they belong to a class whose members are known as endowed with these particular properties in the already existing rational order of reality. But what use I shall make of objects endowed with these properties in my present practical activity, after having found that my view of them is theoretically justified, is a purely practical problem.

The whole question is the same when it concerns relations, processes, or groups of interrelated objects and series of processes included in a situation. I can, for example, test theoretically the assumption that a certain process is the cause of another process; how to make use of this knowledge in practice, how to construct a situation in which this causal relation will be actually realized and, being realized, will contribute to the attainment of a definite end, is not a matter of knowledge, and my success or failure has nothing to do with the truth or falsity of my theoretic idea. All the determinations of things, processes, relations, constituting a practical situation may be each separately tested by theoretic reflection, and they are thus tested in building a perfect plan; but how this plan can be practically fulfilled in its totality, whether all this information of detail is so combined in the plan as to make the planned situation practically solvable *now* and *here*, is evidently not the business of the science to which we owe this information.

Our theoretic control may, indeed, go farther still, and we may test theoretically the objectivity and rationality of the whole situation, the practical method of combining all the theoretically tested elements of the situation, of stating and solving this particular practical problem; we make then a theoretic criticism of the situation. But it is beyond the reach of our theory whether, when, and how this situation, as theoretically tested both with regard to its elements and with regard to their combination, will be practically realized. It is the task of practice to create the auxiliary situations necessary for the construction of this main situation, and it is a practical mistake if we begin to construct a schematically determined situation, whether theoretically tested or not, without having the possibility of preparing all that is necessary for its realization. The same thing repeats itself on higher stages of theoretic control which, to be practically efficient, must be dominated by and subordinated to still wider and more complete practical organizations. When in carrying out a plan all of whose parts have been tested by theoretic reflection, we succeed or fail in attaining the expected result, our success or failure is not a test of the validity of our knowledge, but of our ability to use our knowledge for the given practical purposes; it does not show whether our ideas are practically applicable or not, but whether in the practical construction of our plan, we have selected ideas which are utilizable in the given practical conditions and combined them in a way which makes the whole plan practically realizable within the given sphere of practical reality. Science cannot organize practice: it can only furnish ideas-instruments by using which practice may spontaneously attain at once a higher level of rationality, provided it selects for its planning in each particular case the proper ideas and uses them in the proper way.

Of course, if we take a certain set of practical problems from the standpoint of these problems theoretic ideas may be classified into useful, directly or indirectly, and useless. Thus, from the standpoint of material technique ideas bearing on the physical order of things and processes are directly utilizable, whereas among those concerning the psychological, sociological, ideal orders some can be used only indirectly, and others not at all. Ideas must also express general and permanent empirical characteristics of the reality of a certain order if we want them to be widely and permanently applicable; thus, the idea of a physical property which is seldom found in experience, or that of a psychological datum or attitude which is peculiar to some supernormal or subnormal individuals, is of little practical use. Finally, at a certain level of practical organization only ideas below a certain degree of abstractness are valuable, whereas others whose practical significance would appear only if practical activity reached a systematic unity permitting the subordination of many particular situations and schemes to a common fundamental dogma, remain provisionally classed as purely speculative, that is, as having no other significance than that of helping to systematize theoretic ideas. Thus, when material technique in Greece was disconnected and chaotic, as is social technique at the present moment, the speculations of philosophers about the composition of matter had no practical interest whatever; whereas now the discussion between atomism and energetism assumes more and more practical importance as bearing on the way of stating and solving theoretic problems which in the present condition of technique evidently are or will be practically utilized.

The effects which the practical application of scientific ideas has upon the development of the practical organization of reality is thus due not to a substitution of theoretic activity for practical activity in organizing situations, schemes, and systems of schemes, but to the fact that practical activity, by using the results of theoretic activity as instruments for planning, can reach more rapidly a higher degree of rationality in the organization which it gives to its object-matter. The rôle of the idea is exactly similar in this respect to that of any other instrument: it does not diminish the demands put on practical creation; it does not allow us to dispense with any practical organizing efforts; but it helps to increase the efficiency of these efforts and thus, on the one hand, to economize innumerable trials and repetitions in reaching a certain organization, and on the other hand to widen the sphere of possible achievements.

The scientific idea or system of ideas corresponds in every field, as we have seen, to the highest degree of rational perfection which the practical organization of reality has reached in the given line; more than this, not satisfied with the rational order already produced, it gives practical activity the incentive to create still more perfect systems, by having it prepare with the help of practical instruments—collect, classify, isolate—fragments of reality for theoretic observation, and particularly by inducing it to experiment. In this way, when in planning a practical situation we use theoretic definitions for the objects included in it, when in creating a scheme we define theoretically in advance the situations in which it will be realized, when in producing a dogmatic system of schemes we express those schemes in abstract theoretic concepts instead of limiting ourselves to practical concrete experiences and activities, in each of these cases we shape the constitutive parts of our present practical organization in accordance with a rational model and are thus able to give them at once a definiteness, a generality, and a permanence of determination which otherwise they could attain only after numerous repeated practical attempts. Compare, for instance, the rapidity with which any new branch of mechanical technique reaches now an almost perfect rational organization with the slow perfecting of all industries in primitive societies or even, using a modern example, of agriculture everywhere until a hundred years ago.

The second effect of the use of ideas, the widening of the range of practical creation, is directly due to the scientific systematization of knowledge. This systematization in each science unifies in a body a vast complexity of rational forms of reality which in the historical world are scattered all over concrete duration and extension and half-absorbed in the irrational chaos of experience. It offers thus for each practical task a large choice of ready models, easily accessible and easily understood in their reciprocal rational connections. Precisely because scientific idealization of practical reality does not follow the pre-existing real order, but takes its own object-matter, practically simple or practically complicated, without regard to the practical system to which it belongs, and puts it into connection with others with which it never was connected practically, scientific ideas when used in planning make an unlimited number of new practical combinations possible. By their scientific meaning which they obtain while being theoretically connected with other ideas, they suggest to the practical worker such possibilities of reshaping and intercombining given practical objects and practical systems as the already existing practical organization of reality could never suggest. The practical organization left alone would tend to a perfect stability, to an exclusion of all imprevisible change as antirational. But when it begins to use theoretic ideas as its object-matter, it finds there a rational order completely different from its own and yet bearing upon its own, which allows it to produce new types of organization, by their very appearance substituting themselves in active experience for the old types without, however, annihilating the systematic order of the latter which, once constructed, cannot cease to exist. Thus, not only the rationalization of any new practical system is incomparably more rapid, owing to the use of ideas, but the rapidity with which new systems appear increases in an enormous proportion with the growing application of theory to practice. Compare the record of technical inventions now and a thousand years ago, or the development of material technique with that of social technique.

But besides these well-known utilitarian consequences, the practical application of theoretic ideas has a less popularly emphasized but not less important effect in bringing step by step a progressive, though imperfect, practical realization of the theoretic orders in the empirical historical world. We have seen that the degree of reality which a theoretic order can acquire in being imposed upon empirical reality by theoretic thought cannot become very high as compared either with the old concrete complexes of historical objects or with the highly real instrumental organization of practical systems. When, however, a theoretic generalization of things, situations, schemes, established on the ground of their uniformity, becomes the foundation of a practical reflective tendency to treat in the future these things, situations, schemes, as uniform in various practical systems, then the theoretic class is something more, besides being a product and a ground of scientific reflection: it is a constitutive element of some practical scheme. When further a theoretic system of ideas becomes practically used to establish repeatedly between objects, situations, schemes of various classes, such connections as exist between their ideas, the system is something more than a theory: it is also a constitutive part of some practical dogma. In this way, the theoretic order becomes imposed upon the world by practice with the help of practical instruments. This imposition is indeed fragmentary and proceeds not from the higher theoretic generalizations down to particular concepts and ideas, but from particular ideas and concepts of a very limited complexity up to those more comprehensive generalizations which practical life at a given stage of its development can already use for planning. It is impossible to study this evolution thoroughly without going into much historical detail; but its significance will be sufficiently suggested by a few considerations.

On the ground of practical organization alone there is no reason why, for instance, in an industrial system the technical schemes should be treated as belonging more closely together than the economic or legal schemes actually used and without which the continual working of the given system of industry would be as impossible as without proper technical methods. Furthermore, from the practical standpoint there certainly is no original connection whatever between the technical schemes used in different industries and in various countries. But science creates the concept of a purely material reality to which economic and legal schemes as such do not belong, and scientific theories of material reality are used as instruments for practical planning. This brings with it the creation of new practical connections. The scientific methodological conception of one material reality subjected to one order, a conception developed in the details of scientific research and systematization, becomes the ground of a practical tendency to treat various technical schemes as bearing upon the same domain of reality, and therefore as interconnected with each other more closely than with economic or legal schemes, independently of the actual organization of particular, empirically given, industrial systems. The idea of *one material technique* arises as an expression of this tendency; there is a new practical dogma more or less clearly formulated and resulting in the establishment of innumerable practical connections between the technical organizations of various industries, in various countries, under various economic conditions; technique slowly becomes practically, not only theoretically, one domain; and reality as object-matter of technique becomes also in some measure one material world from the practical standpoint.

Furthermore, the possibility of practically substituting in some cases purely technical schemes for a combination of technical and social schemes, that is, of introducing machine work instead of human work, generalized by the growing application of science and theoretically founded on the conception of the methodological unity and formal homogeneity of physical nature, leads to a conscious practical tendency, manifesting itself all through technical life: the tendency to substitute everywhere machine work for human work and to exclude almost entirely social schemes from industrial activities. A parallel tendency working in the social field, at this moment rather inadequately expressed in the socialistic ideal, permits us to foresee a gradual practical separation of problems concerning control of nature from those concerning control of society. Such a separation, in so far as effected, will realize in practice the theoretic distinction of the physical from the social order, and result in a deeper and deeper systematic practical organization of the former in accordance with the postulates of physical science.

Similar examples are found in the sphere of personal life. Psychological reflection, when applied to the solution of practical personal problems, produces a rationalization of personal experiences completely different from their original practical organization; see, for instance, the practical influence of ancient stoical and epicurean doctrines. Perhaps the most striking case of practical realization of a theoretic order is the fact that the very concept of psychological consciousness as of a distinct domain of reality has been so generally accepted as a practical dogma and has such a high degree of reality that philosophical reflection may show its relativity without being able to counterbalance its influence on practical life. However, in this case we have certainly to discount the rôle of religious factors.

It is evident, in general, that only a long empirical investigation can show to what a degree in any given domain theoretic thought has succeeded not only in superimposing its order over the practical organization of reality as a purely "mental" systematization of experience, but also in imposing, though only fragmentarily, its order upon the results of practical activity by having its ideas and systems realized as components of practical systems and with the help of practical instruments. But, whether more or less far-reaching, the realization of the theoretic order in practice is possible only because of the fact that fragments of this order—ideas and systems of ideas—are the object-matter of practical activity, are isolated from their ideal content, incorporated into dynamic practical systems and used by practical reflection for practical purposes as instruments of planning. In the same way, as we have seen, the idealization of the practical organization of reality is possible only because fragments of this organization—objects and systems of objects—are the object-matter of theoretic activity, are isolated from their real content and incorporated into theoretic systems. The relation between the theoretic and the practical rationality of the world is strictly reciprocal. Each influences the other, but only by being passively used as instrument or as material for the other's construction and development.

CHAPTER VI

THE PROBLEM OF APPRECIATION

The rational systems of reality, practical and theoretic, whose construction we have investigated are, as we know, superimposed directly or indirectly upon the concrete chaos of the historical reality, are built from concrete historical objects and complexes by active determination and systematization. Even in their totality they do not exhaust the concrete wealth of contents and meanings which the historical world possesses; no concrete historical object is entirely analyzable into objectively determined things and psychological data; no concrete complex is entirely reducible to a rational situation or set of situations. The empirical reality in its full extension and duration always is the dynamic background, indefinite, changing, chaotic, upon which many rationally simplified and stable figures are outlined without ever covering the background.

Furthermore, all systematic organization of reality, with these very characteristics of definiteness, rational simplicity, and stability, by which it is opposed to its concrete historical background, is not only constructed, but maintained above the historical chaos, prevented from dissolving again into the concrete extension and duration from which it arose, by a continued effort of human activity which, by a natural illusion, accepts as given any order which it is led by its own presuppositions to expect, without realizing that it is its implicit tendency to have its expectations fulfilled which makes it reconstruct this order in each particular case for each particular purpose.

But this is not all. The rationally determined and systematized reality, even when created and maintained, does not remain an immovable superstructure built upon the reality of concrete experience. Though there is more and more rationality in the empirical world, this does not mean that the empirical world passes from a chaotic and historical to an organized and scientific stage, that, speaking in terms of old idealism, there is a progressive realization of Reason in experience, a progressive exclusion of irrationality whose ultimate limit would be complete substitution of a definite plurality of perfect systems for the original chaos.

If this idealistic dream could ever come true, the real world would lose its historical character, since, all systems being ready and each rationally determined within itself, there would be no place for the creative becoming and the irrational multiplicity of historical duration and extension. But even then reality would remain concrete, since all these systems never could combine, as we have seen, in one rational system. And even if we imagined that, with the growth of some, now unforeseen, new method of rationalization such a single rational system could ever be constructed over the many and various particular systems, still the latter would preserve their peculiarities, would be incorporated into this new system only mediately, by a hierarchy of intermediary orders, and a concrete object or a concrete complex of objects would never be rationally exhausted from one standpoint, but would have to be treated in various aspects by various systems. But modern idealism has almost ceased to claim that the dream of a perfectly rational world can be more than a progressively realizable, but never attainable, ideal. And from this standpoint, a reality which should only *tend* to be converted from a full concrete chaos of historical objects into a limited non-historical plurality of systems subordinated to some universal system, would still preserve *during* this evolution, that is, during all its empirical existence, some of its primary historical characteristics, though in a continually decreasing measure. This conception of a gradual passage of reality from an irrational to a rational status, when analyzed proves thus to represent the minimum of what an ontological rationalism can demand; it is the last intrenchment of the rationalistic doctrine which, starting with the absolute, realistic monism of the Eleates, is driven step by step to the idealistic conception of a partially unified pluralism to be realized in an infinite future.

But even this minimum of rationalistic claims cannot be conceded. For every component of the rational organization of reality, every practical thing, situation, scheme or dogma, every theoretic idea or system of ideas, however limited and however wide, with all its rationality, is reintroduced as a concrete object into the historical becoming from which it emerged as a system or part of a system. Its total rational organization is then its content, and this more or less systematic content varies when viewed in various historical complexes by various individuals; its meaning is given to it not with reference to its rational relation to other components of the rational organization of reality, but with regard to its dynamic actual connection with any objects whatever with which it may be coupled for present purposes. A thing, a practical situation, a scheme, a system of schemes, a scientific idea, a theory, the entire body of science, may become an aesthetic, a hedonistic, a religious, an economic, a political object, or all of these, by becoming the object-matter of various individual activities. They are differently experienced and differently reproduced at various *here*'s and *now*'s and mean something else for everyone according to the actual use which he makes of them. As concrete objects, they are again parts of the concrete extension and duration, and grow or decrease in reality, or are diversified or stabilized, just as any historical object.

This reintroduction of rationally determined objects and systems into the historical reality is, however, not the result of unintentional, unorganized activity as is the establishment of many other connecuons between actually given contents in the concrete course of experience and reflection. A component of the rational organization of reality is not originally and accidentally experienced as a content, or if it is, then its experiencing does not include its rational determination or its systematic order. Thus, in unintentional experience a certain particular thing is not given as a rationally determined element of a situation or, still less, as a part of the rational physical reality: it is given only as an immediately sensual content with some actually realizable suggestions. A situation if unintentionally objectified is not given as a system of interrelated things or, still less, as a part of the psychological reality, but as a rather vague complexity with a few outstanding contents and meanings not systematically ordered at all. A scientific theory when unintentionally given is represented by a vaguely limited content including symbols, a few "representative" objects symbolized, perhaps one or two suggestions of theoretic analysis or synthesis, and a vague plurality of indefinite possible experiences and acts behind all this. The rational determination of a thing as of an element of a situation or of the physical order, the rational systematic organization of a situation, the rational systematic order of ideas in a scientific theory, or of concrete experience as object-matter of this theory, are given as essential characteristics of their content when they become incorporated into historical reality, only if and in so far as this thing, situation, theory, theoretic order, are intentionally used as historical, empirical objects for the purpose of creating new objects in concrete, dynamically organized activity. For example, when the statically determined characteristics of the thing are being utilized for a hedonistic purpose; when the practical organization of things in an individually constructed situation is taken as a ground for altruistic activity which, by helping the individual solve this situation, will result in a moral value; when the rational perfection of a

scientific theory is counted upon as an asset for social per-
suasion which is expected to facilitate a political revolution:
then the rationality of the thing, of the practical situation, of
the theory, belongs essentially to their content as historical
values, since if they did not have the determination or the
organization which they do possess, they could not be utilized as they are for the purposes of hedonistic, moral, political
creation.

In fact, we have already spoken, when discussing the
practical organization of reality, about the objectivation of
practical systems as elements of other, wider systems, and in
the last section of the preceding chapter we saw how theoretic
ideas become instruments for practical planning. But we
have treated this reintroduction of ready fragments of rationalized reality into the dynamic development of activity only
from the standpoint of the progress of rational organization
to which they may be made to contribute. This is, however,
only one side of the question. Every increase of rationality
is always and necessarily accompanied by a corresponding
increase of the historical chaos. Any fragment of the rationalized reality, by being used to construct a new rational system, becomes thereby an element of historical reality, and the
wider its rational use, the greater its concrete historical variety of content and meaning. Whatever is thought and done
in the world, even the development of rational order, con-
tributes to the growth of chaotic historical reality.

Now, such objects or systems as are reintroduced from the
rationally organized reality into historical reality by being
used as concrete objects for dynamic creative action, and
which, when turned into objects, preserve their rationality
as essential part of their content, possess as a consequence of
this a different meaning than the primary historical objects
whose content does not include any rational determination.
It is evidently a completely different matter whether we treat
a stone or a tree just as it is primarily given to us in actuality

or whether we take it into account with those rational determinations which it possesses for industry as technical material or for science as a physical thing; and the meaning which a legal institution possesses for a casual observer who sees the building, the men, and a few actions performed by those men is certainly not at all similar to that which a criminal, a moral reformer, or a scientist gives to it when connecting it with his hedonistic, moral, or theoretic aim, and conscious of the rational organization of legal schemes which are behind the direct empirical data.

We can therefore make a distinction between the *primary* historical object, that is, a concrete object whose content is constituted by that which is given directly in individual actualities, and the *secondary* historical object, a concrete object which is not entirely reducible to direct data, because it contains also a rational qualification whose existence is due to the determination which this object has acquired by becoming a component of the practical or theoretic organization of reality. The stone, the tree, the painting, the legal institution, the scientific theory, are primary historical objects in so far as the content of each of them is simply the totality of that which various individuals at various moments have actually experienced when these objects were given in various concrete connections. But the same stone or tree is a secondary historical object when its content includes the rational determination which has been imposed upon it by technique or science.

This determination cannot indeed be realized actually in its full rationality unless we reproduce the scientific or technical system in which it has been acquired; when the stone or the tree is used outside of this system, as a concrete historical object, serving some other intentional activity, the rationality which it possesses as a physical or technical thing can be experienced only indirectly. We qualify the empirically given content by the suggestion of a rational order in which certain of its characters are founded, whereas other characters lack this foundation. Similarly, the painting is a secondary historical object if its content is critically qualified with an implicit reference to an aesthetic system, a style of which it is an example, instead of being naïvely observed as a representation of some reality. The legal institution is a secondary historical object if that which is directly given in casual observation is qualified by the suggestion of a system of political schemes existing behind the actually appearing things, men, and actions, so that in view of this qualification certain of these directly perceived phenomena seem essential, rooted in the objective political order, others accidental, due merely to the fact that the institution is being observed at a certain moment and from a certain individual standpoint. The scientific theory is a secondary historical value when the whole complexity of symbols and symbolized objects which is actually given when "we think about" it, is qualified by the suggestion of a rational, systematic order of ideas which constitutes objectively this theory as part of the ideal reality, so that certain of the experiences which we have when thinking about this theory appear as having a foundation in this suggested rational order, whereas others are included in our experience only as a consequence of the connections in which the theory is given to us *here* and *now*.

By this qualification, the content of a secondary historical object is in a sense divided into a rationally fixed nucleus which appears as essential for this object, and a nebula of nonessential characters which have no foundation in any systematic order. Of course, this rational nucleus is in fact also historical, varying from individual to individual and from moment to moment, since even those characters of the object which are rationally founded appear different in each actual experience and the suggestion of rational order behind them varies from case to case. But there always is the possibility of actually reconstructing this rational order, of turning the given historical object again into a rationally determined object or a rationally organized system, and thus the nucleus, even though varying in fact, seems always and everywhere the same in principle, imposes itself upon every actual experience as absolutely independent of this experience, as the reality *per se*, the thing-in-itself underlying the actual data.

Consequently, the secondary historical object cannot be used as freely for any actual purposes as the primary historical object. When we want to create some new object with its help, we find that we do not control it; our present activity can in no way change its rationally fixed nucleus—unless, of course, we reconstruct and modify the whole rational system in which this nucleus is founded—and by introducing it into our action we have not only made use of its actually experienced content and meaning, but we have made the progress of our activity dependent on its transcendent character; we have implicitly subjected the accomplishment of our intention, in so far as the latter is already defined, to the conditions imposed by a rational order which is entirely beyond the reach of our actual influence, and which may either contribute to the definition and realization of our aim much more than any actually given primary object-matter of our present activity, however real historically it may be, could do by itself, or put in our way much more efficient hindrances than the mere lack of the necessary materials or instruments within our present sphere of reality. Under these circumstances, the secondary historical object becomes from the standpoint of the present dogmatically organized activity an object of *positive or negative appreciation*, a positive or negative *value*.

This opens before us a new and wide field of problems which, however, cannot be adequately stated and solved within the limits of the present work. Realistic philosophy has always tried, indeed, to treat the positiveness and negativeness of values as explicable on the ground of a theory of reality alone, either conceiving them as absolute characteristics of objects, which are then taken as being in themselves, by virtue of their objective essence, good or bad, beautiful or ugly, sacred or impure, true or false, or taking them as results of synthetic connections between natural, social, ideal realities on the one hand and psychological realities on the other; that is, between things and personal (sometimes even social) feelings, emotions, desires, etc.

But it is evident that neither of these methods is adequate. For objective reality by itself is never positive or negative; we make it positive or negative by using it for some active purpose, even if this use should be only "mental." Positiveness and negativeness are not characteristics that we discover in objects, but characteristics that we give to objects. Indeed, the rational constitution of these objects as real systems or parts of systems is a ground for our appreciation, but only a partial ground, since there is no object whatever which, while remaining the same in its rational constitution, may not be subjected by different individuals and different moments to opposite appreciations. This is the reason why realism, having searched in vain for absolute values, was forced to make appreciation dependent not only on the rational constitution of the object, but also on the condition of the psychological subject. But this is merely a restatement of the fact that the appreciation of an object varies from individual to individual (or group) and from moment to moment. And an explanation of these variations on the psychological ground tells us nothing about the objective conditions on which they depend, so that the psychological "theory of values" gives up not only absoluteness, but also objectivity; it resigns all possibility of studying the economic, political, moral, aesthetic, theoretic—in general, the objective—factors of relative appreciations.[1]

[1] Compare for the problem of relative values, my article "The Principle of Relativity and Philosophical Absolutism," *The Philosophical Review*, March, 1915.

For, if the appreciation of an object varies, though the rational constitution of the object remains invariable, it is because it depends on the dynamic, actually constructed system of values with which it is put in connection for the determination and realization of an aim. The object is not a positive value at a given moment and for a given individual because it provokes in this individual pleasure or pain, desire or aversion, but it provokes pleasure or pain, desire or aversion because it is positive or negative from the standpoint of the dynamic organization which the individual intentionally constructs at the given moment. Since a value by its objective rational constitution may help the creation of one object and hinder that of a different object, it is clear that in the first case it will be positive, in the second negative; and since its rôle will depend on the nature of the object which is being created and of the materials and instruments on the ground of which it is being created, there are real objective reasons for both its positiveness in some connections and its negativeness in others. On the other hand, a value can help or hinder creation by its pre-existing rationality only as long as activity is still in progress, as long as it has not yet constructed a ready system of objects. For when the system is once constructed, the value will be either excluded from it or included in it; in the former case it will no longer count at all from the standpoint of the system, whereas in the latter case it will be an element of the system, completely determined within its limits with regard to its other elements, and any rational determination it may have possessed outside of this system will be either irrelevant for the latter or converted into a determination within the system. In other words, as part of a ready system of reality the value is no longer an object of appreciation because everything in its content which could affect the organization of the system has been already taken into account in constructing the system, belongs to the system as an objective component. The actual existence of the positive or negative character which a value acquires with reference to a certain dynamic organization of objects depends thus on the fundamental tendency and logical systematization of the activity which is actually connecting this value in its objective rationality with other actually selected and dynamically organized objects. Therefore a study of values as positive or negative cannot be made except on the ground of a theory of creative activity.

The problem of valuation is thus the unifying link between the problem of reality and the problem of active thought. The existence of positive and negative values is the common result of the rational organization of reality and the logical organization of activity. It cannot be explained by either of these organizations alone. In so far as the theory of reality takes values into account, it needs to be supplemented by a theory of activity. And every type of science of reality has to deal in some measure and in some form with empirical values. This is quite evident with reference to the sciences of the ideal order; every dogmatic system of schemes, political, economic, moral, aesthetic, religious, theoretic, is empirically used as a standard of appreciation by all the individuals who accept it as the basis of the practical organization of their experiences in a certain line. Social realities as object-matter of social theory possess on the one hand the character of criteria of values when statically treated, in so far as individual experience and activity are required to conform with them and, by actually following or not this requirement, are positively or negatively appreciated; and on the other hand each of these criteria is itself a value when viewed from the dynamic point of view, whenever in the course of social evolution it is positively or negatively appreciated relatively to other components of social civilization, as corresponding or not to actual experiences and attitudes of the members of the given group. In the static psychological order personal experiences are values, when regarded from the standpoint of their actual conformity or non-conformity with the standards imposed by natural reality, and in the dynamic psychological order appreciation is involved in the actual appearance of every attitude and the object with regard to which the attitude is taken is a value.   Even in the physical order the distinction between the physically real and the physically unreal implies valuation as manifested in the course of actual practical organization or theoretic research, though reduced to a minimum.

A science of reality can ignore the existence of values only as long as it remains within the limits of an abstractly isolated, closed, ready, perfectly rational real system.   As soon as it extends its investigation beyond these limits, attempts to put the system on the wider ground of concrete, imperfectly rational reality, or tries to find some connection between it and the rest of the world, even if only in order to reach at the end of this investigation a rational relation between this system and some other, also perfectly rational, system, it meets inevitably the problem of appreciation in its way, in the form of a number of empirical values which it may finally succeed in analyzing and explaining away but which, by the very fact that they must be explained away, remind it continually of the part played by human activity in constructing and maintaining all rational order.   The knowledge of reality would be self-sufficient if it were completely ready and its entire object-matter were given at once in a perfectly achieved rational order.   But because it is and always will be a knowledge in becoming, because it has to rationalize its object-matter step by step, because any rational order it wants to construct in a perfect form exists objectively as an imperfectly rational organization of innumerable imperfect and chaotically interconnected systems, all immersed and becoming in the ceaselessly evolving stream of historical reality from which they must be taken out in the very course of scientific investigation, the knowledge of reality will be never sufficient to itself.   It needs continually to be supplemented by some knowledge which is not a theory of reality as rational. Each of its static results is, indeed, perfectly valid within itself and, in so far as achieved, reconstructs adequately the rational aspect of reality upon which it bears. But in its dynamic development, in its tendency to transcend any given results, to widen indefinitely every rational order, it meets at every step the creatively growing side of the world which it cannot grasp. In a word, the knowledge of reality must be supplemented by some other type of knowledge, not because of the imperfection of its doctrines, but because of the specific character of its researches which, while pursuing any theoretic problem, must exclude progressively, in order to reach any rational solution, all these features of their object-matter which are founded not in rational stabilization, but in creative development.

It can be supplemented, needless to repeat, only by an empirical theory of activity, if such a theory is possible; and an empirical theory of activity must be identical with philosophy. For, on the one hand, we have seen that there is no place left for philosophy in the entire domain of the knowledge of reality and that, on the other hand, all particular sciences are sciences of reality and there is none whose object-matter could include active thought. Moreover, philosophy has always had the ambition of being a theory of the world as a whole and thus creating, as "queen of sciences," an objective unity of knowledge. But no unity of knowledge can be reached in the field of reality: therefore, assuming that a theory of activity is possible, it is the only domain in which the old ideal of a synthesis of all knowledge might still have some objective significance.

INDEX

INDEX

Absolute, 266 ff.

Absolute experience criticized, 28

Absolute meanings, philosophy of, 90, 91

Absolute subject (ego), rejected, 28–29, 133, 264 ff.

Absolute values, 12 ff., 22, 90, 91, 346 ff.

Abstraction, 234 ff.

Abstractness: of contents denied, 58, 59; of ideas, 234 ff.

Acquaintance: opposed to knowledge, 231; aim of history, 322

Act: of reflection, 40 ff.; producing connections, 65 ff.; as creative, 118, 169; instrumental distinguished from mental, 177 ff.; starting a process, 205, 206; not a cause, 225, 226; objectivated as idea, 233 ff.

Action: practical, 154–69; in physics, 253

Activity: in general, xii, 24 ff., 349; identified with thought, 42 ff.; individual range of, 129 ff.; theoretic, 152, 230 ff.; practical, constructing systems and producing objects, 155 ff., 326 ff.; instrumental, 177 ff., 308, 326 ff.; mental, 178 ff., 198, 308, 326 ff.

Actuality: of experience, 35 ff.; of reflection, 40 ff.; final definition of, 50; and personality, 51, 52

Adaptation: of active being to environment criticized, 17, 18, 131, 132, 163 ff., 274; between new object and pre-existing reality in practice, 165 ff.

Aesthetic complex as reality, 81, 82

Aesthetic object: as example of historical object, 99 ff.; its concrete extension, 113–14; as value, 345

Aim, 160, 161, 169, 182 ff.

Analysis, scientific, 237 ff.

Application: of theory in practice, xiv–xvi, 2, 3, 4, 325 ff.

Appreciation, 87 ff., 346 ff.

Approximation, scientific principle of, 244 ff.

Aristotelism, mediaeval, 10

Aristotle: logic, 44, 185; conception of actuality, 116; history of philosophy, 301

Art: applied, illustrating multiplication of objects, 99 ff.; as practical organization of reality for the production of new objects, 168, 183, 186, 189–92; distinguished from history, 324; as object-matter of theory, 299 ff.

Association of data of experience, 36 ff., 65 ff., 80

Atomism, 333

Attitude: concept of, in psychology, 280 ff.; in sociology, 295 ff.

Attribute, 247, 252

Automatization of activity, 260

Auxiliary actions, 193 ff.

Auxiliary situations, 194 ff.; their unification, 208 ff.

Axiological selection in history, 323

Becoming: of experience, 37 ff.; of reality, 117 ff.

Beginning: of reality in time, 119 ff.

Behaviorism, 274

Bergson, x, xii, 123, 148, 152, 268

Biological: presuppositions in theory of knowledge, 3 ff.; in psychology, 272–74; in sociology, 287, 288

Body: organic, as instrument, 73, 74, 172, 187; as historical product, 131, 132; in psychology, 273

Categories: traditional, in practice, 185 ff.; in theory, 245, 246, 255 ff.

Causality: as concrete connection, 75–77; inapplicable to historical evolution, 122 ff.; as practical relation, 208, 225 ff.; as theoretic principle, 244, 245, 257 ff.; psychological, 274, note, 280, 281; psycho-physical, 278; sociological, 295 ff.

Cause: final, 208; efficient, 225 ff.; as functional dependence, 258

Change: of content denied, 60, 61; as practical form, 206; as theoretic form, 249, 253, 254

Civilization: past reconstructed, 135 ff.; defined as culture of a territorially localized group, 293

Classification: of sciences, 245 ff., 318 ff.; psychological, 277; sociological, 293

Common-sense reality, 81, 100, 145, 146, 228, 229

Communication, social, 138 ff., 292

Complex, system of objects with a minimum of rationality, 64, 79, 97 ff., 149 ff.

Complexity: of contents denied, 59, 60; of practical organization, 217; of ideas, 237, 238; of social reality, 293 ff.

Concept, 237 ff.

Concreteness: of contents denied, 58, 59; of historical objects, 79 ff., 94 ff.; and rationality in science, 244, 282, 297

Connection: theory of, 64 ff.; objectivated as relation, 184, 185

Consciousness, 27, 30, 31, 43, 51, 52, 263, 264, 271 ff.

Conservatism: in practical life, 227, 228; overcome by science, 334, 335

Construction of systems, 154 ff.

Consumption of food as example of practical activity, 157, 158

Content: as datum and subject-matter of reflection, 56 ff.; and meaning, in realistic and idealistic philosophies, 87 ff.; its relation to meaning in the practical instrument, 170, 175, 176; of the idea drawn from reality, 230, 232 ff.

Continuity: of the course of experience, 29 ff.; of historical evolution, 120, 121

Control: of reality by active thought, 210 ff., 221 ff., 228, 229, 304, 310; of practice by theory, 152, 328 ff.

Co-operation, social, 141 ff.

Creation: concept of, in modern philosophy, x ff.; as condition of personal life, 50–52; unorganized, of historical reality, 119 ff.; organized, 154 ff.; of new types of processes, 259 ff.; of ideas, 230, 231; in historiography, 320 ff.

Culturalism, formulation of, 15 ff.

Culture: in the traditional sense, as special part of reality, 8 ff., 55, 111, 112, 122, 138; in the sense of the present work, covering the entire reality in so far as produced and determined by human activities, 15 ff., 24, 25, 44 f., 53, 54, *passim*

355